D0554013

Living with the Dead

Living with the Dead
Mortuary Ritual in Mesoamerica

EDITED BY JAMES L. FITZSIMMONS AND
IZUMI SHIMADA

The University of Arizona Press   Tucson

The University of Arizona Press
© 2011 The Arizona Board of Regents
All rights reserved

www.uapress.arizona.edu

Library of Congress Cataloging-in-Publication Data

Living with the dead : mortuary ritual in Mesoamerica / edited by
James L. Fitzsimmons and Izumi Shimada.
    p.   cm.
    Includes bibliographical references and index.
    ISBN 978-0-8165-2976-6 (cloth : alk. paper)
    1. Mayas—Funeral customs and rites.   2. Indians of Mexico—Funeral
customs and rites.   3. Indians of Central America—Funeral customs and
rites.   4. Human remains (Archaeology)—Mexico.   5. Human remains
(Archaeology)—Central America.   6. Mexico—Antiquities.   7. Central
America—Antiquities.   I. Fitzsimmons, James L.   II. Shimada, Izumi.
    F1435.3.M6L58   2011
    972′.01—dc22   2010050571

Manufactured in the United States of America on acid-free, archival-
quality paper containing a minimum of 30% post-consumer waste and
processed chlorine free.

16   15   14   13   12   11   6   5   4   3   2   1

Contents

Living with the Dead

CHAPTER 1

Introduction

JAMES L. FITZSIMMONS AND IZUMI SHIMADA

STUDIES OF FUNERARY BEHAVIOR have long been at the forefront of the anthropology of Mesoamerica. From the pioneering works of such figures as Edward Thompson (1896) and Oliver Ricketson (1925) to the present day, research on death in the Americas has focused on burials— and associated material culture—as a means of understanding not only the dead themselves but also the mind-set of the living. Cataloguing grave goods, examining evidence for trauma, observing ceramic change or similar archaeological activity has commonly guided the force of analysis toward moments of death and subsequent interment. The funeral is, often correctly, set as one of only a handful of supreme moments in which sociopolitical activities are expressed and relationships initiated, renewed, or reinforced. For the region in question, however, death is almost never accompanied by the immediate extinction of the social persona. It is more the beginning of a process than an end in itself, often the first step in a series of relationships—some of them long-term—between the living and the dead.

This book documents the various manners in which the dead and the living interact in prehistoric and historic Mesoamerica. Together with its upcoming complementary volume on living with the dead in the Andes, it views this interaction from cross-disciplinary and diachronic perspectives. Written by a host of scholars from different backgrounds in the humanities and social sciences, the chapters of this volume offer synergistic insights into the enduring and varied articulation between the dead and those who survived them. From physically opening the tombs of their ancestors and carrying ancestral heirlooms, to periodic feasts, sacrifices, and other lavish ceremonies, the heirs mentioned in this volume revisit death on a regular basis. The range of activities attributable to the dead, moreover, range from passive definitions of territorial boundaries to more active exploits, from "dancing" at weddings to "witnessing" royal accessions. The dead were—and continue to be—a vital part of everyday life.

The rituals and practices surrounding the dead were more than just commemorative events honoring ancestors. The bones of captives, whether prayed to or proudly displayed as spoils of war, were not simple trophies. Instead, we might view these activities and actions as points during which a particular event—for example, the death of a king—is remembered, reviewed, and reinterpreted. Over time, the activities and actions themselves become memories, subject to interpretation and potentially passed on to others in ways that change their significance.[1] The reason why memory is important to the study of death involves such changes. As both archaeologists and ethnographers have noted cross-culturally, mortuary ritual is an opportunity for identity and social memory to be constructed, tested, and renegotiated (e.g., see Bloch 1982; Chesson 2001; Gillespie 2001, 2002; Metcalf and Huntington 1991; O'Shea 1996; Weiner 1976). In other words, it involves social drama. Given that the dead were literally omnipresent in ancient Mesoamerica, from the tombs of Classic Maya temple-pyramids to the crypts beneath the floors of Zapotec houses, we might say that the opportunities for social drama were frequent and perhaps ongoing. The clash between, and pull of, different personalities in mortuary behavior is thus something that we should keep in mind.

Information on the interplay between the living and the dead comes from a variety of sources. Although prehispanic written sources are, by and large, extant for the Mesoamerican cultures in this volume, the types of surviving information recorded by ancient scribes widely vary. Classic Maya (200–900 CE) rulers, for example, recorded elaborate rites of death, burial, and exhumation in far greater detail than their contemporaries in Central Mexico. Nevertheless, such lengthy descriptions come from only a handful of Maya sites, with diverse nobles in time and space choosing far different subject matter to highlight in their inscriptions. Perhaps, as suggested by several chapters in this volume, the political expediency of the dead relative to other concerns played a role in how and when they surfaced in Maya ritual.

Historical sources, from the colonial period and beyond, are likewise invaluable in the interpretation of mortuary practices, particularly with regard to the Mexica and other peoples who encountered the first wave of European exploration in the fifteenth century. Where possible, moreover, the authors of the papers in this volume have drawn upon comparative literature in art history, anthropology, sociology, and other disciplines. Estella Weiss-Krejci, for example, argues that Maya treatment of the dead can be placed within a larger world context, with comparisons to mortuary activities in diverse parts of Europe and Asia. By comparison, the chapter by Elizabeth Baquedano draws upon ethnohistory to inform upon the art of the Aztec world. As a rule, however, material culture and archaeological context provide not only the bulk of information on funerary behavior but also the common threads tying each of the cultures of this volume together.

Several major developments over the last ten years have greatly influenced the timing and production of this volume, itself an outgrowth of a 2005 SAA session in Salt Lake City entitled, "Between the Living and the Dead: Cross-Cultural and Diachronic Perspectives," organized by James L. Fitzsimmons and Izumi Shimada. In Mesoamerica, the discovery of the language of Classic Maya inscriptions (Houston et al. 2000, 2001) has, coupled with further refinements in the deciphering of Maya hieroglyphic writing, allowed for a theoretical broadening of Maya epigraphy. Works on the body, senses, emotions, and even psychology of the Classic Maya have recently emerged, one of the most noteworthy being *The Memory of Bones: Body, Being and Experience Among the Classic Maya* (Houston et al. 2006). Another major development in Mesoamerica includes the initially grudging, then rapid (re)acceptance of Teotihuacan's presence in southern Mesoamerica and the interconnectedness between the Maya area and this northern giant, with its enclaves of Maya, Zapotec, and other ethnic groups (e.g., Braswell 2003; Sugiyama and Cabrera Castro 2003; Taube 2003). Likewise, recent syntheses of burial practices in several regions of Mesoamerica have appeared, from the Maya area (Ciudad Ruiz et al. 2003; Eberl 1999; Fitzsimmons 2009; Tiesler Blos and Cucina 2006) to the Valley of Oaxaca (Martínez López et al. 1995; Winter 2002; Winter et al. 1995), as well as a series of refinements to our knowledge of indigenous concepts of the afterlife in Central Mexico and beyond (e.g., Joyce 2001; López Luján 2005; Taube 2004; Wells and Davis-Salazar 2007). These works would not have been possible, of course, without a wealth of previous literature on death and the body in several parts of Mesoamerica (e.g., Furst 1995; López Austin 1984; Ruz Lhuillier 1968; Schele and Mathews 1998; Storey 1992;

Welsh 1988). At present, a body of literature on postfunerary mortuary behavior is building for West Mexico, particularly with regard to the Postclassic Tarascans at Tzintzuntzan and at Epiclassic Urichu (e.g., see Cabrera Castro 1977–1978; Haskell 2008; Pollard and Cahue 1999), where tombs appear to be reused and reentered in ways similar to those discussed by the multiple authors of this volume. This is an encouraging development, and one that will doubtless contribute to discussions of Mesoamerican mortuary behavior in the years to come.

Combined with ongoing regional publications into the archaeology, anthropology, and art history of death, the majority of recent literature has increasingly tended to stress the interconnectedness of the peoples and cultures of Mesoamerica. The present volume is no exception. This is not to say that the cultures described herein were all in constant, direct contact or to promote — together with the complementary volume on living with the dead in the Andes — a hyperdiffusionist, pan-indigenous model for the Americas. Rather, the similarities and differences in mortuary ritual presented here were the result of a widespread system of interaction or world system whose boundaries shifted with the waxing and waning of local political and economic institutions. Although the nature of this system has been — and will doubtless continue to be — a topic of debate for some time (Blanton and Feinman 1984; Carmack and Gossen 2006; Kepecs 2005; Moberg 1988; Robertson 2001; Santley and Alexander 1996; Smith and Berdan 2000, 2003; Wallerstein 1976), it is clear that regional interaction and cultural exchange could and did occur. This work offers a comparative perspective informed by the reality of this interaction and elucidates a variety of shared or persistent rituals and beliefs that have not been recognized; it explores cross-cultural explanations in addition to highlighting unambiguously local developments.

The chapters at the beginning of the book provide background material for comparison with several cultures of Mesoamerica, including the Lowland Maya, Zapotec, Mixtec, Teotihuacano, and Aztec. Each of the chapters combines regional synthesis with site-oriented discussion, highlighting recent archaeological, epigraphic, or artistic analysis at these locations. The chapters by Jeffrey Blomster, Saburo Sugiyama, and Diane and Arlen Chase, for example, set data from Etlatongo, Teotihuacan, and Caracol, respectively, within a larger geographic and archaeological framework.

FIGURE 1.1. Map of Mesoamerica.

Temporally, the different cultures of Mesoamerica (Evans 2004) in this volume follow separate but overlapping archaeological chronologies (fig. 1.1). The general chronology corresponds to Formative or Preclassic (1500 BCE–250 CE), Classic (250–1000 CE), and Postclassic (1000–1500 CE) periods, although each of these is traditionally divided into two or more facets. For the purposes of this volume, the Formative period is divided into Early (1500–1000 BCE), Middle (1000–400 BCE), and Late (400 BCE–250 CE) phases, while the Classic period is divided into Early Classic (250–600 CE), Late Classic (600–800 CE), and Terminal Classic (800–1000 CE). Although the Postclassic is not divided in the chapter by Baquedano, it is typically divided into Early (1000–1250 CE) and Late (1250–1521 CE) periods; the period of Aztec hegemony in Postclassic Mesoamerica roughly corresponds to what some archaeologists term the Late Aztec period, or 1400–1521 CE (Smith 2002).

Given that several themes run continuously through the papers presented here, this volume is organized primarily along rough chronological and geographic lines. The first few chapters on the Classic Maya span epigraphic, archaeological, and cross-cultural comparisons (Fitzsimmons,

Weiss-Krejci, and Chase and Chase). We then turn northward, looking at the development of mortuary traditions in the Valley of Oaxaca (Blomster), particularly with regard to the Mixteca Alta, as well as contemporary activities at the vast Central Mexican metropolis of Teotihuacan (Sugiyama). Continuing on in the Valley of Mexico, we look at Aztec concepts of death and sacrifice at Tenochtitlan and other sites in the final years before European colonization (Baquedano). This is followed by a discussion of common themes in the archaeology, art history, and ethnohistory of living–dead interactions in Mesoamerica (McAnany).

The themes of this work can largely be divided into topical and theoretical categories. Topically, several of the authors in this volume highlight the ways in which the dead were politicized; human remains and other memorabilia were, in these case studies, used by the living as a means of demonstrating and reinforcing status. The chapters by Estella Weiss-Krejci and James L. Fitzsimmons specifically center on this theme. Weiss-Krejci draws upon several struggles over choices of burial places—and even corpses themselves—from societies worldwide in her "The Role of Dead Bodies in Late Classic Maya Politics." She documents the ways in which the bodies of the rich, famous, and even anonymous have been exhumed, reburied, and desecrated "in order to elevate or degrade the status of their owners, to construct new affiliations between groups, or to rewrite history and retrieve social memory." Building upon this world literature, she then explores the politicization of human remains among the Classic Maya; ultimately, Weiss-Krejci sets their behavior within larger models of postinterment body manipulations and highlights the political role that bones may have played among the Maya. Fitzsimmons touches upon this latter theme in his "Perspectives on Death and Transformation in Ancient Maya Society." In examining the evidence for the utilitarian and ritual use of ancestral and sacrificial human remains, Fitzsimmons explores the idea that human remains were considered to be efficacious by the ancient Maya, involved in the dedication of buildings and hieroglyphic monuments as well as key to the conjuring of ancestors, gods, and other supernaturals. Beyond objects, he argues, human remains and other heirlooms were embodiments of ancestral identity and considered—in a sense—to be alive. Although the evidence for this stems largely from epigraphic and iconographic sources, Fitzsimmons presents several archaeological case examples that suggest the pervasiveness of these beliefs during the Classic period.

One of the most common topical themes of the papers in this volume involves the dead defining social space and creating—as well as renewing—social and familial ties. The chapters by Jeffrey Blomster and Diane and Arlen Chase each employ these themes. Echoing the papers by Weiss-Krejci and Fitzsimmons, Blomster's "Bodies, Bones, and Burials" looks at how the possession and display of bodies, particularly select parts, provided legitimacy to Oaxacan elites, particularly in the Postclassic Mixteca Alta. More importantly, however, he explores changing patterns in the mortuary behavior of Zapotec and Mixtec communities over time, from Formative expressions at sites like Etlatongo to the early years of the colonial period at Yanhuitlán. In doing so, he defines how corpses materialized social spaces and identities, serving—as in the Maya area—as the "generative and legitimizing force of ancestors" in precolumbian Oaxaca.

Chase and Chase also deal with the "social compact" between the dead and the living reflected in burials, in their "Ghosts Amid the Ruins." There the dead are integrated within the household, buried beneath the floors of residences; those of the highest status were set within a specific building within each residential group that was dedicated to mortuary ritual. Occasionally the tombs of the dead at Caracol were purposefully reentered, with the intent being to redefine and reify the relationships between the living and the dead. Chase and Chase suggest a cyclical nature to these activities. As in the paper by Blomster, Chase and Chase are viewing the corpse as a means of maintaining social status and reinforcing political relationships; they view reentry, moreover, as having the capacity to "alter" the contract between the dead and their descendants.

The sacrifice of war captives was an integral part of mortuary ritual in Mesoamerica, and even parts of Central America (Coe 1962). As Houston et al. (2006) have noted, such sacrifice often had two very different sides. One involved humiliation: Maya captors, for example, often went through great length to denigrate their captives prior to their deaths. Yet notions of honor and prestige also play a major role in human sacrifice, a point made clear by Saburo Sugiyama in "Interactions between the Living and the Dead at Major Monuments in Teotihuacan." Outlining the rich history of excavations at Teotihuacan, Mexico, over the last two decades, Sugiyama contrasts the seemingly honored, militaristic sac-rifices of the Feathered Serpent Pyramid with the discovery of several burial complexes in the Temple of the Moon; there "respected" human sacrifices occur along with bound victims, decapitated heads, and head-less bodies. He reconstructs the mortuary rituals taking place at the moment of monumental construction and explores the meanings and functions of the intended interactions between the sacrificed peoples and the living authorities in charge of the event. As with the other burials of this volume, Sugiyama argues that each was prepared by the living to communicate power, transmitting specific politico-religious messages to all present.

Elizabeth Baquedano likewise engages concepts surrounding human sacrifice in her "Concepts of Death and the Afterlife in Central Mexico." Employing both Spanish and native chronicles of Aztec beliefs about the dead, she combines art history, ethnography, ethnohistory, and archaeol-ogy to outline concepts of the Mesoamerican afterlife at the time of the conquest. Specifically, she highlights the disparity between the afterlives available to those who died average, unremarkable deaths and to those who were courageous on the battlefield or dutiful in civil society. Baque-dano notes the importance attached to death by sacrifice, citing it as the death that "most preoccupied the minds of native peoples and the conquistadors." Human sacrifice was more than just a normalized death within indigenous thought; theoretically, it was preferred to death with-out distinction, a "good death" in the Aztec mind-set.

In addition to the above topical themes, this book confronts several major theoretical issues. One of these involves the notion of a "good death" itself: what was the "good death" for the prehispanic peoples of Mesoamerica? Baquedano highlights remarkable deaths, deaths that had meaning and thereby became attached to one of the choicer afterlives. As she and other scholars note in the following pages, however, even the physicality of the remarkable death was not all ancient Mesoamericans were concerned with. Surely a "good death" encapsulated more than just physicality and the final moments of life. But if we view the good death as more than simply a preferred mode of expiration, then do we draw a dichotomy between being, on the one hand, socially and bio-logically alive and, on the other hand, socially and biologically dead? Of course not. But where to draw this line for Aztecs, as with other peoples of ancient Mesoamerica, is always a difficult question, and one that deserves contemplation in the reading of this volume. Mesoamerican captives, as per Houston et al. (2006), certainly reached a point when they were socially dead and biologically alive, a social chasm away from groups who would likely dispatch them. What if the reverse—being biologically dead but socially alive—was not only possible but also part of normal relations between the living and the dead (Hallam et al. 1999)?

A good death meant being remembered. It meant that the social persona would be perpetuated and that one's memory would, at least in the immediate sense, be cared for. The good death guaranteed a future for the dead, an extension of identity that was both subordinate to and determinative of living society.[2] As Baquedano notes, the living could both seek a "peerless afterlife" informed by the deaths of paramount citizens and manipulate those same deaths to suit a particular political or ideological goal. The sacrifice of a captive seems to have involved similar factors, although ultimately the only identity preserved involved—as far as the captor was concerned—one connected to perpetual subordination. Continuity—of a sort—was assured.

Many of the theoretical ideas presented in this book are connected with liminal aspects of mortuary behavior. Perhaps most closely associated with the works of Arnold van Gennep (1961) in Madagascar and Victor Turner (1967, 1969) among the Ndembu of southern Africa, liminality in funerary ritual has been defined as a transitional state wherein the deceased is between normal societal roles. It can be explained in terms of change, process, and passage (Metcalf and Huntington 1991:33); ultimately it is a transitional state wherein the dead move from one social status to another. Theoretically, these concepts overlap with the works of scholars like Robert Hertz (1960) in Indonesia, who examined periods in which the body was considered neither fully alive nor dead. The ritual process included secondary burials as well as feasting, with the intent being to change the status of the deceased from a defunct person into an ancestor; his attention to the ways in which the changing state of the body reflected the changing state of the soul, together with his focus on the ritual process, formed the backbone of many mortuary studies to come.

The change from defunct body to ancestor is, as Hertz and others have argued, oftentimes informed by the idea that society not only has lost a member but also has been presented with a threat to its existence, in the "very principle of its life" (Hertz 1960:78; Metcalf and Huntington 1991), that must be adequately dealt with by the living. The dead body "highlights the passage of time, the inevitability of physical transformation, and thereby acts as a powerful reminder that the self is subject to change" (Hallam et al. 1999:5). As Foucault has noted, even the moment of death itself is a setting wherein the monotony of life is transcended; a life that is otherwise dull, ordinary, or routine takes on an extraordinary, dramatic character, with interpersonal relationships between the living and the dead laid bare (Foucault in Miller 1991). Each of these considerations is particularly salient in the case of the elite body in Mesoamerica, where the body in a moment of crisis forms a site where notions of the self and its relationship to a functioning society are highlighted (e.g., see Fitzsimmons 2009). Several of the authors deal with the threat and subsequent resolution to societal existence that elite (particularly royal) death provides. For example, the chapter by Blomster looks at how dominant ancestors were "deployed" by elites to reinforce their political and religious legitimacy in Oaxaca; bones and images of ancestors were, in precolumbian Oaxaca, not only objects of reverence but also a means to a sociopolitical end. Ancestors became ritually "reintegrated" into society as symbols of authority in Oaxaca much as they were in other parts of Mesoamerica. We might see the elites of these papers replaying the crisis of death time and again, with its successful resolution both the prerogative and (partial) source of their power.

Yet giving primacy to the "resolution" of death over the "success" of Mesoamerican elites in times of crisis perhaps bestows too finite a nature to mortuary ritual. As several scholars have noted, much of the early anthropological work on death was so focused on beginnings, on middles, and on endings that ritual itself was viewed as something finite, and the ritual process clearly definable; of course ritual, mortuary or otherwise, is more complex than this and can lack clear spatial or temporal boundaries (e.g., Bell 1992; Hallam et al. 1999; Parkin 1992; Seremetakis 1991). Examples abound in the archaeology, anthropology, and ethnohistory of Mesoamerica where the boundaries between ritual and routine social activities are blurred—why should mortuary ritual be any different? And if we take the position that applying a rigid, clearly defined model for ritual behavior in Mesoamerica is mistaken, what does this mean for the finality or resolution of death as applied to the creation of ancestors? In line with Seremetakis, acknowledging "the problematic nature of discrete beginnings and endings also assumes that there is never a full restoration of social stability; that death, its representation, its discourses, and its performative elaboration can haunt society and become an essential collective metaphor of social experience beyond the margins of ceremonial performance" (1991:48). We might see death as never truly "resolved" in the Mesoamerican context. Certainly, Mesoamerican elites, such as the Oaxacans mentioned above, performed mortuary rituals with clearly defined end points. But the ability to revisit death, as is described in this volume time and again, stems from a fundamental lack of theoretical finality. We might view death as having two aspects or levels: acute, represented by the point of expiration or the (more or less) bounded rituals undertaken by descendants, and chronic, represented by the ability of death and the dead to resurface time and again. The Mesoamerican elites of this volume revisit the acute aspects of death by virtue of its chronic features. It is the paradoxical fact that death as an event is both over and never truly over that makes ancestors so powerful in the Mesoamerican context. Some social theorists have described the western conception of the body as a being in the process of becoming, recognizing a gradual finishing process leading toward death informed by social as well as biological considerations ranging from the ongoing production of self-identity to wrinkles, scarring, and clothing (Giddens 1991; Shilling 1993). Physical death is, however, separate from social death, and in the latter case, western-style "finishing" becomes blurred: as Hallam et al. (1999:49) have noted, the social body is made "*atemporal* in preserved images of the live body in fitness and health" as well as in paintings, photographs, and other representations of the self. When we look at the papers in this volume, however, we are dealing not only with the purposeful continuation of the social body through images but also with the interaction between the living and ancestral human remains. Many of the items under consideration in this volume, bone or otherwise, were considered to be more than simply objects. Oftentimes they were considered to be animate, bearing either the identity of the deceased or a new, imposed character. We might therefore say that the body in ancient Mesoamerica was never truly "finished."

Notes

1. Indeed, as Rosemary Joyce (2001) has noted, these events are informed by a set of practices and behaviors that begin long before the individual is actually deceased.

2. We might view the good death, in addition to commemorative rituals in various forms, as fundamentally prospective or forward-looking. As K. M. George (1996:200) has noted, proper mortuary behavior offers a "structure of anticipation" in which individuals are told—by virtue of their participation in the belief or practice—how things were, how they are, and how they will (or should) be.

Works Cited

Beetz, Carl P., and Linton Sattherthwaite
1981   Monuments and Inscriptions of Caracol, Belize. Monograph 44. University of Pennsylvania, University Museum, Philadelphia.
Bell, Catherine
1992   Ritual Theory, Ritual Practice. Oxford University Press, New York.
Blanton, Richard E., and Gary Feinman
1984   Mesoamerican World System. American Anthropologist 86(3):673–682.
Bloch, Maurice
1982   Death, Women and Power. In Death and the Regeneration of Life, edited by Maurice Bloch and Jonathan Parry, pp. 211–230. Cambridge University Press, Cambridge.
Braswell, Geoffrey E. (editor)
2003   The Maya and Teotihuacan: Reinterpreting Early Classic Interaction. University of Texas Press, Austin.
Cabrera Castro, Rubén
1977–   Exploraciones en Tzintzuntzan, Michoacán: Décima temporada de excavaciones.
1978   Instituto Nacional de Antropología e Historia, Mexico City.
Carmack, Robert M., and Gary Gossen
2006   The Legacy of Mesoamerica: History and Culture of a Native American Civilization. 2nd ed. Prentice Hall, Upper Saddle River, New Jersey.
Chesson, Meredith S. (editor)
2001   Social Memory, Identity, and Death: Anthropological Perspectives on Mortuary Rituals. Archaeological Papers of the American Anthropological Association No. 10. University of California Press, Berkeley.
Ciudad Ruiz, Andrés, Mario Humberto Ruz Sosa, and María Josefa Iglesias Ponce de León (editors)
2003   Antropología de la eternidad: La muerte en la cultura maya. Sociedad Española de Estudios Mayas, Madrid.
Coe, Michael
1962   Costa Rican archaeology and Mesoamerica. Southwestern Journal of Anthropology 18(2):170–183.

Eberl, Markus
1999   Tod und begräbnis in der klassischen Maya-Kultur. Unpublished Master's thesis, Philosophische Fakultät, Rheinische Friedrich-Wilhelms-Universität, Bonn.
Evans, Susan T.
2004   Ancient Mexico and Central America: Archaeology and Culture History. Thames and Hudson, New York.
Fitzsimmons, James L.
2009   Death and the Classic Maya Kings. University of Texas Press, Austin.
Furst, Jill L.
1995   Natural History of the Soul in Ancient Mexico. Yale University Press, New Haven.
George, Kenneth M.
1996   Showing Signs of Violence: The Cultural Politics of a Twentieth-Century Head-hunting Ritual. University of California Press, Berkeley.
Giddens, Anthony
1991   Modernity and Self-Identity: Self and Society in the Late Modern Age. Polity Press, Cambridge.
Gillespie, Susan
2001   Personhood, Agency, and Mortuary Ritual: A Case Study from the Ancient Maya. Journal of Anthropological Archaeology 20:73–112.
2002   Body and Soul among the Maya: Keeping the Spirits in Place. In The Space and Place of Death, edited by Helaine Silverman and David B. Small, pp. 67–78. Archaeological Papers of the AAA No. 11. University of California Press, Berkeley.
Graham, Ian, and Eric Von Euw
1977   Corpus of Maya Hieroglyphic Inscriptions 3(1): Yaxchilan. Harvard University, Peabody Museum of Archaeology and Ethnology, Cambridge.
Hallam, Elizabeth, Jenny Hockey, and Glennys Howarth
1999   Beyond the Body: Death and Social Identity. Routledge, London.
Haskell, David L.
2008   The cultural logic of hierarchy in the Tarascan state: History as ideology in the Relación de Michoacán. Ancient Mesoamerica 19(2):231–242.
Hertz, Robert
1960   A Contribution to the Study of the Collective Representation of Death. In Death and the Right Hand, edited by Rodney Needham and Claudia Needham. Free Press, New York.
Houston, Stephen D., John Robertson, and David Stuart
2000   The Language of Classic Maya Inscriptions. Current Anthropology 41(3):321–356.
2001   More on the Language of Classic Maya Inscriptions. Current Anthropology 42(4):558–559.
Houston, Stephen D., David Stuart, and Karl Taube
2006   The Memory of Bones: Body, Being and Experience Among the Classic Maya. University of Texas Press, Austin.

Joyce, Rosemary

2001   Burying the Dead at Tlatilco: Social Memory and Social Identities. In *Social Memory, Identity, and Death: Anthropological Perspectives on Mortuary Rituals*, edited by Meredith S. Chesson, pp. 12–26. Archaeological Papers of the American Anthropological Association No. 10. University of California Press, Berkeley.

Kepecs, Susan

2005   Mayas, Spaniards, and Salt: World Systems Shifts in Sixteenth-Century Yucatan. In *The Postclassic to Spanish-Era Transition in Mesoamerica: Archaeological Perspectives*, edited by Susan Kepecs and Rani T. Alexander, pp. 117–138. University of New Mexico Press, Albuquerque.

López Austin, Alfredo

1984   Cuerpo humano e ideología: Las concepciones de los antiguos Nahuas. Serie Antropológica 39. Universidad Nacional Autónoma de México, Instituto de Investigaciones Antropológicas, Mexico.

López Luján, Leonardo

2005   *The Offerings of the Templo Mayor of Tenochtitlan*. University of New Mexico Press, Albuquerque.

Martínez López, Cira, Marcus Winter, and Pedro Antonio Juárez

1995   Entierros humanos del Proyecto Especial Monte Albán 1992–1994. In *Entierros humanos de Monte Albán: Dos estudios*, edited by Marcus Winter, pp. 79–244. Proyecto Especial Monte Alban 1992–1994, Contribución No. 7. Centro Instituto Nacional de Antropología e Historia, Oaxaca.

Metcalf, Peter, and Richard Huntington

1991   *Celebrations of Death: The Anthropology of Mortuary Ritual*. 2nd ed. Cambridge University Press, Cambridge.

Miller, Mary E.

1991   On the eve of collapse: Maya art of the eighth century. In *Lowland Maya Civilization in the Eighth Century*, edited by Jeremy Sabloff and John Henderson, pp. 355–414. Dumbarton Oaks Research Library and Collections, Washington, D.C.

Moberg, Mark A.

1988   Between Agency and Dependence: Belizean Households in a Changing World System. Unpublished Ph.D. dissertation, University of California, Los Angeles, Department of Anthropology, Los Angeles.

O'Shea, John

1996   *Villagers of the Maros: A Portrait of an Early Bronze Age Society*. Springer Verlag, New York.

Parkin, David

1992   Ritual as spatial direction and bodily division. In *Understanding Rituals*, edited by David De Coppet, pp. 11–25. Routledge, London.

Pollard, Helen P., and Laura Calue

1999   Mortuary patterns of regional elites in the Lake Patzcuaro Basin of western Mexico. *Latin American Antiquity* 10(3):259–280.

Ricketson, Oliver
1925   Burials in the Maya Area. *American Anthropologist* 27(3):381–401.

Robertson, William I.
2001   Transnational Processes, Development Studies and Changing Social Hierarchies in the World System: A Central American Case Study. *Third World Quarterly* 22(4):529–563.

Ruz Lhuillier, Alberto
1968   *Costumbres funerarias de los antiguos Mayas*. Universidad Nacional Autonoma de México, Mexico.

Santley, Robert S., and Rani T. Alexander
1996   Teotihuacán and Middle Classic Mesoamerica: A Pre-Columbian World System? In *Arqueología mesoamericana: Homenaje a William T. Sanders*, edited by Alba Guadalupe Mastache, Jeffrey R. Parsons, Robert S. Santley, and Mari Carmen Serra Puche, pp. 173–194. Instituto Nacional de Antropología e Historia, Mexico.

Schele, Linda, and Peter Mathews
1998   *The Code of Kings: The Language of Seven Sacred Maya Temples and Tombs*. Scribner, New York.

Seremetakis, C. Nadia
1991   *The Last Word: Women, Death and Divination in Inner Mani*. University of Chicago Press, Chicago.

Shilling, Chris
1993   *The Body and Social Theory*. Sage Press, London.

Smith, Michael E.
2002   *Aztecs*. Blackwell, Oxford.

Smith, Michael E., and Frances F. Berdan
2000   Postclassic Mesoamerican World System. *Current Anthropology* 41(2):283–286.
2003   Spatial Structure of the Mesoamerican World System. In *The Postclassic Mesoamerican World*, edited by Michael E. Smith and Frances F. Berdan, pp. 21–34.

Storey, Rebecca
1992   *Life and Death in the Ancient City of Teotihuacan: A Modern Paleodemographic Study*. University of Alabama Press, Tuscaloosa.

Sugiyama, Saburo, and Rubén Cabrera Castro
2003   Hallazgos recientes en la Pirámide de la Luna. *Arqueología Mexicana* 11(64):42–49.

Taube, Karl
2003   Maws of Heaven and Hell: The Symbolism of the Centipede and Serpent in Classic Maya Religion. In *Antropología de la eternidad: La muerte en la cultura maya*, edited by A. Ciudad Ruiz, Mario Humberto Ruz Sosa, and María Josefa Iglesias Ponce de Léon, pp. 405–442. Sociedad Española de Estudios Mayas, Madrid.
2004   Flower Mountain: Concepts of life, Beauty, and Paradise Among the Classic Maya. *RES: Anthropology and Aesthetics* 45:69–98.

Thompson, Edward
1896   *Ancient Tombs of Palenque*. Charles Hamilton, Worcester, Mass.
Tiesler Blos, Vera, and Andrea Cucina (editors)
2006   *Janaab' Pakal of Palenque: Reconstructing the Life and Death of a Maya Ruler*. University of Arizona Press, Tucson.
Turner, Victor
1967   *The Forest of Symbols: Aspects of Ndembu Ritual*. Cornell University Press, Ithaca.
1969   *The Ritual Process: Structure and Anti-Structure*. Walter de Gruyter, New York.
Van Gennep, Arnold
1961/   *The Rites of Passage*. Translated by Monika Vizdom and Gabrielle L. Caffee.
[1909] University of Chicago Press, Chicago.
Wallerstein, Immanuel
1976   *The Modern World-System*. Academic Press, New York.
Weiner, Annette B.
1976   *Women of Value, Men of Renown: New Perspectives in Trobriand Exchange*. University of Texas Press, Austin.
Wells, Christian E., and Karla L. Davis-Salazar
2007   *Mesoamerican Ritual Economy: Archaeological and Ethnological Perspectives*. University of Colorado Press, Boulder.
Welsh, W.B.M.
1988   *An Analysis of Classic Lowland Maya Burials*. BAR International Series 409. British Archaeological Reports, Oxford.
Winter, Marcus
2002   Monte Albán: Mortuary Practices as Domestic Ritual and Their Relation to Community Religion. *Domestic Ritual in Ancient Mesoamerica*, edited by Patricia Plunket, pp. 67–82. Costen Institute of Archaeology, University of California, Los Angeles.
Winter, Marcus, William O. Autry, Jr., Richard G. Wilkinson, and Cira Martínez López
1995   Entierros humanos en una area residencial de Monte Albán: Temporadas 1972–1973. In *Entierros humanos de Monte Albán: Dos estudios*, edited by Marcus Winter, pp. 11–78. Proyecto Especial Monte Alban 1992–1994, Contribución No. 7. Centro Instituto Nacional de Antropología e Historia, Oaxaca.

CHAPTER 2

The Role of Dead Bodies in Late Classic Maya Politics

Cross-Cultural Reflections on the Meaning of Tikal Altar 5

ESTELLA WEISS-KREJCI

DEAD BODIES HAVE PLAYED and still play a tremendous role in politics. Struggles over the choice of burial place and fights over corpses have been documented from various time periods and parts of the world (Fox 1987; Robson 2003; Waterson 1995). These include the historic and legendary competitions over the corpses of Oedipus, Martin of Tours, Francis of Assisi, Ansfrid of Utrecht, Francis of Sales, and German-Roman king Albert II (Meyer 2000:160; Ohler 1990:95–99; Verdery 1999:1). Disputes over the role of participants in the funeral arose after the death of French king Henri IV (Giesey 1960:123–124), German-Roman emperor Maximilian I (Schmid 1997:205), and the British Queen Mother in 2002, during whose lying-in-state—according to sections of the British press— then prime minister Tony Blair assumed an improper role.

Ownership claims to dead bodies are made not only with regard to the newly deceased, but also to those who have been defunct for quite some time. Mortal remains of famous people as well as anonymous dead have been exhumed, reburied, or desecrated in order to elevate or degrade the status of their owners, to construct new affiliations between groups, and to rewrite history and retrieve social memory (Verdery 1999:1–3; Johnson 2004). In Guatemala exhumation and reburial of massacre victims was central in the process of democratization. Desecration of graves (e.g., Jewish graves), destruction of shrines (e.g., a Shiite shrine in Samarra), rallies at monuments and tombs of venerated idols by far-right organizations (e.g., William of Orange in Delft), and the continuous conflict between scientists and indigenous and spiritual groups over repatriation, restoration, and nondisturbance of human remains confirm that dead bodies play a very important and active role in our modern world.

This article is inspired by Katherine Verdery's (1999) study of dead-body politics in postsocialist Eastern Europe. In the 1990s in Russia, Romania, Hungary, Bulgaria, Poland, Ukraine, and the former Yugoslavia, a variety of exhumations and reburials of named and famous as well as anonymous dead played an essential role in the process of political and social renewal. Not only dead bodies but also statues and monuments—another kind of dead people—were moved.

These manipulations of dead bodies and monuments in Eastern Europe happened at a time of major social and political transformation. Verdery argues that dead bodies become especially important whenever "worlds" are being reordered and changes in social relations, political ideas, behavior, worldviews, and religious ideas take place. "World" for Verdery is a combination between worldview and associated action in the world. People's ideas and actions constantly influence each other in a dynamic way. "Beliefs and ideas materialized in action" is Verdery's definition of culture, which she draws from Bourdieu (1977).

> In moments of major transformations, people may find that new forms of action are more productive than the ones they are used to, or that older forms make sense in a different way, or that ideals they could only aspire to before are now realizable. Such moments lead to reconfiguring one's world; the process can be individual and collective, and is often driven by the activities of would-be elites (in competition with one another). (Verdery 1999:34)

Although Verdery considers the manipulation of dead bodies in the postsocialist context as unique, especially because of the magnitude and speed of change, the use of the dead for political purposes is quite common throughout the world. Dead bodies are highly effective political symbols. Bones, coffins, urns, statues, and monuments that represent dead people can be moved around. They can be displayed and strategically located in specific places to localize a claim. Dead people's life stories can be used by different people to very different ends. Additionally, dead bodies have a concreteness that transcends time and evokes the awe associated with cosmic concerns such as the meaning of life and death. This lends them an extra sacred quality (Verdery 1999:27–31).

Dead Body Manipulations among the Ancient Maya

The hieroglyphic inscriptions on monuments and many of the tombs and skeletons themselves suggest that the ancient Maya, who once lived in the region that is now southern Mexico, Guatemala, Belize, northwestern Honduras, and northern El Salvador (fig. 2.1), used the dead in a variety of ways. Ancient reentries, not only to place bodies but to remove bones and artifacts—and in some instances burning—have been archaeologically recorded at several sites. Texts on altars and stelae also refer to tomb visits, tomb censing, and exhumation and reburial (Chase and Chase 1996, 2003; Eberl 2005; Fitzsimmons 1998, 2006; Houston et al. 1998; Martin and Grube 2000; McAnany 1995, 1998; Stuart 1998; Wagner 2006). Many of these rites have been interpreted as protracted burial rites, secondary rituals, or ancestor cult (Chase and Chase 1996; Eberl 2005; McAnany 1995, 1998). In this chapter I try to show that specific types of exhumations existed among the ancient Maya that were primarily of a political nature.

Robert Hertz (1907, 1960) and Arnold Van Gennep (1909, 1960) first discussed depositions of corpses that are not the end point in the funeral but form stages in a mortuary program comprising exhumation and reburial (see also Metcalf and Huntington 1991). Hertz saw these secondary rites as embedded in an ideology in which the passage of a person from life to death is only a gradual one. Using the example of extended burial rituals in Indonesia, he drew attention to the parallel processes of decay, mourning, and the changing state of the soul. The body of the deceased, while awaiting a second burial, is temporarily deposited in a place distinct from the final one. Once the corpse has decomposed and the bones are dry, the final funeral is held. The soul can enter the land of the dead, and the mourning is over.

However, temporary storage and exhumation can take place for a variety of reasons unrelated to ideas of prolonged dying, a necessity for completion of putrefaction, or a journey of the soul. The long time period that usually elapses between first disposal and the final funeral may allow the survivors to reorganize their social relations. The timing of second funerals can also be strongly caused by economic considerations (Hutchinson and Aragon 2002:30; Miles 1965). When buildings, crypts,

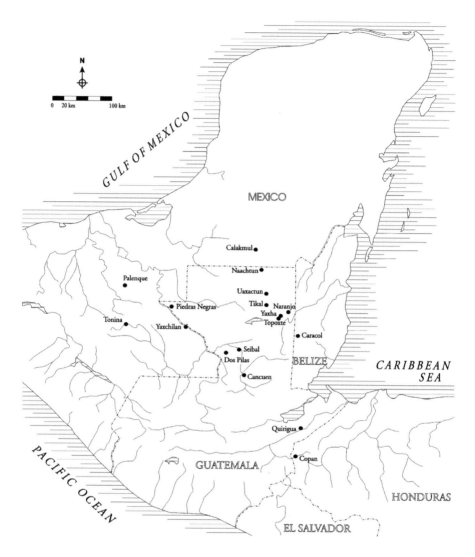

FIGURE 2.1. Map of the Maya Area.

or tombs are not yet ready to house the mortal remains, corpses may also be stored and later reburied. If somebody dies in a distant area and needs to be transported back home, considerable delays between death and final deposition are possible (Weiss-Krejci 2005). Among the Merina of Madagascar, a reburial ceremony (*famadihana*) is usually held to return

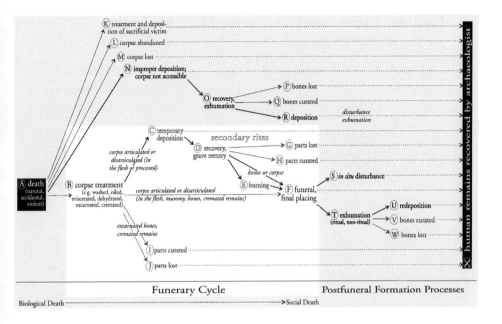

FIGURE 2.2. Schema of post- and extrafuneral exhumations and redepositions.

to the ancestral tomb a corpse that has originally been buried elsewhere. Bloch points out that, in contrast to Indonesian practices, Merina funerals are also completed without a famadihana, and that these reburials are not thought to change the nature of the soul (Bloch 1971:146, 162).

Figure 2.2 depicts the main processes that bodies may go through after death. All the rites described above follow through stages B-C-D-(E)-F. They belong within the funerary cycle, although—as in the case of prolonged body storage—the boundary between funeral and postfuneral mortuary ritual can become blurred. However, there exist other types of exhumations that are not embedded in the funerary ritual at all. They are not related to temporary storage and do not constitute secondary burial rites. They lie beyond the funerary cycle, but discussing them in terms of ancestor cult would also fall short of the complexity associated with them. They usually follow very different motivations and attract a lot of public attention. Figure 2.2 shows their possible stages (F-S, F-T-U, or N-O-R). These post- and extrafuneral depositions are the topic of this chapter.

Post- and Extrafuneral Rites in the Maya Lowlands during the Late Classic

The majority of historically and archaeologically recorded dead-body manipulations in the Maya area took place in the seventh and eighth centuries AD (Eberl 2005; Fitzsimmons 1998, 2006; Martin and Grube 2000). These were times of frequent wars and dynastic struggles in the Central Lowlands (Tikal, Calakmul, Naranjo, Caracol, etc.), in the western region (Piedras Negras, Yaxchilan, Palenque, Tonina), and in the south (Copan and Quirigua) (fig. 2.1; Demarest 2004; Martin and Grube 2000, 2008). It appears that during these times dead bodies became vehicles for the expression of political identities and legitimization of power. This process probably originated in the second half of the sixth century, when major political transformations started to take place in the Maya Lowlands. It led to the reordering of the entire Maya "universe" in the sense of Verdery. I will try to outline this process and its consequences for the dead using the example of the site of Tikal.

Tikal's Political Development from the Sixth to the Eighth Centuries

From the middle of the sixth century on, fundamental changes took place in the Maya Lowlands. Teotihuacan in central Mexico, which had close ties to the Maya Lowlands in the Early Classic, collapsed, and interregional wars, internal struggles for succession, and military defeat plunged the once powerful city of Tikal into a "dark age" (Martin and Grube 2000:39). An attack by an enemy site in AD 562 probably cost Tikal's king Wak Chan K'awiil his life and initiated the "Hiatus," a period of 130 years in which no Tikal monument was carved (AD 562–692) (Houston 1991; Martin 2003; Moholy-Nagy 2003a). Tikal's history during this time is mainly known through the inscriptions from other sites.

While Tikal declined, its biggest rival, Calakmul, flourished. This center in the north (fig. 2.1) established alliances with a variety of kingdoms (e.g., Caracol, Cancuen, and Dos Pilas) and instigated a series of wars against Tikal throughout the seventh century. Under the auspices of Calakmul, the Petexbatun site of Dos Pilas and its king, who directly descended from the Tikal line and used the Tikal emblem glyph, defeated his own relatives in AD 679 (Boot 2002; Demarest 2004:226–238; Guenter 2003; Martin 2003:25–30).

Only at the end of the seventh century did Tikal regain its original strength, after Jasaw Chan K'awiil I (reign AD 682–734) won a decisive victory over Calakmul in AD 695. With him the period of silence and the Hiatus ended. Although the wars continued throughout the eighth century, Tikal's situation seems more stable during the reign of this king, as well as under his successor, Yik'in Chan K'awiil (reign AD 734–746), who fully restored Tikal's power (Martin and Grube 2000:44–50).

Tikal North Acropolis in the Seventh Century: Reburial of Stelae and Bones

The first extensive dead-body manipulations happened at Tikal in the seventh century AD (early Late Classic period) and coincided with the Hiatus. In the North Acropolis, the burial place of many of the Tikal kings, redeposition of Early Classic (AD 250–600) bones on the one hand and stone monuments[1] on the other formed part of a massive construction program which took place between 9.8.0.0.0 and 9.12.0.0.0 (= AD 593–672, North Acropolis Time Span 5) (Coe 1990:840–846). These ritual activities seemed to commemorate two specific Early Classic dynasties, the dynasty of K'inich Muwaan Jol, thirteenth ruler of Tikal (fourth century), and the succeeding dynasty, which started with the fifteenth ruler Yax Nuun Ahiin I and held the power from the late fourth to the early sixth century (Martin and Grube 2000:26–32).

Toward the middle of the seventh century, during the reign of the unknown Tikal rulers 23 and 24, the fifth-century Stela 31 was entombed beneath Temple 33 (Coe 1990:756–759). It is dedicated to the Early Classic lord Sihyaj Chan K'awiil II, sixteenth ruler of Tikal, son of Yax Nuun Ahiin I and grandson of the central Mexican lord Spearthrower Owl. Also around the same time, Stela 1—another stela of Sihyaj Chan K'awiil II— was reset in front of Structure 26 (Coe 1990:782–783), and Problematical Deposit 22 (PD 22) was buried in close proximity. Coe (1990:324–327) believes that it holds the cleared-out remains of a burial. PD 22 included Early Classic and Intermediate Classic vessel sherds (Culbert 1993:figs. 123–126). One of these sherds carries the name of the nineteenth ruler in line, Kaloomte' B'alam, consort of Lady of Tikal, who belonged to the Yax Nuun Ahiin patri-line (Martin 2003:20). PD 22 also contained various fragments of Early Classic monuments; human cranial, mandible, and dental parts of an adult male, along with major long bones and numerous bones of hands and feet, many altered by fire; Early Classic types of eccentric chert and obsidian; one metate; jade and shell beads and mosaic elements; one fragmentary imitation stingray spine; several unmodified marine shells; one deer antler and metapodial; a dog tooth; land turtle shell fragments and a turtle foot; crocodile scutes; and a quail humerus (Coe 1990:324–327; Moholy-Nagy 2003b:Appendix F, 2008).[2] Around the middle of the seventh century, two royal tombs, Burials 23 and 24 (Coe 1990:536–543), were also placed in close proximity to Sihyaj Chan K'awiil II's grave in Temple 33. They probably held the remains of Tikal rulers 23 and 24 (Martin 2003:25).

The last Hiatus king is Nuun Ujol Chaak, the twenty-fifth ruler of Tikal, who enters history in AD 657 and ruled until at least AD 679. The bitter dynastic feud with his brother B'alaj Chan K'awiil of Dos Pilas dominated Tikal's politics during the second part of the seventh century (Boot 2002; Guenter 2003; Houston 1993; Martin 2003:26). During his reign the smashed Early Classic Stela 26, attributed to the fourth-century ruler Chak Tok Ich'aak I, fourteenth Tikal ruler and son of K'inich Muwaan Jol (Martin and Grube 2000:28), was buried under an altar in Temple 34, together with four caches (Coe 1990:744–745). Caches 14A, 14B, and 14D contained human finger bones and a variety of animal bones.[3] The shattered Stela 26, which was covered with cinnabar, resembled the state of the bones in several Maya royal tombs. The reburial of Stela 26 took place in the temple that covers Burial 10. According to Coggins (1975) this tomb holds the remains of Chak Tok Ich'aak's immediate successor, Nuun Yax Ahiin I, the son of the Teotihuacan king Spearthrower Owl, who founded a new Tikal dynastic line.

The Use of the Dead by Jasaw Chan K'awiil I and His Successors

Tikal's revitalization at the end of the seventh and in the eighth century, during the reign of Rulers 26 to 29, the son, grandson, and great-grandsons of Nuun Ujol Chaak (Jasaw Chan Kawiil I, Yik'in Chan K'awiil, Ruler 28, and Yax Nuun Ahiin II; see Martin and Grube 2008), was once again accompanied by extensive commemoration of the dead and elaborate deposition rituals. However, in addition to reburying bones like their predecessors of the Hiatus period, these Late Classic kings applied a wider range of strategies of dead-body use. They recorded their commemoration of the dead on wooden lintels and stone monuments and also made references to royal dead persons from other dynasties and places. These rites often took place in conjunction with anniversaries and served to draw connections between foreign polities and the Tikal kingdom. Tikal's victory over Calakmul in AD 695, for example, was commemorated on a wooden lintel in Temple 1. The day selected for commemoration was the 13 *k'atun* (13 × 7,200 days) death anniversary of Spearthrower Owl, who had died in AD 439 (Martin and Grube 2000:45). Jasaw Chan K'awiil I was buried deep beneath this impressive temple in Burial 116, together with a collection of 37 incised bones. A number of the carved bones record the death dates of royal individuals from other kingdoms (Coggins 1975; Martin and Grube 2000:47).

The so-called twin-pyramid groups also developed during this time period. These groups comprised twin eastern and western stepped pyramids, with a variable number of pairs of plain stelae and altars in front of the eastern pyramid, a southern range structure with nine doors, and a northern enclosure with a carved stela and an altar pair (see fig. 2.3A). The northern monuments carry *k'atun* ending dates (one k'atun is a period of 20 years, or 7,200 days) (Ashmore 1991; Houston et al. 2006:83; Jones 1969; Rice 2004:121–124). The earliest recorded date in a twin-pyramid complex, 9.13.0.0.0. (AD 692, group 3D-1, Altar 14), falls into the reign of Jasaw Chan K'awiil I; the latest recorded date, 9.18.0.0.0. (AD 790, group 4E-3, Stela 19), dates to the reign of Yax Nuun Ahiin II.[4]

Twin-pyramid groups contain living and dead bodies in many shapes and forms (Weiss-Krejci 2010). When carved, the northern stela always bears the portrait of the current ruler in the act of performing a scattering ritual. A *k'altuun* glyph, which means the act of "stone binding," is legible on Stelae 16, 20, and 22. Houston et al. (2006:83–84) suppose that the purpose of this ritual was to protect and contain the divine essence held within the stones that embodied time and its movement. The substela deposits usually hold sets of flints and obsidians symbolizing Maya deities, as well as human skulls, teeth, and long bones, deer leg bones, and snake vertebrae. The predominance of human skulls and long bones as

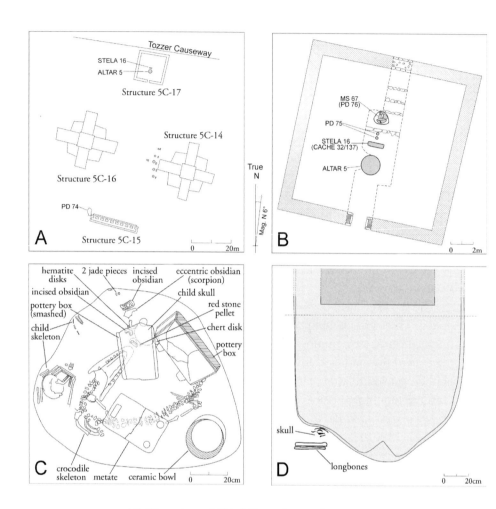

FIGURE 2.3. (A) Plan view of Tikal Twin-Pyramid Group N (Group 5C-1) and Problematical Deposit PD 74 (after Jones 1969:fig. 6). (B) Plan view of Str. 5C-17 with Stela 16, Altar 5, and Problematical Deposits 75 and Miscellaneous Monument MS 67, which covered PD 76. Based on field drawing D47 and sketch in Christopher Jones's unpublished notebook (Jones 1963:34). (C) Plan view of Problematical Deposit 76 without MS 67 (Jones 1963:D17). (D) Human skull and long bones (Cache 137) from below Stela 16 (after unpublished drawing by Sally Bates in Jones 1963:D2; courtesy of Penn Museum).

well as specific animal species suggests that these played a particular role in the *k'altuun* rituals. As among many groups throughout the world, the Maya saw the head as the essential manifestation of the body (Houston et al. 2006:68). Deer are associated with fertility and life renewal, and it is out of the maw of the snake that the ancestors are reborn (Emery 2004:105). Beyond the stela deposits, a variety of worked and unworked animal bones belonging to other sacred animals, such as crocodile, turtle, opossum, peccary, dog, and jaguar, were also encountered in these types of groups. Thirteen artifacts made from human bone derive from the southern building of Group 5C-1 (Moholy-Nagy 2003b:Appendix F).

Bodies also loom large on the associated altars. Altars 8, 10, and 6 (*k'atuns* 16, 17, and 18) display bound captives. The earlier Altar 5 shows Jasaw Chan K'awiil I and a lord from another power sphere exhuming and redepositing the bones of a noble lady, eight years after her death and 31 days before the completion of the fourteenth *k'atun* in AD 711. Altar 5 is located in Group 5C-1 (fig. 2.3A), also known as Twin-Pyramid complex N. This group marks the beginning of a new era in twin-pyramid group construction based on both the architecture and the types of ritual deposits (Jones 1969:111–112).[5]

Altar 5

The Context of Altar 5

Tikal Altar 5 is one of the most outstanding examples of eighth-century dead-body use. This monument emphasizes the alliance between Tikal and the kingdom of Maasal, two polities that did not always entertain friendly relationships (Martin and Grube 2000:37). Altar 5 is coupled with Stela 16 (Jones and Satterthwaite 1982:37), which depicts Jasaw Chan K'awiil I performing the k'altuun ritual of 9.14.0.0.0. (= AD 711). Both monuments were discovered by Teobert Maler in 1904 (Maler 1911:85–90) on the centerline of the northern building 5C-17 (figs. 2.3A and 2.3B).

During the excavation of the center trench in 1963, Christopher Jones encountered three formal human remains deposits. Problematical Deposit 75 (fig. 2.3B) held the weathered scraps of two separate adult skulls and seven adult teeth (one incisor probably filed) associated with pottery fragments, unworked deer bones, flint and obsidian flakes and

limestone monument pieces (Op. 43C, Lot 17; Object Catalogue Card/
Human Bone, 43C-59/60).

About 1.75 meters north of Stela 16, Jones found a pit that had been
dug into the construction fill, Problematical Deposit 76 (Op. 43C, Lot 26).
The bottom of the pit was occupied by a large river crocodile with its
head pointing north (fig. 2.3C). The crocodile was complete and articulated and apparently had been sacrificed and deposited on its back.[6] In
the same layer and to the north of the reptile's nose were several flint
and obsidian eccentrics and flakes, two incised obsidians depicting Maya
deities (Moholy-Nagy 2008:figs. 20c, 49a), jade, pyrite, and shell mosaic
elements, a scarcely altered oyster, and a badly preserved youth's skull
(Tikal Archives, Object Catalogue Card/Human Bone, 43C-21). In the
layer above the crocodile there were one ceramic bowl and two pottery
boxes (one badly smashed, the other containing dark, powdery organic
fill) (Culbert 1993:fig. 133c), a complete sandstone tripod metate (upside
down) (Moholy-Nagy 2003b:fig. 85d), and—to the west—a disarticulated,
incomplete child skeleton, approximately six years of age, mixed with a
few unidentified animal remains (Object Catalogue Card/Human Bone,
43C-20). The whole deposit was covered by a broken but complete, thin
disk of chalky, bedded limestone (MS 67; Jones 1963:34; Jones and Satterthwaite 1982:90). While PD 75 apparently postdates the setting of Altar 5
and Stela 16, PD 76 was probably deposited around the same time.

Another human remains deposit derives from the cache below Stela 16.
A part of the cache that contained eccentric flints and incised obsidians (Cache 32; Kidder 1947:21–23, figs. 8, 70, 72c; see also Moholy-Nagy
2008:fig. 45) had been partially removed in 1930 by General Eduardo
Hay from the Boundary Commission (Jones and Satterthwaite 1982:37;
Morley 1938:268, 341). In 1963 Jones continued this excavation, uncover-
ing a beer bottle from the 1930s and the rest of the cache (Op. 43C, Lots
32, 33). It consisted of flint and obsidian flakes and human bones pertaining to one individual between 12 and 20 years (Cache 137, fig. 2.3D). He
(or she) was missing one and a half molars, four premolars, one incisor,
and one canine. While small human bone fragments, skull fragments,
and long-bone fragments were present, ribs, vertebrae, and phalanges
were absent. Of the remaining 21 teeth, one upper incisor was notched
(Romero 1970, type B4); other front incisors may have been filed down
(Tikal Archives, Object Catalogue Card/Human Bone, 43C-7). Stuart

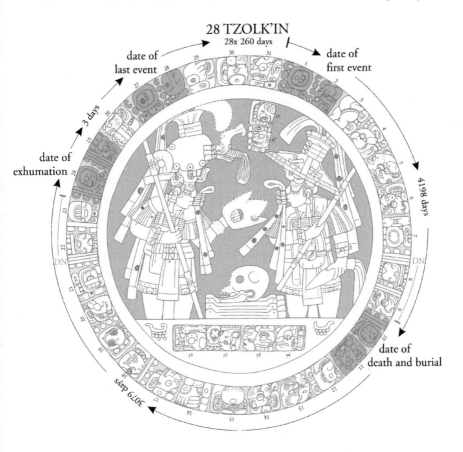

FIGURE 2.4. Tikal Altar 5 in Twin-Pyramid Complex N, eighth century AD (dark glyphs indicate Calendar Round dates); courtesy of the Penn Museum.

(1998:408) suggests that the human skull and long bones from below Stela 16 belong to the person whose exhumation is the topic of Altar 5. The strong resemblance between the position and orientation of the skull and long bones from below Stela 16 in Sally Bates's field drawing (fig. 2.3D) and on Tikal Altar 5 (fig. 2.4) strongly supports this hypothesis.

The Story on Altar 5

The story on the altar starts on 1 Muluk 2 Muwan 9.12.19.12.9 (November 25, AD 691) (fig. 2.4, position 1–2; dates in Morley 1938:339). On this specific day some unidentified event happened in the life of a lady named "Tuun Kayawak" (her name in fig. 2.4, glyphs 5–6, after Fitzsimmons 2002). The as yet undeciphered verb (glyph 3) consists of a headless, fat, and walking body and a *ya*-suffix. A distance number (DN) of 4,198 days (18.11.11) (fig. 2.4, position 8–9) indicates the time difference between the first event and the second event, which took place 11.5 years later, on 13 Manik' o Xul 9.13.11.6.7 (May 25, AD 703) (position 10–11). On this day, Lady Tuun Kayawak (her name in position 13–14) died (*chamiiy*, position 12) and was buried (*muhkaj*, position 17) in the "Nine Lord House" (position 18). The funeral was supervised by the Lord of Maasal (glyphs 19–20). A second distance number of 3,079 days (19.9.8) (fig. 2.4, position 22–23) leads to the date 11 Kimi 19 Mak 9.13.19.16.6 (October 29 AD 711, glyphs 24–25). On this day bones were exhumed (fig. 2.4, glyph 26 "it is opened" *pasaj*, glyph y1 "her bone"). The text underneath the skull and bones (position y2–y4) speaks of a lady whose name is not the same as the lady mentioned in the ring of glyphs. However, the text undoubtedly refers to the same dead person (Eberl 2005:99; Grube and Schele 1994:2). Three days later, on 1 Muluk 2 K'ank'in 9.13.19.16.9 (November 1, AD 711, glyphs 27–28), something (glyph 29, probably an arrival) happened in the company of the Kalo'mte' (glyphs 30–31). The depiction on Altar 5 clearly indicates the nature of this event. Tikal's king Jasaw Chan K'awiil I on the left and a lord from Maasal on the right (Martin and Grube 2008:46) are exhuming and reburying the skull and long bones of the noble lady. The story finally ends on Stela 16, which portrays Jasaw Chan K'awiil I completing the fourteenth *k'atun* on 6 Ahaw 13 Muwan (December 2, AD 711), 31 days after the last event on Altar 5.

Martin and Grube (2000:46) consider the scene on Altar 5 evidence for increased influence of Tikal to its north. Maasal shows consistent ties with Tikal's enemy Calakmul and is probably identical with the site of Naachtun (fig. 2.1). The exhumation and joint reburial of the noble lady by the king of Tikal and the king of Maasal in AD 711, and the emphasis on the alliance between these two kingdoms, may indicate an important shift in the power relations of the central lowlands after the main war of AD 695.

However, several questions remain. Who was the lady, where was she originally buried, why was she exhumed, where was she reburied, and what is the relationship between the two main actors on Altar 5? Are PD 76 and the substela cache of Stela 16 directly related to each other, and part of one ritual? What is the meaning and purpose of this ritual? While at present it is not possible to answer all of these questions (see also Fitzsimmons 2006:38), I will try to address some of them.

The Structure of Post- and Extrafuneral Exhumations

During an extensive analysis of historically documented exhumations from all over the world, I was able to identify four basic types of extrafuneral and postfuneral dead-body manipulations: (a) desecration, (b) rescue exhumation, (c) reconciliation exhumation, and (d) staged exhumation.

Type A: Desecration

Disturbance and desecration of graves and monuments are quite common throughout the world and frequent during wars and crisis (fig. 2.2, Process F-S, Process F-T-U). One quite recent example is the massive attack that was launched on the burial shrine of two revered leaders of Shiite Islam in Samarra, Iraq, in February 2006. In European history major desecration of tombs took place during wars and riots, for example, the Turkish wars, the Thirty Years' War, the French Revolution, and campaigns under Napoleon. Usually the bones or whatever was left were later reburied in their original graves (Brown 1985; Weiss-Krejci 2005). Desecration of graves during warfare was not uncommon among the ancient Maya either. Naranjo Stela 23 refers to the hostile opening of a grave and scattering of bones of the Yaxha king Yax B'olon Chaak in AD 710 a few months after Naranjo's victory over Yaxha (Eberl 2005:161; Martin and Grube 2000:76).

Type B: Rescue Exhumation

Rescue exhumations usually take place when the body is in some kind of danger of being destroyed, stolen, or simply coming under the dominance of an enemy force (fig. 2.2, Process F-T-U). Famous historic examples of rescue exhumations are the exhumations and reburials of Christopher Columbus and Galileo Galilei. Columbus, who died in 1506, was exhumed and reburied many times: first from Valladolid to La Cartuja at Seville, and then from Seville to Santo Domingo in 1537, where he lay till 1795. When the Spanish ceded the island to France, they decided that Columbus's remains should not fall into the hands of foreigners. So a set of remains that the Spaniards believed to be Columbus's were shipped to Havana and, when the Spanish-American War broke out in 1898, back to Seville (Donaldson and Donaldson 1989:39–41). The removals of Columbus's bones from Santo Domingo to Cuba in 1795 and from Cuba to Spain in 1898 were rescue exhumations directly caused by changing political conditions.

Galileo Galilei died a heretic, in 1642, for holding the Copernican view that the sun was the center of the universe. Since Pope Urban VIII denied the request of the city of Florence in Tuscany to honor the astronomer with a monument in Santa Croce, the body was laid to rest in the basement of the church (Donaldson and Donaldson 1989:71). In 1735, an arrangement was made among Austria, France, England, and the Netherlands that Tuscany should become part of the Habsburg Empire. To save the body from the Austrians, Gian Gastone, the last Medici ruler of Tuscany, commissioned a memorial in the church of Santa Croce. Before Austrian troops occupied Tuscany, Galileo's remains were transferred to the monument. During the exhumation on March 12, 1737, a devotee cut off Galileo's middle finger of the right hand. While the body was buried into the monument, the finger "with which the illustrious hand covered the heavens and indicated their immense space" (part of the text on the container that holds the finger) was not reburied (fig. 2.2, Process F-T-V). Today it is on display in the Florence Institute and Museum of the History of Science.

Type C: Reconciliation Exhumation

A third type of exhumation and reburial is reconciliation exhumation (fig. 2.2, Process N-O-R). These exhumations concern persons who have been either executed or murdered, did not receive a proper funeral, or are simply buried in the wrong place. In this group we find political icons like Che Guevara and Tsar Nicholas II, executed royals like Mary, Queen of Scots, Louis XVI, and Marie Antoinette (Weiss-Krejci 2008), and also the early Christian martyrs and anonymous dead like the victims of massacres and genocides.

Che Guevara and six of his companions were killed on October 9, 1967, and buried at a secret location in Bolivia. After the exhumation in July 1997, Che Guevara and his companions were reburied three months later in Cuba, in a huge public ceremony (Dosal 2004; Hart 2003). The Romanovs were killed during the night of July 16–17, 1918, in Yekaterinburg and hidden in the ground. The bodies were exhumed in 1991 and reburied in St. Petersburg, July 17, 1998, in the presence of Russian president Boris Yeltsin (Follath 1998). While reburial of Che Guevara in Cuba was a powerful political drama that celebrated the Cuban Revolution and emphasized the continuity of the socialist system, the reburial of the Russian tsar in 1998, on the other hand, celebrated its end. The funeral for the Romanovs was a way to pay respect to the representatives of a regime that had been brought down by the Russian Revolution.

Reconciliation exhumations and reburials are of a highly political and public nature, and the dead are often subject to complex political negotiations. Famous individuals as well as anonymous dead in this group play an important role in processes of the creation of collective, historic, and national identities. They have a high chance of being reburied more than just once. Postmortem status of individuals in this group can be elevated. The veneration of Che Guevara at Vallegrande, Bolivia, where he was shot, has reached dimensions that are comparable to the devotion to a saint (Dosal 2004; Taibo 2003).

Type D: Staged Exhumation

The fourth type is the staged exhumation, in which no real immediate threat to the corpse or necessity for exhumation exists (fig. 2.2, Process F-T-U). These people have died a proper death and received a proper funeral. However, like reconciliation exhumations, staged exhumations are highly political, and the postmortem status of the exhumed is transformed.

Translations of saints who are not martyrs are staged exhumations. While the relics of Christian martyrs were exhumed from the early Middle Ages on and distributed throughout Europe, in the later Middle Ages revered individuals and even some royal corpses achieved saintly status too. Once canonized, the bodies were exhumed in the ritual of *translatio,* and the relics were moved to a holier, more honorable position

(Finucane 1981:52–53). Nowadays, exhumations often serve to draw attention to a specific dead body and thus pave the way for beatification and canonization. The mechanisms for the selection of saints have often followed and still follow highly political objectives.

There also exist other kinds of staged exhumations that are not translation rituals. One of the best historical examples is the exhumation and reburial of the Duke of Reichstadt, the son of Napoleon. Napoleon was Austria's worst enemy and led warfare against it since 1796. When Napoleon occupied Vienna in 1809, the hand of the eldest daughter of Austrian emperor Francis I, Marie Louise, was the price for the peace treaty of Schönbrunn (Macartney 1968:193). Through intermarriage with the daughter of the former German-Roman emperor, Napoleon legitimized his right to rule.[7] The only son from the marriage was born in 1811 as Napoleon II, "king of Rome" but never ruled and therefore received the title of "Duke of Reichstadt." After his death in 1832 in Schönbrunn Castle at age 22, the duke was buried beside his grandfather in the Capuchin Vault in Vienna, the burial crypt of the House of Habsburg.

After resting at the Capuchin Vault for 108 years, the coffin with the body was removed on December 15, 1940, by order of Adolf Hitler.[8] It was transported from Vienna to Paris by train and deposited beside Napoleon's tomb on December 16 (Hawlik-van de Water 1993:213–218). Hitler's intentions were simple. The coffin was not only a tribute to the dead Napoleon but also a present to Marshal Philippe Pétain, the leader of the recently installed Vichy regime. It served to enforce the political ties between France and Germany. The date for the exhumation was also well chosen. It was the hundredth anniversary of the reburial of Napoleon at Les Invalides in Paris (Benoit 2007).

In this staged exhumation the corpse of Napoleon's son, a person of rather low political status, served to reverse history and connect two powerful people and places with each other: Pétain's France, formerly Napoleon's empire, with Hitler's Third Reich. Austria—until 1804 part of the German-Roman Empire—had been annexed by Hitler in 1938.

The Use of Anniversaries

Reconciliation (type c) and staged (type d) exhumations are specific ways to commemorate the dead or to bring them back into the public memory.

Therefore, it is hardly surprising that these types of exhumations and reburials usually happen on anniversaries. Desecrations (type a) are more sporadic, though in modern times they are also sometimes tied to anniversaries, as for example the attacks on Jewish graves on Hitler's birthday. Rescue exhumations (type b), on the other hand, are usually not associated with anniversaries.

Reconciliation exhumations (type c) often take place at death anniversaries. Che Guevara's reburial was connected to his thirtieth death anniversary; the Romanovs were reburied exactly 80 years after their death. On July 11, 2005, hundreds of victims were reburied in Srebrenica on the tenth anniversary of the massacre. All these reburials took place on dates that can be multiplied by ten. On the other hand, Mexican revolution hero Emiliano Zapata was exhumed and reburied on his thirteenth death anniversary, on April 10, 1932 (Brunk 2004:155). Thirteen is a number that played a special role in ancient Mexico's calendric systems.

In reconciliation exhumations round dates and anniversaries put a special emphasis on the fact that the acts of the past and those who committed them were wrong. Exhumation and reburial reverse the process of improper death and burial. Staged exhumations (type d) can also take place on death anniversaries, but are usually more constructed as in the case of Napoleon's son, who was exhumed on the hundredth anniversary of the reburial of his father.

Many Maya dead-body manipulations are also tied to anniversaries. The time units are always multiples of *tzolk'in* (1 *tzolk'in* is a period of 260 days), *tun* (360 days), *haab* (365 days), and *k'atun* (7,200 days). Most anniversaries in the Maya area, especially those from Piedras Negras and Tonina, are death anniversaries (Fitzsimmons 1998). Several small disk altars from Tonina record "tomb firing" rituals 260 days after the death of the individuals portrayed on them (Stuart 1998:397). Such rituals did not involve exhumation and reburial of the dead. Since they followed more or less regular patterns and took place not too long after death, they were probably part of the funerary cycle (fig. 2.2). In contrast, rituals that took place a long time after death, in some instances decades or centuries later, are not related to the initial mortuary rites. Despite their highly ritualistic nature, these events formed strategic postfuneral manipulations and served primarily political goals. Piedras Negras Stela 40, for example, shows Ruler 4 performing a ceremony at a tomb in AD 746—probably his mother's—83 tzolk'in after the death of Ruler 2 in AD 686 (Eberl 2005:153). Since Ruler 4 was not Ruler 3's son, the reference to Ruler 2 may have had special importance for the legitimization of his right to rule (for more examples, see Fitzsimmons 1998, 2006).

Ideas of Properness

Ideas of proper treatment and deposition of the dead loom large in reconciliation exhumations (type c) but generally play a role in all four exhumation types. To give a proper burial to a dead body is always a strong motivation to rebury a corpse. Rescue events (type b) create proper burial places for those whose bodies are endangered. Columbus and Galilei were in danger of falling into the hands of foreign polities. Galileo additionally had not been properly buried to begin with, because he had died as a heretic and the pope denied burial in a monument in the upper part of Santa Croce. Some individuals who were part of reconciliation exhumations (type c) never received a funeral. The murdered tsar and his family and Che and his companions had been hidden in the ground. And even in the case of a staged exhumation (type d), properness plays a role. The postmortem status change of a saint calls for a change of burial place. The bones are the material representative of the soul, and the physical translation is also a spiritual one. Hitler also corrected a mistake of improper burial by shipping off the Duke of Reichstadt to France. As a Bonaparte, the duke should have been buried in France in the first place, not in Austria. Finally, desecration (type a) is also connected to these ideas because the mortuary remains are purposely treated in an improper way.

The cross-cultural examples that I have given so far primarily derive from the Western World. However, proper treatment of the corpse and proper deposition have been important in many time periods and various regions of the world. In ancient Egypt, for example, proper treatment and deposition of the corpse was seen as a precondition for a successful journey of the soul and for rebirth (Meskell and Joyce 2003; Taylor 2001). Vice versa, improper burial can cause trouble for the living and endanger the souls of the dead. It can also have severe economic and political consequences. Among the Sa'dan Toraja of highland South Sulawesi, members of a descent group (*tongkonan*, the house) have the right to be buried into the collective house tomb (*liang*), which is often referred to as "the house of the ancestors." If a body is placed in the "wrong" tomb, that is, in a tomb where it has no right to be, it can happen that, years later, the body will be retrieved and placed in its own family liang (Waterson 1995:208–210). Since in the larger Austronesian world the association between a corpse and the other ancestors in the tomb serves as a basis for defining kinship groupings (Fox 1987; Waterson 1995), improper burial in a wrong tomb may eventually lead to improper claims to social position, land, and property by the descendants.

The Symbolic Meaning of Altar 5

Beliefs in a direct connection between the fate of the soul and the corpse, and the idea that the tomb serves as a point of departure for the soul of the dead, also existed among the ancient Maya (e.g., Fitzsimmons 1998; Gillespie 2002; Hull 2006; Reentz-Budet et al. 2004; Weiss-Krejci 2006). Taube (2004a, 2004b) suggests that the ideal of Maya afterlife was not the dark and threatening underworld, but a lovely paradise called Flower Mountain, which appears widely in ancient Maya art. Resurrection was the ideal end to a person's life.

Altar 5 might reflect these ideas. The Maya scribe arranged Lady Tuun Kayawak's exhumation as her resurrection and entry into the Maya paradise. The order of the text and dates shows that from her death (starting with the distance number DN in position 8–9, fig. 2.4) till her exhumation (DN in position 22–23), Lady Tuun Kayawak was in the underworld. Through her exhumation from the "House of the Nine Lords" and redeposition at Tikal, she reached a different state of being. The artist has placed the death date (10–11) exactly opposite from the exhumation verb (glyph 26), which is enclosed by the two exhumation Calendar Round dates (24–25 and 27–28). Lady Tuun Kayawak's exhumation is the opposite of her death and burial; in a way her exhumation reverses death. The skull and bones, which are a symbol of rebirth in Mesoamerica (Carlson 1981:193; McAnany 1995:47), support this idea. The lady's resurrection would also explain her name change (fig. 2.4, position y2–y4). During her lifetime and during her stay in the underworld, she was Lady Tuun Kayawak, but after the exhumation she is called new and different names, a clear sign for some elevated postexhumation status. Comparable to the translation rituals of martyrs and saints in Europe, the exhumation and redeposition of her relics serve as metaphors for a spiritual change.

The two distance numbers (DN, fig. 2.5A) which mark the borders between the date of her death and burial and the date of her exhumation additionally separate the altar into two parts, a lower one relating to the underworld, and an upper one relating to life and rebirth. The arrangement on Altar 5 actually mirrors the symbolism of the twin-pyramid group (fig. 2.3A) in which the pyramids on the east and west represent sunrise and sunset and separate the group into a northern and southern part.[9]

The two-part division on Altar 5 is also similar to an early Late Classic plate from a burial vault in Pyramid E (= construction phase 8) of Structure A-I at Uaxactun (Smith 1937:207). The plate dates to the seventh century (ceramic style Tepeu I) (Smith 1955:fig. 72f) and depicts a funerary procession or possibly even an exhumation and reburial. In the lower section two jaguars reach out for a fleshed corpse that is in the Underworld (fig. 2.5B) (Valverde Valdés 2004:80). Like the two kings on Altar 5, the person on the right is partially standing (or dancing) in the Underworld.

The plate was buried a few meters away from a Tepeu I style vase (fig. 2.6; Smith 1955:fig. 72b). The event on the vase takes place in a distant past, on 7.5.0.0.0 (256 BC), and shows nobles in funeral attire and a jaguar presenting a lidded pot, which resembles Late Preclassic (300 BC–AD 250) cache pots, to a king. Two pairs of such redware bowls with flaring sides set lip to lip were discovered close to a disarticulated corpse beside the second step of the stairway of Late Preclassic pyramid B (= construction phase 2), which lies buried deep below Structure A-I of Uaxactun (Smith 1937:219). Possibly the Late Classic vase commemorates a Preclassic reburial event that took place in the same building. Two individuals on the vase (fig. 2.6) carry the same trident stone objects as the king of Tikal on Altar 5. These objects probably played an important role during tomb reentry, exhumation, and redeposition. The distinctive costume assemblages, which combine Jaguar God characteristics, long fire drill staffs, and trident flints or obsidians can be traced to several monuments, for example, Naranjo Stela 30 and Lintel 2 in Temple III at Tikal. The text on Naranjo Stela 30 states that on 7 Ahaw 3 Kumk'u (= 9.13.10.0.0 AD 702) "his person is in darkness" (Stuart 1998:407). The time difference between this Calendar Round date and another one inscribed on

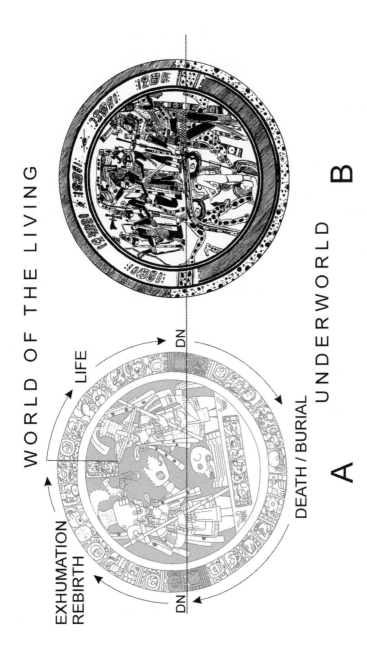

WORLD OF THE LIVING

LIFE

EXHUMATION
REBIRTH

DN

DN

DEATH / BURIAL

UNDERWORLD

A

B

FIGURE 2.5. (A) Distance Numbers on Tikal Altar 5 (after Jones and Satterthwaite 1982:fig. 23). (B) Seventh-century polychrome plate (Tepeu I) from Uaxactun Structure A-I (Smith 1932:fig. 8).

Long Count date 7.5.0.0.0 (256 BC)

Preclassic cache pot   Trident obsidians

FIGURE 2.6. A seventh-century polychrome vase (Tepeu I) from Uaxactun Structure A-I (Smith 1932:fig. 9).

the drill staff (7 Ahaw 18 K'ank'in = 9.14.3.0.0 AD 714) is exactly 13 *tun* (13 × 360 days = 4,680 days = ca. 12 years).

Altar 5 also carries an anniversary. The first event on the altar and the last event are exactly 28 *tzolk'in* (28 × 260 days = ca. 20 years) apart (fig. 2.4). Though the first event was probably of some political significance for the polity of Tikal, the anniversary looks very constructed. The date commemorates an event during Lady Tuun Kayawak's lifetime.

Problematical Deposit 76

In this context PD 76 of Group 5C-1 also becomes especially puzzling. As already mentioned, the crocodile in this deposit was buried at the bottom of the pit and on its back. Although the close relation between Early Classic crocodiles at Tikal and the name of the founder of one of Tikal's Early Classic dynasties, Yax Nuun Ahiin (*ahiin* means "crocodile") suggests the use of this specific animal as a sort of dynastic symbol, I believe that the reptile in PD 76 played a different role. It is probably associated with the resurrection ritual of Lady Tuun Kayawak and the *k'atun* celebrations.

According to Taube (1989), in Late Postclassic and Early Colonial Yucatan crocodiles denoted the surface of the earth and were used in fire-walking ceremonies, which began with the preparation and painting of a caiman. The ceremonies were the reenactment of the cosmogonic flood. In the *Dresden Codex* a crocodile is vomiting huge scrolls of water. In the Postclassic period crocodiles also seemed to have a particular calendri-cal and cosmological significance embodying the concept of completion and subsequent renewal. At several Late Postclassic sites the depictions of crocodiles were accompanied by day signs and numerical coefficients.

The crocodile metaphor was also present among the Classic Maya. Bench 1 from Palenque, which derives from the south subterranean building of Palenque's Palace, is decorated with the "Starry Deer Croco-dile," formerly known as the "Celestial Monster," which symbolizes the night sky (Stuart 2003, 2005). Hieroglyphic platform of Temple XIX at Palenque narrates the sacrifice of the Starry Deer Crocodile in an ear-lier creation cycle. First God GI is enthroned under the supervision of Itzamnaaj; a few years later a crocodile is sacrificed. The text refers to this creature as "Hole-Backed Caiman, Painted-Back Caiman." Actions that involve fluid—probably blood—fire drilling, and the placing of an object also take place (Stuart 2005; Houston et al. 2006:92). The entire passage of Temple XIX alludes to a destruction event in mythic time, probably by flooding followed by subsequent renewal. Velásquez García (2006) points out that in a number of Late Classic depictions the Starry Deer Crocodile vomits a torrential liquid decorated with conch shells, jade beads, small bones, rows of dots, completion signs, and K'AN and YAX logograms. PD 76 could represent the physical remains of the reenactment of such a scene. The objects in front of the crocodile's snout (fig. 2.3C) are flint eccentrics and flakes; obsidian eccentrics and incised obsidians; jade, pyrite, and shell mosaic elements; jade beads; an oyster shell; and human bones. They resemble the vomited objects of the iconographic depictions.

Conclusions

Although the texts on both Altar 5 and Stela 16 are silent on that mat-ter, the close resemblance between the arrangement of the bones in

Cache 137 (fig. 2.3D) and the pile of bones surmounted by the human skull on Altar 5 (fig. 2.4) very strongly suggests that the bottom of Stela 16 was indeed Lady Tuun Kayawak's final deposition place. Her original burial place remains unidentified. Grube and Schele (1994) have suggested that the woman mentioned on Altar 5 had originally been buried at Topoxte and that the reason for her exhumation was a pending threat by attacking enemies. The lady's bones had to be rescued by the Tikal king to protect them from the kingdom of Naranjo, whose king had desecrated the grave of a king of the neighboring Yaxha (Martin and Grube 2000:76; Eberl 2005:161).

Based on the cross-cultural analysis of postfuneral exhumations, I have come to the conclusion that Lady Tuun Kayawak's exhumation was probably not a rescue from attacking enemies. The emphasis on her resurrection in conjunction with the constructed anniversary suggests that Altar 5 depicts a reconciliation or even a staged exhumation and redeposition event (type c or type d). Maybe something about the lady's death, treatment of her corpse, or the location of her first burial was improper, and therefore, if she had not been reburied, Lady Tuun Kayawak would have had to remain in the Underworld. Alternatively, her exhumation and reburial could have just been motivated by political considerations. Both her exhumation and reburial are associated with her postmortem spiritual transformation and probably formed part of a large public multistage drama that could have lasted for weeks or even months. The sacrifice and deposition of the crocodile as a symbol of destruction and subsequent renewal and a fire drilling ceremony may have formed highlights in this spectacle.

Although the lady's mortal remains were obviously precious and of political relevance, this does not imply that she was a Tikal queen, as proposed by Harrison (1999:139). By helping to redeposit her bones at Tikal and thus symbolically taking her out of the Underworld, the lord of Maasal probably presented a very valuable gift to the king of Tikal, assuring his loyalty and friendship. The first event mentioned on the altar took place four years before Tikal's important victory over Calakmul in AD 695. The exhumation in AD 711 indicates a power shift in political alliances that started to take place at the beginning of the eighth century. As suggested by Martin and Grube (2008:46), by this time the kingdom of Maasal had probably become an ally of Tikal. Through the dead lady who could have been a blood or affinal relative, the two kings were able to strengthen their ties and forget their past enmities.

Altar 5 is a unique monument, created in a very specific historic context. However, the many fragmentary human bones in Twin-Group 5C-1 as well as other contexts of Late Classic Tikal suggest that Lady Tuun Kayawak was neither the first nor the last person to be exhumed and redeposited. There exists plenty of evidence that in the troubled seventh and eighth centuries, in times of tremendous political transformation, the political elite introduced new rituals, modified older forms, and extensively used dead bodies to legitimize their right to rule and to overcome dynastic crisis. By linking tombs and dead people in time units within their calendar and number system, the ancient Maya forged ties among living people, places, and people of the past. They used a strategy that is common throughout the world.

Acknowledgments

This chapter is based on a paper I first presented at the Annual Meeting of the Society for American Archaeology 2005 in Salt Lake City. I thank the Portuguese Science Fund FCT (Grant SFRH/BPD/8608/2002) for partially funding my participation in this event. Since then, the paper has been considerably rewritten. I would like to express my gratitude to the Austrian Science Fund FWF (Grant P18949-G02) for the ongoing financial support of my dead-body politics project, including the funds for a research month in Philadelphia in 2008. My special thanks go to Christopher Jones and Alex Pezzati from the University of Pennsylvania Museum of Archaeology and Anthropology. They gave me access to unpublished documentation materials of Tikal deposits, and Chris helped me find my way through the Tikal archives. Thanks are also due to Simon Martin for drawing my attention to important and new literature and for discussing Altar 5 with me; to Daniel Graña Behrens for his extensive comments and suggestions; to Karl Taube and Hattula Moholy-Nagy for contributing literature; and to one anonymous reviewer for his or her extensive comments and helpful suggestions. Finally, I want to thank the organizers of the SAA 2005 session and editors of this two-volume series, James Fitzsimmons and Izumi Shimada.

Notes

1. The ancient Maya considered stones as filled with vital essence. "Stelae, like rulers, possessed this divine soul-like quality (what Tzotzil Maya today call *ch'ulel*) and were in some way considered living things invested with *k'uh*" (Houston et al. 2006:83–84).

2. Quails and crocodiles are extremely rare at Tikal. Complete specimens in burials and caches are a hallmark of the Early Classic. Quails were included with Burial 48, the grave of Sihyaj Chan K'awiil II in Temple 33 (Coe 1990:122). Complete crocodiles were

discovered in Burial 10 (the grave of Yax Nuun Ahiin I in Temple 34) (see Wright 2005:91) and in the sixth-century Caches 86 and 140, which date to the reign of Lady of Tikal and her consort Kaloomte' B'alam. One articulated crocodile was also found in the Late Classic Problematical Deposit 76 of Twin-Pyramid Group 5C-1, which I discuss in this chapter (see also Moholy-Nagy 2003b, Appendix F).

3. Caches 14A–14D held a variety of objects such as eccentric and incised obsidian objects, jade and shell mosaic pieces, stingray spines, fish vertebrae, and unmodified marine shells (Coe 1990:490–491).

4. The earliest evidence for twin pyramids derives from below the East Plaza ball court (Group 5E-Sub. 1). Based on the ceramic evidence, the two pyramids date to the sixth century. Monuments and the southern and northern structures are lacking. The next known "twin-pyramid complex" (4D-2) has been given a tentative date of AD 652; it comprises only one north and one east stela. The third group (5B-1), which contains one northern stela/altar set and two eastern stelae and altars but also lacks the northern enclosure and the southern building, probably dates to AD 672 (Jones 1969, 1991:114, 119; Moholy-Nagy 2003a:80; Weiss-Krejci 2010).

5. Deposits found beneath the eastern stelae P44, P49, and P45, located in front of the eastern building 5C-14, held teeth and fragmentary bones of adults and children, together with vertebrae of snakes and fish, one oyster, and eccentric flints and obsidians (Ops. 43A, Lots 3, 5, 6; Moholy-Nagy 2003b:Appendix F; 2008). Approximately one meter from the northwestern corner of the southern building Str. 5C-15 (fig. 2.3A), Jennifer Balch discovered a pit (Problematical Deposit 74) that contained the partially burned, fragmentary, and commingled remains of at least five individuals (adults and children) (Tikal Archives, Object Catalogue Card/Human Bone, 43F-15), mixed with Early Classic ceramic sherds (Culbert 1993:figs. 134–138), green obsidian blades, flint bifaces, charcoal-laden earth, animal bones, etc. (Tikal Archives, Object Lot Card, Op. 43F, Lot 17). The animal bones consisted of worked (charred) and unworked deer antlers and deer bones, bones of opossum, mandibles of cavy and agouti, a dog skull, turtle shell and bones, and one turkey tarsometatarsus (Object Catalogue Cards/Animal Bone, 43F-16, 43F-74, 43F-75; see Moholy-Nagy 2003b:Appendix F). Although the ceramics in PD 74 are Early Classic, the nature of the deposit and its close resemblance to PD 22 of the North Acropolis (Coggins 1973) make an early Late Classic deposition date probable. However, PD 74 probably predates the construction of the southern twin-pyramid group building 5C-15.

6. Like all crocodiles at Tikal, it was either a *Crocodylus acutus* or *Crocodylus moreleti*. Although both are river forms, *C. moreleti* occurs only in the lakes and aguadas of the Peten, whereas *C. acutus* could also derive from Pacific Mexico or South America (Stuart 1968).

7. Five days after Napoleon had been crowned emperor of France on December 2, 1804, German-Roman Emperor Francis II renounced the Holy Roman crown and became Francis I, emperor of Austria.

8. Following the occupation of France in June 1940, Hitler visited Paris for the first and only time. Among the sites he chose to see was Napoleon's tomb at Les Invalides. As a tribute to the dead emperor, Hitler ordered the remains of Napoleon's son to be moved from Vienna to rest beside his father.

9. According to Ashmore (1991:201), the northern enclosure is the celestial realm. In her opinion the ruler who is portrayed on the northern stela stands in the sky and thus in a position of consummate power. One could also consider the northern enclosure as a portal into Flower Mountain, the paradise inhabited by resurrected people. Alternatively (personal communication by Laura Sotelo and María del Carmen Valverde), it could represent the night sky and a portal to the underworld. The single-room building to the south with the nine doorways possibly is associated with the nine Lords of the Night.

Works Cited

Ashmore, Wendy
1991   Site-Planning Principles and Concepts of Directionality among the Ancient Maya. *Latin American Antiquity* 2:199–226.

Benoit, Christian
2007   La nécropole des Invalides. *Revue de la Société des Amis du Musée de l'armée* 133:27–43.

Bloch, Maurice
1971   *Placing the Dead: Tombs, Ancestral Villages, and Kinship Organization in Madagascar.* Seminar Press, London.

Boot, Erik
2002   The Dos Pilas–Tikal Wars from the Perspective of Dos Pilas Hieroglyphic Stairway 4. Electronic document, http://www.mesoweb.com/features/boot/DPLHS4.pdf, accessed August 27, 2010.

Bourdieu, Pierre
1977   *Outline of a Theory of Practice.* Cambridge University Press, Cambridge.

Brown, Elizabeth A. R.
1985   Burying and Unburying the Kings of France. In *Persons in Groups*, edited by Richard C. Trexler, pp. 241–266. Medieval and Renaissance Texts and Studies 36. Binghamton, New York, Center for Medieval and Renaissance Studies.

Brunk, Samuel
2004   The Mortal Remains of Emiliano Zapata. In *Death, Dismemberment, and Memory: Body Politics in Latin America*, edited by Lyman L. Johnson, pp. 141–178. University of New Mexico Press, Albuquerque.

Carlson, John B.
1981   A Geomantic Model for the Interpretation of Mesoamerican Sites: An Essay in Cross-Cultural Comparison. In *Mesoamerican Sites and World-Views*, edited by Elizabeth P. Benson, pp. 143–215. Dumbarton Oaks, Washington, D.C.

Chase, Diane Z., and Arlen F. Chase
1996   Maya Multiples: Individuals, Entries, and Tombs in Structure A34 of Caracol, Belize. *Latin American Antiquity* 7:61–79.
2003   Secular, sagrado y "revisitado": La profanación, alteración y reconsagración de los antiguos entierros Mayas. In *Antropología de la eternidad. La muerte en la cultura maya*, edited by Andrés Ciudad Ruiz, Mario Humberto Ruz Sosa, and

María Josefa Iglesias Ponce de León, pp. 255–277. Sociedad Española de Estudios Mayas y Centro de Estudios Mayas, Madrid.

Coe, William R.

1990   *Excavations in the Great Plaza, North Terrace, and North Acropolis of Tikal.* Tikal Report 14. University Museum Monograph, 61. University Museum, University of Pennsylvania, Philadelphia.

Coggins, Clemency

1973   Unpublished communication to Christopher Jones, General Index Card/Problematical Deposit 74, Operation 43F, Lots 17/18, Tikal Archives, University of Pennsylvania Museum of Archaeology and Anthropology, Philadelphia.

1975   *Painting and Drawing Styles at Tikal: A Historical and Iconographic Reconstruction.* Unpublished Ph.D. dissertation, Department of Art History, Harvard University, Cambridge.

Culbert, T. Patrick

1993   *The Ceramics of Tikal: Vessels from the Burials, Caches and Problematical Deposits.* Tikal Report 25A. Monograph 81. University Museum, University of Pennsylvania, Philadelphia.

Demarest, Arthur

2004   *Ancient Maya: The Rise and Fall of a Rainforest Civilization.* Cambridge University Press, Cambridge.

Donaldson, Norman, and Betty Donaldson

1989   *How Did They Die?* St. Martin's Press, New York.

Dosal, Paul J.

2004   San Ernesto de la Higuera: The Resurrection of Che Guevara. In *Death, Dismemberment, and Memory: Body Politics in Latin America,* edited by Lyman L. Johnson, pp. 317–341. University of New Mexico Press, Albuquerque.

Eberl, Markus

2005   *Muerte, entierro y ascensión. Ritos funerarios entre los antiguos Mayas.* Ediciones de la Universidad Autónoma de Yucatán, Mérida, Mexico.

Emery, Kitty F.

2004   Animals from the Maya Underworld: Reconstructing Elite Maya Ritual at the Cueva de los Quetzales, Guatemala. In *Behavior Behind Bones: The Zooarchaeology of Ritual, Religion, Status and Identity.* Proceedings of the 9th Conference of the International Council of Archaeozoology, Durham August 2002, edited by Sharyn Jones O'Day, Wim Van Neer, and Anton Ervynck, pp. 101–113. Oxbow Books, Oxford.

Finucane, Ronald C.

1981   Sacred Corpse, Profane Carrion: Social Ideals and Death Rituals in the Later Middle Ages. In *Mirrors of Mortality,* edited by Joachim Whaley, pp. 40–60. Europa Publications, London.

Fitzsimmons, James L.

1998   Classic Maya Mortuary Anniversaries at Piedras Negras, Guatemala. *Ancient Mesoamerica* 9:271–278.

2002   Death and the Maya: Language and Archaeology in Classic Maya Mortuary Ceremonialism. Ph.D. dissertation, Department of Anthropology, Harvard University, Cambridge.

2006   Classic Maya Tomb Re-Entry. In *Jaws of the Underworld: Life, Death, and Rebirth among the Ancient Maya*. Proceedings of the 7th European Maya Conference, British Museum, London, edited by Pierre R. Colas, Geneviève LeFort, and Bodil Liljefors Persson, pp. 33–40. Acta Mesoamericana Vol. 16. Verlag Anton Saurwein, Markt Schwaben.

Follath, Erich

1998   Verrat, Feigheit, Betrug. *Der Spiegel* 30:118–119.

Fox, James

1987   The House as a Type of Social Organization on the Island of Roti, Indonesia. In *De la hutte au palais: Sociétés "à maison" en Asie du Sud-Est insulaire*, edited by Charles Macdonald, pp. 171–178. Editions du CNRS, Paris.

Giesey, Ralph E.

1960   *The Royal Funeral Ceremony in Renaissance France*. Droz: Geneva.

Gillespie, Susan D.

2002   Body and Soul Among the Maya: Keeping the Spirits in Place. In *The Space and Place of Death*, edited by Helaine Silverman and David B. Small, pp. 67–78. Archaeological Papers No. 11. American Anthropological Association, Arlington, Va.

Grube, Nikolai, and Linda Schele

1994   Tikal Altar 5. *Texas Notes on Precolumbian Art, Writing and Culture* 66:1–6.

Guenter, Stanley

2003   The Inscriptions of Dos Pilas Associated with B'ajlaj Chan K'awiil. Electronic document, http://www.mesoweb.com/features/guenter/DosPilas.pdf, accessed August 27, 2010.

Harrison, Peter D.

1999   *The Lords of Tikal: Rulers of an Ancient Maya City*. Thames and Hudson, London.

Hart, Joseph (editor)

2003   *Che: The Life, Death, and Afterlife of a Revolutionary*. Thunder's Mouth Press, New York.

Hawlik-van de Water, Magdalena

1993   *Die Kapuzinergruft*. Herder, Vienna.

Hertz, Robert

1907   Contribution à une étude sur la représentation collective de la mort. *Année Sociologique* 10:48–137.

1960   A Contribution to the Study of the Collective Representation of Death. In *Death and the Right Hand*, edited by Rodney Needham and Claudia Needham, pp. 27–86. Cohen and West, New York.

Houston, Stephen D.

1991   Caracol "Altar 21." Appendix to "Cycles of Time: Caracol in the Maya Realm." In *Sixth Palenque Round Table, 1986*, edited by Merle Greene Robertson and

Virginia M. Fields, pp. 38–42. Palenque Round Table series Vol. 7. University of Oklahoma Press, Norman.

1993   *Hieroglyphs and History at Dos Pilas: Dynastic Politics of the Classic Maya*. University of Texas Press, Austin.

Houston, Stephen D., Héctor L. Escobedo, Donald Forsyth, Perry Hardin, David Webster, and Lori Wright

1998   On the River of Ruins: Explorations at Piedras Negras, Guatemala, 1997. *Mexicon* 20:16–22.

Houston, Stephen D., David Stuart, and Karl Taube

2006   *The Memory of Bones: Body, Being, and Experience Among the Classic Maya*. University of Texas Press, Austin.

Hull, Kerry

2006   Journey from the Ancient Maya Tomb: Ropes, Roads, and the Point of Departure. In *Jaws of the Underworld: Life, Death, and Rebirth Among the Ancient Maya*. Proceedings of the 7th European Maya Conference, edited by Pierre R. Colas, Geneviève LeFort, and Bodil Liljefors Persson, pp. 43–52. Acta Mesoamericana Vol. 16. Verlag Anton Saurwein, Markt Schwaben.

Hutchinson, Dale L., and Lorraine V. Aragon

2002   Collective Burials and Community Memories: Interpreting the Placement of the Dead in the Southeastern and Mid-Atlantic United States with Reference to Ethnographic Cases from Indonesia. In *The Space and Place of Death*, edited by Helaine Silverman and David B. Small, pp. 27–54. Archaeological Papers No. 11. American Anthropological Association, Arlington, Va.

Johnson, Lyman L. (editor)

2004   *Death, Dismemberment, and Memory: Body Politics in Latin America*. University of New Mexico Press, Albuquerque.

Jones, Christopher

1963   Unpublished Field Notes of Christopher Jones. Tikal Archives, University of Pennsylvania Museum of Archaeology and Anthropology, Philadelphia.

1969   The Twin-Pyramid Group Pattern: A Classic Maya Architectural Assemblage at Tikal, Guatemala. Unpublished Ph.D. dissertation, University of Pennsylvania, Philadelphia.

1991   Cycles of Growth at Tikal. In *Classic Maya Political History*, edited by T. Patrick Culbert, pp. 102–127. Cambridge University Press, Cambridge.

Jones, Christopher, and Linton Satterthwaite

1982   *The Monuments and Inscriptions of Tikal: The Carved Monuments*. Tikal Report 33, Pt. A. University Museum Monograph 44. University Museum, University of Pennsylvania, Philadelphia.

Kidder, Alfred V.

1947   *The Artifacts of Uaxactun, Guatemala*. Publication No. 576. Carnegie Institution of Washington, Washington, D.C.

Macartney, C. A.

1968   *The Habsburg Empire 1790–1918*. Weidenfeld and Nicolson, London.

Maler, Teobert
1911   *Explorations in the Department of Peten, Guatemala: Tikal. Report of Explora-*
        tions for the Museum. Memoirs Vol. 5, No. 1. Peabody Museum of American
        Archaeology and Ethnology, Harvard University, Cambridge.

Martin, Simon
2003   In the Line of the Founder: A View of Dynastic Politics at Tikal. In *Tikal: Dynas-*
        ties, Foreigners and Affairs of State, edited by Jeremy A. Sabloff, pp. 3–45. School
        of American Research Press, Santa Fe.

Martin, Simon, and Nikolai Grube
2000   *Chronicle of the Maya Kings and Queens.* Thames and Hudson, London.
2008   *Chronicle of the Maya Kings and Queens: Deciphering the Dynasties of the*
        Ancient Maya. Rev. ed. Thames and Hudson, London.

McAnany, Patricia
1995   *Living with the Ancestors: Kinship and Kingship in Ancient Maya Society.* Univer-
        sity of Texas Press, Austin.
1998   Ancestors and the Classic Maya Built Environment. In *Function and Meaning in*
        Classic Maya Architecture, edited by Stephen D. Houston, pp. 271–298. Dumbar-
        ton Oaks Research Library and Collection, Washington, D.C.

Meskell, Lynn M., and Rosemary A. Joyce
2003   *Embodied Lives: Figuring Ancient Maya and Egyptian Experience.* Routledge,
        London.

Metcalf, Peter, and Richard Huntington
1991   *Celebrations of Death: The Anthropology of Mortuary Ritual.* Cambridge Univer-
        sity Press, Cambridge.

Meyer, Rudolf J.
2000   *Königs- und Kaiserbegräbnisse im Spätmittelalter.* Beihefte zu J. F. Böhmer,
        Regesta Imperii 19. Böhlau, Cologne.

Miles, Douglas
1965   Socio-Economic Aspects of Secondary Burial. *Oceania* 35:161–174.

Moholy-Nagy, Hattula
2003a   The Hiatus at Tikal, Guatemala. *Ancient Mesoamerica* 14:77–83.
2003b   *The Artifacts of Tikal: Utilitarian Artifacts and Unworked Material.* Tikal Report 27,
        Pt. B. University Museum Monograph, 118. University of Pennsylvania Museum
        of Archaeology and Anthropology, Philadelphia.
2008   *The Artifacts of Tikal: Ornamental and Ceremonial Artifacts and Unworked*
        Material. Tikal Report 27, Pt. A. University Museum Monograph 127.
        University of Pennsylvania Museum of Archaeology and Anthropology,
        Philadelphia.

Morley, Sylvanus G.
1938   *The Inscriptions of Peten,* vol. 1. Carnegie Institution of Washington Publication
        No. 437. Carnegie Institution of Washington, Washington, D.C.

Ohler, Norbert
1990   *Sterben und Tod im Mittelalter.* Artemis, Munich.

Reentz-Budet, Dorie, Ronald L. Bishop, and Ellen Bell

2004 Secretos bajo la superfície: La ceramic Maya y las antiguas prácticas funerárias. In *Culto funerário en la sociedad maya: Memoria de la Cuarta Mesa Redonda de Palenque*, edited by Rafael Cobos, pp. 309–331. Instituto Nacional de Antropología e Historia, Mexico.

Rice, Prudence

2004 *Maya Political Science: Time, Astronomy, and the Cosmos*. University of Texas Press, Austin.

Robson, James

2003 A Tang Dynasty Chan Mummy [Roushen] and a Modern Case of *Furta Sacra?* Investigating the Contested Bones of Shitou Xiqian. In *Chan Buddhism in Ritual Context*, edited by Bernard Faure and Robert Stammers, pp. 151–178. Routledge, London.

Romero, Javier

1970 Dental Mutilation, Trephination, and Cranial Deformation. In *Handbook of Middle American Indians: Volume 9. Physical Anthropology*, edited by T. Dale Stewart, pp. 50–67. University of Texas Press, Austin.

Schmid, Peter

1997 Sterben - Tod- Leichenbegängnis König Maximilians I. In *Der Tod des Mächtigen: Kult und Kultur des Todes spätmittelalterlicher Herrscher*, edited by Lothar Kolmer, pp. 185–215. Schöningh, Paderborn.

Smith, A. Ledyard

1932 *Two Recent Ceramic Finds at Uaxactun*. Contributions to American Archaeology Publication 436, pp. 1–25. Carnegie Institution of Washington, Washington, D.C.

Smith, Robert E.

1937 *A Study of Structure A-I Complex at Uaxactun, Peten, Guatemala*. Contributions to American Archaeology Publication 456, No. 19, pp. 189–231. Carnegie Institution of Washington, Washington, D.C.

1955 *Ceramic Sequence at Uaxactun, Guatemala*. Middle American Research Institute Publication 20, Vols. 1 and 2, Tulane University, New Orleans.

Stuart, David

1998 "The Fire Enters His House": Architecture and Ritual in Classic Maya Texts. In *Function and Meaning in Classic Maya Architecture*, edited by Stephen Houston, pp. 373–425. Dumbarton Oaks Research Library and Collection, Washington, D.C.

2003 A Cosmological Throne at Palenque. Electronic document, http://www.mesoweb.com/stuart/notes/Throne.pdf, accessed August 27, 2010.

2005 *The Inscriptions from Temple XIX at Palenque*. Pre-Columbian Art Research Institute. San Francisco

Stuart, L. C.

1968 Communication on Object Catalogue Cards/Animal Bone, 12C-506, 12J-148, and 43C-22; Tikal Archives, University of Pennsylvania Museum of Archaeology and Anthropology, Philadelphia.

Taibo, Paco Ignacio II

2003   Images and Ghosts. In *Che: The Life, Death and Afterlife of a Revolutionary*, edited by Joseph Hart, pp. 425–429. Thunder's Mouth Press, New York.

Taube, Karl

1989   *Itzam Cab Ain: Caimans, Cosmology, and Calendrics in Postclassic Yucatan*. Research Reports on Ancient Maya Writing 26. Center for Maya Research, Washington, D.C.

2004a   Flower Mountain: Concepts of Life, Beauty, and Paradise Among the Classic Maya. *Res: Anthropology and Aesthetics* 45:69–98.

2004b   Structure 10L-16 and Its Early Classic Antecedents: Fire and the Evocation and Resurrection of K'inich Yax K'uk' Mo'. In *Understanding Early Classic Copan*, edited by Ellen E. Bell, Marcello A. Canuto, and Robert J. Sharer, pp. 265–295. University of Pennsylvania, Museum of Archaeology and Anthropology, Philadelphia.

Taylor, John H.

2001   *Death and the Afterlife in Ancient Egypt*. British Museum Press, London.

Valverde Valdés, María del Carmen

2004   *Balam: El jaguar a través de los tempo y los espacios del universo maya*. Universidad Nacional Autónoma de México, Mexico.

Van Gennep, Arnold

1909   *Les rites de passage*. Nourry, Paris.

1960/   *The Rites of Passage*. Translated by Monika Vizdom and Gabrielle L. Caffee.
[1909] University of Chicago Press, Chicago.

Velásquez García, Erik

2006   The Maya Flood Myth and the Decapitation of the Cosmic Caiman. *Pari Journal* 7(1):1–10.

Verdery, Katherine

1999   *The Political Lives of Dead Bodies: Reburial and Post-Socialist Change*. Columbia University Press, New York.

Wagner, Elisabeth

2006   White Earth Bundles—The Symbolic Sealing and Burial of Buildings Among the Ancient Maya. In *Jaws of the Underworld: Life, Death, and Rebirth among the Ancient Maya*. Proceedings of the 7th European Maya Conference, British Museum, London, edited by Pierre R. Colas, Geneviève LeFort, and Bodil Liljefors Persson, pp. 55–69. Acta Mesoamericana Vol. 16. Verlag Anton Saurwein, Markt Schwaben.

Waterson, Roxana

1995   Houses, Graves and the Limits of Kinship Groupings Among the Sa'dan Toraja. *Bijdragen tot de Taal-, Land- en Volkenkunde* 151:194–217.

Weiss-Krejci, Estella

2005   Excarnation, Evisceration, and Exhumation in Medieval and Post-Medieval Europe. In *Interacting with the Dead: Perspectives on Mortuary Archaeology for the New Millennium*, edited by Gordon Rakita, Jane Buikstra, Lane Beck, and Sloan Williams, pp. 155–172. University Press of Florida, Gainesville.

2006   The Maya Corpse: Body Processing from Preclassic to Postclassic Times in the Maya Highlands and Lowlands. In *Jaws of the Underworld: Life, Death, and Rebirth among the Ancient Maya*. Proceedings of the 7th European Maya Conference, British Museum, London, edited by Pierre R. Colas, Geneviève LeFort, and Bodil Liljefors Persson, pp. 71–86. Acta Mesoamericana Vol. 16. Verlag Anton Saurwein, Markt Schwaben.

2008   Unusual Life, Unusual Death and the Fate of the Corpse: A Case Study from Dynastic Europe. In *Deviant Burial in the Archaeological Record*, edited by Eileen M. Murphy, pp. 169–190. Oxbow, Oxford.

2010   Depósitos rituales en los Complejos de Pirámides Gemelas de Tikal. In *El ritual en el mundo maya: De lo privado a lo publico*, edited by Andrés Ciudad, María Josefa Iglesias, y Miguel Sorroche, pp. 83–105. Publicaciones de la SEEM Vol. 9. SEEM, Grupo de Investigación Andalucía-América, CEPHCIS-UNAM, Madrid.

Wright, Lori

2005   In Search of Yax Nuun Ayiin I: Revisiting the Tikal Project's Burial 10. *Ancient Mesoamerica* 16:89–100.

CHAPTER 3

Perspectives on Death and Transformation in Ancient Maya Society

Human Remains as a Means to an End

JAMES L. FITZSIMMONS

ROYAL ANCESTORS IN THE CLASSIC PERIOD (AD 250–850) played a vital role in the religious and political life of ancient Maya society. As opposed to being passive participants in royal ceremonies, ancestors were believed by the Maya to "see" or "witness" a variety of events ranging from accessions to birthdays (Fitzsimmons 1998). On Classic monuments, we find ancestors hovering over the living from celestial paradises, talking to their descendants and behaving much like deities. Occasionally, though, they were subjected to more direct contact. Engaged in ancestor venera- tion, powerful lords at places like Copan, Tonina, and Caracol would often enter the realms of the dead by opening up their tombs and making changes therein (e.g., interring additional individuals, painting bones with cinnabar, or other alterations; see Chase and Chase 1994; Fitzsim- mons 2006, 2009). There is a growing body of evidence for even more personal contact between the dead and the living within Classic Maya society, however, where lords curated ancestral or sacrificial remains as sacred objects. This behavior appears to have been tied to the belief that human remains were ritually efficacious, able to assist in the dedication of monuments as well as ancestral or divine communication. They were not mere objects to be used, however.

Human remains were viewed by ancient Mesoamericans in ways that blur traditional Western distinctions between concepts like "alive" and "dead" or "self" and "other." The dead could be and often were invoked, conjured, and negotiated with. Although dead, they functioned as indis- pensible social actors. To the living, the dead also provided portable objects that could be owned, stored, or even talked to. Such objects were, in a sense, "alive" and could serve as embodiments of identity somewhat equivalent to the images we see of individuals on monuments, pottery, or other formats. Although a given skull or long bone could represent the identity or "self" of the deceased, it could also serve in more complex identity formations. When a Classic Maya warrior wore the skull of a former enemy on his belt, for example, he was not only displaying his prowess in battle but also participating in or absorbing the identity of his captive (Houston et al. 2006:72). To an extent, the captive became part of the captor's "self," with his personal name often reflecting this new arrangement (Houston et al. 2006:79; Stuart 1985). In short, human remains were far more than just bones to the peoples of ancient Mesoamerica. The following pages will address how human remains, beyond burials, were treated by the Classic Maya nobility, bringing together written and archaeological evidence to explore what we do and do not know about this aspect of Classic Maya mortuary ceremonialism.

Animation and Dedication

As Mock (1998) and others have observed, burials of kings and captives alike were often used to animate or ensoul buildings or new construction phases at Maya sites: the prestigious dead served as "seeds" and sources of "regenerative power" in ancient Maya ritual. Similar considerations, involving transferring or transmitting "animateness" to buildings, have been widely observed in Maya archaeology, ethnohistory, and ethnography. Building dedications in the lowlands often seem to have involved the death of a human or surrogate animal, where a degree of animation was transferred from the individual—now dead—to the newborn structure.[1] In fact, as Houston et al. (2006:13) have recently demonstrated, Classic Maya conceptions of the body overlapped with ideas about architecture: in ancient Maya art, buildings are oftentimes depicted as both animate and anthropomorphic, with platforms and other sections of buildings subject to the same stylistic conventions as human hands, feet, or other body parts.

The interplay between body and building goes beyond artistic conventions, however. Throughout precolumbian Mesoamerica, buildings (and other objects) were purified with fire or incense, measured, named,

FIGURE 3.1. Excerpt from Stela A Copan (after Schele and Mathews 1998:161).

fed, clothed, and subjected to clear assertions of ownership, with each component of the ritual an important step in what Brian Stross calls "animating the inanimate" (1998:32). If we consider bodies and buildings to be rough analogues in Classic Maya thought, then habitually pairing the two together—with burials, sacrifices, or both—would seem a natural outcome, as would the substitution of one for the other within ancient Maya ritual. We might view, for example, the "fleshy, blood-enveloping quality" of red pigment on Maya buildings (Houston et al. 2006:14) as functionally equivalent to the red pigment adorning the bodies of prestigious Maya dead in tombs throughout the lowlands. Several authors have gauged the interplay among tombs, houses, caves, and ball courts (e.g., see Coe 1988; Fitzsimmons 2009; Schele and Mathews 1998). To this list we might therefore add the human body.

Beyond animating buildings, moreover, Classic Maya remains could be used to dedicate or erect hieroglyphic monuments, as in a well-known example from Copan Stela H. It describes how the remains of Butz' Chan, the eleventh king of Copan, were "peeled" or "sliced" as part of its dedication ritual in 731 (fig. 3.1). These activities were performed at the behest of the ill-fated king Waxaklajuun Ub'ah K'awiil (e.g., 18 Rabbit, who would meet his demise at the hands of Quirigua seven years later).[2] Perhaps the most famous king of Copan, he interred jade, shell, and portions of a gold statue from the Intermediate Area below Stela H, which were ultimately recovered by Gustav Stromsvik in the early 1940s. These events were so important to Waxaklajuun Ub'ah K'awiil that he referred to them on Stela A, whose erection 60 days later was witnessed by representatives from Tikal, Calakmul, and Palenque (Schele and Mathews 1998:156, 161; Fitzsimmons 2009:306). No human remains were recovered by Stromsvik from either of the substela caches beneath Stelae H and A. But the "peeling" or "slicing" of the bones of Butz' Chan does seem to have been a significant, if not the most significant, aspect of the dedication of Stela H, which was "set up" immediately after those remains were manipulated (Schele and Mathews 1998:157).

Trophies and the Royal Maya "Self"

Human bones served a number of additional roles in ancient Maya society. Apart from animating buildings, they could be prestigious war trophies, craft or utilitarian items, or even part of a ritual "toolkit" used in the conjuring of supernaturals (see also Weiss-Krejci as well as A. Chase and D. Chase in this volume). Trophies occupied somewhat of a special role in Classic Maya society. War captives were literally known as the *b'aak* or "bone(s)" of their owners throughout the inscriptions (fig. 3.2). After death their heads or bones were displayed as trophies on monuments and pottery. As Baudez and Mathews (1978) have observed, images of kings and other lords on monuments show shrunken heads—and even whole, shrunken bodies—being worn by warriors as part of their battle accoutrements. Such practices continued among the Maya into the colonial era: "they considered those who were sacrificed as holy. If the victims were slaves captured in war, their master took their bones, to use them as a trophy in their dances as a token of victory . . . after the victory they took the jaws off the dead bodies and with the flesh cleaned off, they put them on their arms" (Tozzer 1941:120–123). A similar practice of trophy making has been cited for the Aztecs, who believed that the femurs of women who died in childbirth, regarded as deceased warriors, "enhanced the potency of warriors; grieving families had to fight off attempts to steal these women's body parts" (Miller and Martin 2004:172).

Physically, remains of Classic Maya captives—from femurs to trophy skulls—have been recovered with inscriptions and imagery portraying scenes and themes of death, triumph, and humiliation, with some of the well-known bones from Tikal Burial 116 (the burial of Jasaw Chan K'awiil I) providing perhaps the best examples.[3] Easiest to carve when fresh, human remains formed one of a set of bone media that included manatees,

FIGURE 3.2. Yaxchilan Lintel 16 and *aj b'aak* "he of bone(s)" phrase at F4 (Graham and von Euw 1977; reproduced courtesy of the Corpus of Maya Hieroglyphic Inscriptions and the President and Fellows of Harvard College).

peccaries, and other wild animals (Coe and Kerr 1998:140). On a purely material level—and given the dehumanization of captives commonplace in Classic Maya society—one could say that all bone media were more or less equivalent in the eyes of the Classic Maya nobility, all being personal possessions and little else. The Maya attitude toward "trophy" human bones, however, may have been a bit more complex than this.

As Houston et al. (2006:37, 202) have noted, captives in Classic Maya society were both humiliated and, for prestige purposes only, exalted figures: they are among the only individuals who physically touch other human beings in Classic Maya imagery. We might say that there is little to no social space between captor and captive in such imagery, because the identity of one is being literally absorbed by the other; as noted earlier, the captive even provides a titular number or name to the captor (Stuart 1985). The victim is dehumanized and, to an extent, in a liminal role, only to emerge as part of the identity of the victor in a manner echoing arguments by Igor Kopytoff (1982) and Victor Turner (1969): the captive undergoes a social death, a disenfranchisement from status, freedom, and family, long before he or she is actually killed. Whatever is left belongs to the victor.

If captive bodies and body parts indeed "belonged to others" (Houston et al. 2006:204), with their identities (to an extent) absorbed by their captors, then it would stand to reason that captives' bones were not viewed simply as trophies. Rather, such bones—as the remains of "absorbed" victims—were part of the captor's identity. To some extent, the trophies were part of who the victor was and how the victor defined himself. So long as the origins of a given bone remained clear, it would be both a reminder of conquest as well as a part of its owner's identity. In a royal context, we might hypothesize that the remains of well-remembered captives would, to some degree, become (more) powerful by continuous association with the king and his person, an extension of the royal personage: the king was, for all purposes, divine. His person and image were holy.

Theoretically, one could take this argument further and extend it to many royal, sacred personal objects. The argument of personal possessions as "royal extensions" may indeed sufficiently explain the attitudes of rulers (and their court) toward specialized items like masks, *k'awiil* scepters, and other objects—including artifacts composed of human remains—habitually employed in the rites of ancient Maya kingship. To be sure, such objects fundamentally depend upon both context (e.g., where or when they were used) and memory (e.g., the circumstances of their origins) to function as extensions of royal identity or what we might call the royal "self."

But how do we define "self" in the Maya royal context? After all, conceptions of "self" can change over time and can even vary with the situation, as has been observed with Classic Maya naming practices. For ancient Maya rulers, "multiple names represent different relationships between humans and the supernatural, each investing the self with a complex identity from different vantage points" (Houston et al. 2006:70). In other words, each king had several different potential identities, depending upon who he was dealing with and what he wanted to demonstrate. His identity was manufactured and, as the sociologist Glenn Vernon (1970:24) has observed, probably involved a complex interaction of definitions and symbols: "The pattern in which the same individual is both the defined and the definer is characteristic of *all* self-definitions, and every individual has a tremendous storehouse of definitions from which he selects particular labels to place upon himself at the appropriate time. Each individual is able to conceive of himself in any number of different conditions." We certainly find Classic Maya rulers selectively adopting different titles, costumes, and objects in their monumental portraits and inscriptions as well as in burials: these are symbols through which a given lord defines himself and, depending upon the occasion, imparts meaning to others. As Vernon notes, symbols usually acquire an existence independent of their originators: the poem and the poet or, in a Classic Maya case, the portrait of a ruler and the ruler himself are not the same thing. They acquire, in this view, an existence independent of their creators. This view of symbolism is somewhat opposed to the way in which ancient Maya rulers actually conceived of material objects: there was considerable overlap between "image and subject in Maya belief" (Houston et al. 2006:74), such that the image of a king—inert in stone— was literally part of the identity of the living, breathing king and could even interact with others as a social being. If we view portraits and other royal monuments as parts of the "extendable self," essential elements of royal personhood, then I see no reason why certain essential portable goods, including those of human bone, should be excluded from Vernon's "storehouse of definitions" for the self.

Why would human remains, out of all of the potential portable goods carried by a ruler, be special items in the "storehouse"? Unlike other objects, human remains already have a definable identity before becoming part of a royal artifact assemblage. The captor–captive relationship, by definition, makes such items special. Metaphorically speaking, we might also say that all human remains are the product of a narrative.

Whether it is particularly violent, involving the capture, sacrifice, and body processing of an ancient Maya noble, as with the trophies mentioned above, or a more peaceful one, concerning the death of a ruler and his exhumation by kin, we might say that the narrative is central to the way in which human remains are viewed. As the sociologist Robert Fulton (1965) has observed, death "asks us for our identity," and in doing so it forces us to (re)create ourselves in relationship to the dead. In the Classic Maya sense, it is the very act of this creation that separates human remains from other categories of artifacts.[4] In the case of a trophy, there is a specific, defining event with a clear outcome and implications for how the victor views himself and is viewed by others. The captor (re)creates himself in relationship to the dead simply by wearing or holding the object. Such creation, of course, assumes that the *memory* of the original event and the identity of the bone material, as human, is retained. As the memories fade, the objects degrade, or the bones are transferred to new locations or individuals, trophies acquire new roles and lose their original meanings.

Bone Industries and Utilitarian Items

There are a number of archaeologically recognizable craft industries, or what Joseph Michels has called "exotica craft assemblages" (Michels 1979:161–163) in the Maya area, and only some of these were clearly involved in the production of trophies as described above. Exotica craft items, after all, can range from objects that are recognizably from human sources—such as modified crania—to those that have been worked so drastically that they are visually indistinguishable from faunal remains. Some are even utilitarian in function. Should we consider the utilitarian items comprised of human remains to be part of the "storehouse of definitions" and subject to the same considerations and beliefs outlined above?

   To address this question, we can briefly examine the industries themselves. One broad-based practice involves using cut human long bones for rattles, awls, punches, or other utilitarian objects. The most extensive samples for this behavior in the Maya area come from Early Classic Uaxactun (Ricketson and Ricketson in Kidder 1947:58–59) and Tikal (Moholy-Nagy and Ladd 1992:131; see fig. 3.3), although worked human

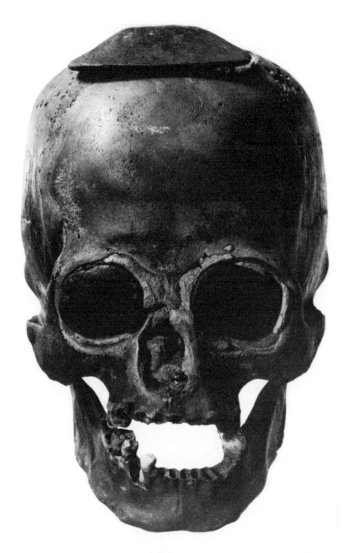

FIGURE 3.3. Human skull incense burner from Chichen Itza (in Coggins 1992: fig. 5.49; reproduced courtesy of the President and Fellows of Harvard College).

long bones have been found at many Maya sites, with Middle Classic Kaminaljuyu, Terminal Classic San Jose, and Postclassic Chichen Itza as well as Mayapan providing some of the clearest examples (Michels 1979:163; Moholy-Nagy and Ladd 1992:130–131; Proskouriakoff 1962:375; Thompson 1939:pl. 30). As Ricketson and Ricketson have noted, one

Early Classic practice at Uaxactun—typically using the bones of adult males—seems to have involved ringing the proximal and distal ends of a femur, tibia, fibula, humerus, ulna, or radius and subsequently cutting them off. Longitudinal cuts were then made in the shaft to extract large bands of bone, which were then fashioned into awls or punches. The sawn proximal and distal ends then were either discarded or employed in decorative or ceremonial ways: noting that "femur heads were set like bosses in the plastered walls of the inner chamber of the buried temple in the Castillo at Chichen Itza," Kidder (1947:59) has suggested the latter possibility. Joseph Michels has noted a similar practice at Middle Classic Kaminaljuyu, where the elite household 46-22-079 was apparently producing, in addition to high-quality ceramics, worked artifacts of human bones. Discarded articular ends of femurs similar to those recovered at Uaxacatun appear, as Michels states (1979:165), to be the products of low-ranking artisans "constrained to ply their craft on the premises of the [elite] individual for whom they worked."

Other recognizable industries involving long bones include the production of rattles and so-called beveled-end bones, objects of unknown function that are split, rounded off, beveled on one end and subsequently polished. Such objects, as well as the more recognizably utilitarian awls and punches mentioned above, can be made of human or animal bone and have been found in Classic period contexts at Barton Ramie (Willey et al. 1965:496), Holmul (Merwin and Vaillant 1932:89), Chiapa de Corzo (Lee 1969:162), Tikal (Moholy-Nagy and Ladd 1992:131), and San José (Thompson 1939:pl. 30). Others are, not surprisingly, of indeterminate origin.

That utilitarian objects do not have to be manufactured from human remains (indeed, most are not) would suggest that human remains—when modified in this way—are no more "special" than faunal remains. However, given what we know about the relationship between captors and captives in ancient Maya society, the use of bones as trophies, and the belief in the supernatural properties of human remains prevalent in elite Maya culture (even the remains of royal individuals, as with Butz' Chan at Copan), it seems unlikely to the author that awls, tubes, rattles, and other objects made from human bone were viewed this way at *the time of their manufacture*. I argue that the very knowledge that a given tool is from a captive or another individual automatically creates a relationship between the living and the dead. Whether that relationship persists—or if the source of the bone is even remembered to be human—depends upon the memory and value of the object. The members of the elite households commissioning bone awls and punches at Uaxactun, for example, had to know in part where the raw material for their specialized industry was ultimately coming from and were even using the discarded parts as decorations. They would seem to be employing an extension of the captor–captive relationship and, as such, playing with notions of self-definition and status similar to that which I have outlined for trophies. It would be a stretch, however, to unequivocally say that the motivations and beliefs represented for trophies are the same as those for utilitarian items. More likely, ideas about such items contributing to one's sense of "self" varied on a case-by-case basis.

Sainted Remains, Royal Bones, and *Pars Pro Toto*

Apart from utilitarian items and trophies there are, of course, all manner of isolated human remains in the archaeological record. Disembodied jaws, skulls, femurs, fingers, and even teeth are relatively common in excavations, from the famous skull pit at Colha' to the "finger-bowl" caches of Caracol (e.g., see Ricketson and Ricketson 1937; Welsh 1988; Massey and Steele 1997; Chase and Chase 1994). Some are plainly the result of sacrifice and probably were war trophies at one time. Most are the product of unknown circumstances and could be from war captives, events like tomb reentry, or even taphonomy.

Looking at how the ancient Maya treated isolated bones in their art and writing, we find that disarticulated skeletal elements are commonplace on ceramic vessels but far rarer on monuments. Unfortunately, most such elements are not labeled with names or situations describing their origins. However, we do occasionally find isolated human remains being used as "sainted" or "holy" objects, much as in Colonial period Yucatán (Tozzer 1941:123, 131) or among the Postclassic Mixtecs (Caso 1969:pl. 4) and Mexica (Covarrubias 1957:316; Gonzáles Rul 1961; Matos Moctezuma 1980:772). A ritually charged example from the well-known Yaxchilan Lintel 25 perhaps provides the best visual support for this idea. On this monument Lady K'ab'al Xook uses a skull—possibly that of a royal ancestor, although the context is far from clear—to accomplish the appearance of the ancestral deity Aj K'ahk' O'Chaak (fig. 3.4). A less well known example occurs in the fallen stucco glyphs of Palenque Temple 18. In 1952, Franz Blom excavated this temple and found a number of the stucco glyphs intact; subsequent work by Alberto Ruz Lhuillier and William Ringle has revealed one of the glyphs to have originally read *u jol k'uhil* "his skull god" (Blom 1923; Ringle 1996; Ruz Lhuillier 1958). What this means is unclear, although one cannot help but recall the image of a lady from Yaxchilan holding aloft a human skull to conjure her ancestral deity.

From the above examples, it is difficult to say whether royal or ancestral bones were used, as per the Butz' Chan case, or whether the items in question were the remains of sacrificed individuals or other persons put to royal use. To support the case for royal bone usage, we can proceed from the most circumstantial evidence to more concrete epigraphic and archaeological data. Two major sources for possible bone usage stem from the central Petén at the sites of Uaxactun (Burials C1 and A20) and Tikal (Burial 48), where the heads or faces—and, in the case of Tikal Burial 48, femurs—were removed prior to final interment and mosaic masks placed as substitutes. In the case of Tikal Burial 48, thought to house the body of Siyaj Chan K'awiil II, the king was clearly the product of a secondary interment; his complete lack of a head was probably not the result of taphonomy or absentmindedness! Missing heads and faces are not limited to these sites or to royalty, however: W.B.M. Welsh has noted similar behavior among other populations at Tikal (Burial 85), Altun Ha (C-16/22), and Altar de Sacrificios (Burial 79), and in the northern lowlands at Dzibilchaltun (Burials 450-1, 385-1, 385-2, 385-3, and 57-5; Welsh 1988:216).

How did the Classic Maya conceive of these partial remains? Why were *these* elements missing, and how were they used? To address these questions, we can look to both epigraphy and material culture at Maya sites. As Houston et al. (2006:12–13) have recently demonstrated, Classic Maya depictions of the body are heavily influenced by the idea that neither the body nor its elements (i.e., hands, feet, head, etc.) can be understood apart from the other. That is to say, the visual representation of a body part, such as the word "hand," was never depicted as a "hand" per se, but as a "hand from an arm" or, more properly, a "hand from a body." Houston et al. have used this idea to explain why most Maya

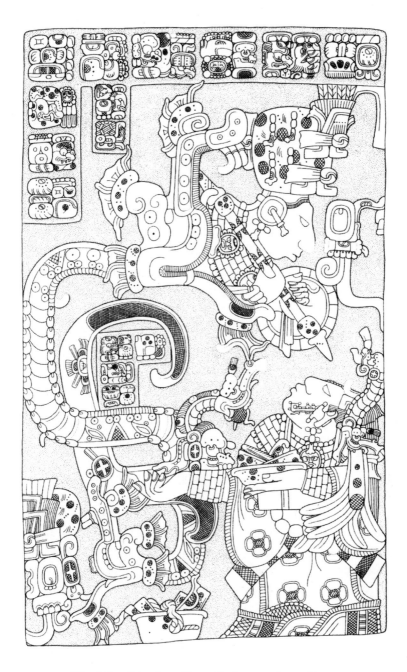

FIGURE 3.4. Yaxchilan Lintel 25 (from Graham and von Euw 1977; reproduced courtesy of the Corpus of Maya Hieroglyphic Inscriptions and the President and Fellows of Harvard College).

glyphs involving body parts, such as the syllables *chi-* or *chu-*, show them as severed from a larger whole: circles of flesh, and occasionally bone, mark where the part has left the whole. In glyphic terms, body parts are represented with a suffix, *-Vl*, that is attached to nouns and adjectives (Houston et al. 2000); John Robertson has noted that this suffix "creates an abstraction, such as English 'whiteness,' and then requires that this quality and whatever it is attached to be imagined as a single thing" (Houston et al. 2006:12). So described, we might say that the Classic Maya were employing a form of metonymy here. Using a single characteristic to identify a more complex concept was not restricted to fleshy body parts, moreover, but was commonplace for bones. The ubiquitous logograph for bone, as an example, is usually depicted as severed and can be represented as possessed with the *-Vl* suffix. As a result, the "missing" bones from Tikal, Altar de Sacrificios, and the other locales mentioned above, were they to be described in text, could be expressed—visually, linguistically, or both—only as part of some greater whole.

We might be tempted here to apply an idea like *pars pro toto*, or "(taking) a part for the whole," to the Classic Maya case; in this scheme any of the "missing" bones above could represent the body and associated concepts such as royal identity or power. But stating that the body and its parts cannot be conceived of as separate does not necessarily mean that one can substitute for the other. While all may serve as portions of identity, some parts—as mentioned earlier—are probably more important than others. Instead, we might look at the types of "missing" bones to gain a more nuanced understanding of how the Maya would have perceived of partial remains.

As attested by Houston et al. (2006) and Clancy (1999), there appears to have been a hierarchy of the body expressed in Classic Maya iconography that placed, not surprisingly, the head at the top: Maya monuments generally enlarge the head and upper body, including upper limbs, at the expense of the lower. Likewise, images to the viewer's right are invariably of higher status than those to the left in Maya art (Houston 1998). Houston et al. (2006:29–30) have made a convincing case that these hierarchies can be applied to individual body parts depending upon their position. There is no reason not to believe that skeletal elements, like their fleshy counterparts, had specific, hierarchical associations. Stuart (2002) as well as Houston et al. (2006:30) have done much to clarify the distinctions made between right and left hands, for example: they have pointed out that the right hand is considered "straight," "correct," or "pure" in some Maya languages, whereas the left is "ill-behaved," "clumsy," "weak," or "crazy." Legs, feet, and other aspects of the body, particularly in the lower half of the body, are a bit more problematic in definitive associations, although one has to wonder whether skeletal elements, being spatially lower, were also of inferior status.

Certainly the head, written as *jol* and the seat of Classic Maya identity, was one of the most significant aspects of the body and one of the most common of the "missing" bones cited above. As Houston et al. (2006:28) have noted, the logograph for *jol* is curiously depicted as a skull missing its jaw and not, as would be expected, a fully fleshed head. That a skull sans mandible served, for the Classic Maya, as a head lends further meaning to the Yaxchilan and Palenque examples above and suggests a lesser importance for the jaw, which seems more an extremity than a crucial part of ancient Maya identity. In fact, the most crucial part of the head, in terms of identity, was the face. As the seat for personality in numerous Mesoamerican cultures, it is not surprising that we find faces removed from Maya interments.

A mosaic mask from Calakmul Tomb 4, thought to be the tomb of Yuknoom Yich'aak K'ahk,' bears a curious inscription. According to Simon Martin and Nikolai Grube, the text describes the mask as the *b'aah* "image" or "face" of Yuknoom Cheen II, father and predecessor of Yuknoom Yich'aak K'ahk' (Martin and Grube 2000). As Stephen Houston and David Stuart (1998:85) have demonstrated, the concept of *b'aah* goes beyond mere associations with faces and images: it is intimately connected to Classic Maya conceptions of the self. Notions of self and image did, in turn, overlap with ideas about the soul in Classic Maya thought—*b'aah* was a term for one's individuality, essence, and personal qualities (Fitzsimmons 2009).

Thus, bearing the "face" and personhood of his deceased father, Yuknoom Yich'aak K'ahk' was laid to rest carrying—or even impersonating—his ancestor. Discoveries like these lend further meaning to the removal of faces and skulls from burials, to the power that "faces" and "images" of the dead had, and to the interplay between mosaic masks and actual, skeletal faces within interments. Theoretically, such items would be interchangeable and consistent with what we know from Classic Maya religion. Given this compatibility, one might obtain the *b'aah* of a deceased individual in a variety of ways (Fitzsimmons 2009), from the removal of actual skeletal elements to their substitution by wooden, jade, or other analogues.

In the majority of the cases of face removal in the Maya area, the individuals are processed or previously buried and then re-interred. Welsh (1988:216) has suggested that faces taken out of interments were removed for the purposes of ancestor veneration, although it seems equally plausible that they are the result of sacrifice, transforming the time-honored potential ancestor to a humiliated captive whose image was co-opted by a victorious captor. Shirley Boteler Mock has argued the latter point, seeing removed skeletal objects as the embodiment of a power or life force comparable to the force encapsulated in the seizure of royal items from captured, disgraced, and sacrificed individuals. She notes that facial mutilation, or the flaying of facial skin in particular, removes personality and transfers power to the living, particularly if they choose to wear the skin/skull as a mask (Mock 1998; Schele and Freidel 1990). Whether veneration or humiliation was involved, the end result was similar: the bones of individuals were kept as meaningful portions of the royal self. That some remains were left while others were retained suggests a hierarchical view of the royal body, with certain elements more "useful" than others in their religious or political contexts. From what evidence we do have, the idea seems to be that the essence of personhood, the essence of ancestry resided, for the Classic Maya, in the head and perhaps some key bones (e.g., it seem plausible that occasionally absent femurs, hands, and feet were of greater importance than other parts of the skeleton for retention) from the postcranial skeleton. This hierarchical view of personhood might, when combined with the absence of a "necessary" bone, require the use of a substitute by kin in cases where a ruler or lord was captured and his bones retained by the victors.

As I have noted elsewhere (Fitzsimmons 2009), the use of royal faces or other skeletal elements by the nobility need not have been tied exclusively to sacrifice. During the Colonial period, the practice of ancestor veneration in the Maya area certainly involved such behavior: Diego de Landa, for example, observed sixteenth-century Yucatec Maya using mortuary effigy boxes, where wooden images of the dead were kept much like relics. According to Landa, elite bones were habitually processed, where the cranial ashes of nobles were housed inside hollow clay statues, placed within jars, and deposited within temples. The cranial fragments of "important people," moreover, were placed within a receptacle in the head of a wooden statue and set "with a great deal of veneration among their idols" (Tozzer 1966:131). Rough parallels can be drawn between these statues and effigy figurines of the Classic period recovered from the Street of the Dead at Teotihuacan; the backs of these figures contain holes for presumably similar materials (Headrick 1999). Both of these effigy types can be considered to be heirlooms, inherited property that McAnany has likened to material symbols of the rights of inheritance, visual evidence of one's ancestry, and proper reverence for the deceased (McAnany 1995:36–37). A. M. Tozzer observed analogously curated cranial bones and wooden effigies among the nineteenth-century Lacandones (Tozzer 1907), documenting a physical care for ancestors that mirrors a spiritual care for the dead in present-day Maya populations (McAnany 1995; Nash 1970; Vogt 1969).

Evidence within the Classic Maya context of royal figures actually using the bones of their own ancestors is admittedly sparse. In addition to the example of Butz' Chan from Copan, the head of K'ahk' U Jol K'inich of Caracol ("Fire His Sun-Faced Head"), for example, is seen here (fig. 3.5) borne by his descendant much like a war trophy; the ancestral head dangles from his belt complemented by a number of celts. As Stephen Houston and others have noted, whether the Caracol ornament is figurative or not, there was clearly a desire for portable representations of ancestors among the Classic Maya, particularly in the use of royal heirloom jewelry (Houston 1999). Such portables are usually decorated with the logograph for ancestor, *mam*, usually depicted as an elderly male missing his teeth and bearing a distinctive tuft of hair, as well as the name of a dead king (Houston et al. 2006:50).

Reentered tombs, frequently missing large numbers of skeletal elements and sparsely populated with scattered grave furniture, present the possibility that the Maya were physically accessing and transporting ancestral remains as a form of ancestor veneration. This is probably the case at Caracol, where Diane and Arlen Chase (see also chapter 4, this volume) have done much to clarify the widespread role of human remains in sacred contexts. Human remains there seem to have been fluid in their transport over the landscape; in the royal sphere they have documented a number of burials that seem to have been repeatedly

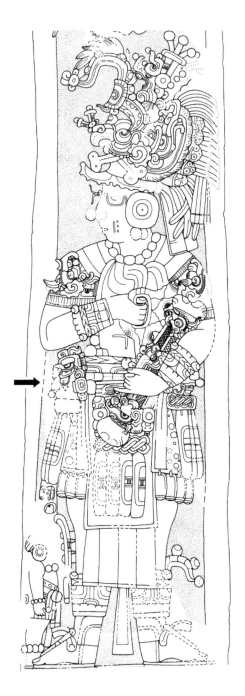

FIGURE 3.5. "Knot Lord" of Caracol wearing the "head" of his ancestor, K'ahk' Ujol K'inich I, as a belt ornament on Caracol Stela 6 (after Beetz and Satterthwaite 1981:fig. 8; courtesy of the Penn Museum).

entered, and human remains removed as well as interred (Chase 1992; Chase 1994; Chase and Chase 1994). Judging from their former connections to royal life and the various uses of human remains, heirlooms, and ancestral images outlined in this work, it seems plausible that royal remains held a special significance for the Classic Maya, useful in royal ritual and ancestral veneration. This seems to have been the case at Terminal Classic Ek' B'alam in the northern lowlands. A recent tomb dating to the 790s bore the remains of a lord, Ukit Kan Le'k, holding a carved human femur (fig. 3.6). Part of the text on this femur states that it was "the (physical) bone" of Ukit Kan Le'k, an individual thought to be the father of the Ek' B'alam lord. Held in the left hand of the deceased, this bone either is an heirloom passed from Ukit Kan Le'k to his son or his own physical remains; in either event, it represents a unique object in the Maya area (Grube et al. 2003). Time will tell if similar, clearly reverential items are recovered among the Southern Classic Maya. Together with the archaeological and epigraphic examples presented in this chapter, the Ek' B'alam bone provides us with evidence of the use of what can only be termed relics in the precolumbian Maya context.

Acknowledgments

I would like to thank all of the staff at the University of Arizona Press for their comments and editing. I would also like to thank Middlebury College, for providing funding for the research of and the support for this publication. Lastly, I would also like to thank Charlene Barrett and Rebecca Bennette.

Notes

1. Indeed, sacrifice is fundamental to how the Maya have perceived habitability since Classic times and has been observed ethnohistorically and ethnographically in numerous incarnations. Guiteras Holmes (1961:26), for example, observed Tzotzil Maya killing chickens and turkeys to make their houses "livable."

2. During the proceedings, he may have identified himself with a supernatural figure called u(y) ek noj k'uh "his black great god," who appears in the text of Stela H just before the name Waxaklajuun Ub'ah K'awiil. The name is similar to that of the so-called vision serpents at Yaxchilan, perhaps alluding to an ancestral conjuring event.

3. There are several types of industries dedicated to trophy production in the Maya area. Some are temporally restricted, such as the carved, cut, or plastered human skulls of the Preclassic and Early Classic (Kidder 1947:57–58; Kidder et al. 1946:153–155; Juarez Muños 1941; Ricketson and Ricketson 1937:145); that industry experienced a revival in the

FIGURE 3.6. Bone from Ek' Balam (after a drawing by Alfonso Lacadena).

Postclassic, however, as exemplified by the possibly plastered (Tozzer 1941:131) incense burner initially encountered by Edward H. Thompson (1891–1926:notes) during his work in the cenote at Chichen Itza. Other industries are not only temporally but also geographically restricted, such as the perforated human teeth—probably used as personal adornments—found in Late Classic contexts at Altun Ha (Pendergast 1979:46–47, 55–56) as well as Early and Late Postclassic contexts at Actun Pobilche (Pendergast 1979:46–47, 55, 56), Chichen Itza (Moholy-Nagy and Ladd 1992:134) and Mayapan (Proskouriakoff 1962:377), respectively. Moholy-Nagy and Ladd (1992:132) have suggested that such materials may be restricted to Belize and the northern lowlands. Nevertheless, we should exercise caution in trying to localize such behavior, for what may appear to be geographic variation may simply be the result of sampling error.

4. There are many items that conceptually overlap with body parts; they would probably receive similar treatment.

Works Cited

Baudez, Claude F., and Peter Mathews

1978   Capture and sacrifice at Palenque. In *Tercera Mesa Redonda de Palenque, 1978,* edited by Merle Greene Robertson and Donnan C. Jeffers, pp. 31–40. Pre-Columbian Art Research Center, Monterrey, California.

Beetz, Carl P., and Linton Satterthwaite

1981   *Monuments and Inscriptions of Caracol, Belize.* University Museum Monograph 44. University Museum, University of Pennsylvania, Philadelphia.

Blom, Franz

1923   *Las ruinas de Palenque.* INAH, Mexico.

Caso, Alfonso

1969   *El tesoro de Monte Alban.* Instituto Nacional de Antropología e Historia, Mexico City.

Chase, Arlen F.

1992   Elites and the Changing Organization of Classic Maya Society. In *Mesoamerican Elites: An Archaeological Assessment,* edited by Diane Z. Chase and Arlen F. Chase, pp. 30–49. University of Oklahoma Press, Norman.

Chase, Diane Z.

1994   Human Osteology, Pathology, and Demography as Represented in the Burials of Caracol, Belize. In *Studies in the Archaeology of Caracol, Belize,* edited by Diane Z. Chase and Arlen F. Chase, pp. 123–138. Monograph 7. Pre-Columbian Art Research Institute, San Francisco.

Chase, Diane Z., and Arlen F. Chase

1994   Maya Veneration of the Dead at Caracol, Belize. In *Septima Mesa Redonda de Palenque, 1989,* vol. 8, edited by Merle Greene Robertson and Virginia Fields. Pre-Columbian Research Institute, San Francisco.

Clancy, Flora S.

1999   *Sculpture in the Ancient Maya Plaza: The Early Classic Period.* University of New Mexico Press, Albuquerque.

Coe, Michael D.

1988   Ideology of the Maya Tomb. In *Maya Iconography*, edited by Elizabeth Benson and Gillett Griffin, pp. 222–235. Princeton University Press, Princeton, N.J.

Coe, Michael D., and Justin Kerr

1998   *The Art of the Maya Scribe*. Harry N. Abrams, New York.

Covarrubias, Miguel

1957   *Indian Art of Mexico and Central America*. Alfred A. Knopf, New York.

Fitzsimmons, James L.

1998   Classic Maya Mortuary Anniversaries at Piedras Negras, Guatemala. *Ancient Mesoamerica* 9:271–278.

2006   Tomb Re-entry among the Classic Maya: Archaeology and Epigraphy in Mortuary Ceremonialism. In *Jaws of the Underworld: Life, Death, and Rebirth among the Ancient Maya*, edited by Pierre R. Colas, Geneviéve LeFort, and Bodil Liljefors Persson, pp. 35–42. Acta Mesoamericana Vol. 16, Verlag Anton Saurwein, Möckmühl, Germany.

2009   *Death and the Classic Maya Kings*. University of Texas Press, Austin.

Fulton, Robert L. (editor)

1965   *Death and Identity*. John Wiley and Sons, New York.

González Rul, Francisco

1961   Trabajos de exploración arqueológica en Tlatelolco. *Anales de Instituto Nacional de Antropología e Historia* 3:10–11.

Graham, Ian, and Eric von Euw

1977   *Corpus of Maya Hieroglyphic Inscriptions, Vol. 3, Part I: Yaxchilan*. Peabody Museum, Harvard University, Cambridge.

Grube, Nikolai, Alfonso Lacadena, and Simon Martin

2003   *Proceedings of the Maya Hieroglyphic Workshop*. Cleveland State University, Cleveland.

Guiteras Holmes, Calixta

1961   *Perils of the Soul: The World View of a Tzotzil Indian*. Free Press, New York.

Headrick, Annabeth

1999   The Street of the Dead . . . It Really Was: Mortuary Bundles at Teotihuacan. *Ancient Mesoamerica* 10(1):69–85.

Houston, Stephen

1998   Classic Maya Depictions of the Built Environment. In *Function and Meaning in Classic Maya Architecture*, edited by Stephen Houston, pp. 333–372. Dumbarton Oaks, Washington, D.C.

1999   Classic Maya Religion: Beliefs and Practices of an Ancient American People. *BYU Studies* 38(4):43–72.

Houston, Stephen, John Robertson, and David Stuart

2000   The Language of Classic Maya Inscriptions. *Current Anthropology* 41(3): 321–356.

Houston, Stephen, and David Stuart

1998   Ancient Maya Self: Personhood and Portraiture in the Classic Period. *RES: Anthropology and Aesthetics* 33:72–101.

Houston, Stephen, David Stuart, and Karl Taube

2006   *The Memory of Bones: Body, Being, and Experience Among the Classic Maya.*
University of Texas Press, Austin.

Juárez Muñoz, J. Fernando

1941   Piezas arqueológicas mayas. In *Los mayas antiguos: Monografías de arqueología,
etnografía y lingüística mayas, publicadas con motivo del Centenario de la Exploración de Yucatán por John L. Stephens y Frederick Catherwood en los años 1841–42,*
pp. 137–142. El Colegio de México, Mexico.

Kidder, Alfred V.

1947   *Artifacts of Uaxactún, Guatemala.* Publication No. 576. Carnegie Institution of
Washington, Washington, D.C.

Kidder, Alfred V., Jesse D. Jennings, and Edwin M. Shook

1946   *Excavations at Kaminaljuyu, Guatemala.* Publication No. 561. Carnegie Institution of Washington, Washington, D.C.

Kopytoff, Igor

1982   Slavery. *Annual Review of Anthropology* 11:207–230.

Lee, Thomas A.

1969   *Artifacts of Chiapa de Corzo, Chiapas, Mexico.* Papers of the New World Archaeological Foundation 26. Brigham Young University, Provo.

Martin, Simon, and Nikolai Grube

2000   *Chronicle of the Maya Kings and Queens: Deciphering the Dynasties of the
Ancient Maya.* Thames and Hudson, London.

Massey, Virginia K., and D. Gentry Steele

1997   A Maya Skull Pit from the Terminal Classic Period, Colha, Belize. In *Bones of
the Maya,* edited by Stephen L. Whittington and David M. Reed, pp. 62–77.
Smithsonian Institution Press, Washington, D.C.

Matos Moctezuma, Eduardo

1980   Teotihuacán: Excavaciones en la Calle de los Muertos (1964). *Anales de Antropología* 17(1):69–90.

McAnany, Patricia A.

1995   *Living with the Ancestors: Kinship and Kingship in Ancient Maya Society.* University of Texas Press, Austin.

Merwin, Raymond E., and George C. Vaillant

1932   *Ruins of Holmul, Guatemala.* Peabody Museum Memoirs Vol. 3, No. 2. Peabody
Museum of Archaeology and Ethnology, Harvard University, Cambridge.

Michels, Joseph W.

1979   *Settlement Pattern Excavations at Kaminaljuyu.* Pennsylvania State University
Press, State College.

Miller, Mary Ellen, and Simon Martin

2004   *Courtly Art of the Ancient Maya.* Thames and Hudson, London.

Mock, Shirley Boteler

1998   Preface. In *The Sowing and the Dawning: Termination, Dedication and Transformation in the Archaeological and Ethnographic Record of Mesoamerica,* edited by
Shirley Boteler Mock. University of New Mexico Press, Albuquerque.

Moholy-Nagy, Háttula, and John M. Ladd

1992   Objects of stone, shell, and bone. In *Artifacts from the Cenote of Sacrifice, Chichen Itza, Yucatan*, edited by Clemency Chase Coggins, pp. 99–151. Peabody Museum Memoirs 10(3). Peabody Museum of Archaeology and Ethnology, Harvard University, Cambridge.

Nash, June

1970   *In the Eyes of the Ancestors: Belief and Behavior in a Maya Community*. Yale University Press, New Haven.

Pendergast, David

1979   *Excavations at Altun Ha, Belize: 1964–1970. Vol. 1*. Royal Ontario Museum: Toronto.

Proskouriakoff, Tatiana

1962   Artifacts of Mayapan. In *Mayapan, Yucatan, Mexico*, edited by Harry E. D. Pollack, pp. 321–442. Publication No. 619. Carnegie Institution of Washington, Washington, D.C.

Ricketson, Oliver G., and Edith B. Ricketson

1937   *Uaxactún, Guatemala: Group E, 1926–1931*. Publication No. 477. Carnegie Institution of Washington, Washington, D.C.

Ringle, William M.

1996   Birds of a Feather: The Fallen Stucco Inscription of Temple XVIII, Palenque, Chiapas. In *Eighth Palenque Round Table, 1993*, edited by Merle Greene Robertson, pp. 45–61. Pre-Columbian Art Research Institute, San Francisco.

Ruz Lhuillier, Alberto

1958   Exploraciones arqueologicas en Palenque 1953–1956. *INAH Anales* 10(39):69–299.

Schele, Linda, and David A. Freidel

1990   *A Forest of Kings: The Untold Story of the Ancient Maya*. William Morrow, New York.

Schele, Linda, and Peter Mathews

1998   *The Code of Kings: The Language of Seven Sacred Maya Temples and Tombs*. Scribner, New York.

Stross, Brian

1998   Seven Ingredients in Mesoamerican Ensoulment: Dedication and Termination in Tenejapa. In *The Sowing and the Dawning*, edited by Shirley Boteler Mock. University of New Mexico Press, Albuquerque.

Stuart, David

1985   The Inscription on Four Shell Plaques from Piedras Negras, Guatemala. In *Fourth Palenque Round Table*, pp. 175–184. Precolumbian Art Research Institute, San Francisco.

2002   Glyphs for "Right" and "Left"? Electronic document, http://www.mesoweb.com/stuart/notes/rightleft.pdf, accessed August 27, 2010.

Thompson, J. Eric S.

1939   *Excavations at San Jose, British Honduras*. Publication No. 506. Carnegie Institution of Washington, Washington, D.C.

Tozzer, Alfred Marston

1907   Survivals of Ancient Forms of Culture among the Mayas of Yucatan and the Lacandones of Chiapas. *Fifteenth International Congress of Americanists, 1906, Quebec, Tome II*, pp. 283–288.

1941   *Landa's Relación de las Cosas de Yucatan*. Papers of the Peabody Museum of American Archaeology and Ethnology Vol. 18. Harvard University, Cambridge.

1966   *Landa's Relación de las Cosas de Yucatán: A Translation*. Kraus Reprint (reprint of 1941 ed.), New York.

Turner, Victor

1969   *The Ritual Process*. University of Chicago Press, Aldine.

Vernon, Glenn

1970   *Sociology of Death: An Analysis of Death-Related Behavior*. Ronald Press, New York.

Vogt, Evon Z.

1969   *Zinacantan: A Maya Community in the Highlands of Chiapas*. Belknap Press of Harvard University Press, Cambridge.

Welsh, W.B.M.

1988   An Analysis of Classic Lowland Maya Burials. *Bar International Series* 409. British Archaeological Reports, Oxford.

Willey, Gordon R., William R. Bullard Jr., John B. Glass, and James C. Gifford

1965   *Prehistoric Maya Settlements in the Belize Valley*. Papers of the Peabody Museum of Archaeology and Ethnology Vol. 54. Peabody Museum of Archaeology and Ethnology, Harvard University, Cambridge.

CHAPTER 4

Ghosts Amid the Ruins

*Analyzing Relationships between the Living
and the Dead among the Ancient Maya at
Caracol, Belize*

DIANE Z. CHASE AND ARLEN F. CHASE

MAYA BURIALS ARE A COMMON part of the archaeological record and a
major resource for the interpretation of ancient Maya beliefs about death
and afterlife. Human interments are encountered with relative frequency
at archaeological sites (Welsh 1988) and are increasingly subjected to
ever more detailed analyses (Wright 2004). While the bulk of evidence
for the consideration of ancient Maya mortuary activity is found in excavations, additional information is available in iconography, epigraphy,
ethnohistory, and contemporary ethnography (Ciudad Ruiz et al. 2003;
Cobos 2004; Tiesler and Cucina 2007). In addition, however, ancient
Maya mortuary activity may be compared with descriptions and theoretical discussions of death ritual worldwide (Metcalf and Huntington 1991)
and expands our understanding of these materials.

Archaeological investigations at Caracol, Belize, have generated substantial information on ancient Maya burial practices; some 282 formal
burials have been recovered during our excavations at Caracol from 1985
through 2008. The ancient Caracol Maya interred their dead in simple
burials, cists, crypts, and tombs (A. Chase and D. Chase 1987:56–57);
human remains also were interred within ritual caches (D. Chase and
A. Chase 1998) or incorporated in residential refuse (D. Chase and
A. Chase 2000). Interments included both single and multiple individuals, and human remains were recovered articulated, disarticulated, and
semi-articulated (D. Chase 1994, 1998). Once thought to have represented a single event or "time capsule" from the past, we now know that
this often is not the case with Maya interments; simple burials and tombs
both show indications of compound burial processes and reentry events

(D. Chase and A. Chase 1996, 2003a). It is the analysis of these burial contexts that provides detailed evidence for a consideration of ancient Maya mortuary systems.

Ancient Maya mortuary and ritual patterns outlined within this chapter indicate the potential of cyclic, as opposed to individual-oriented, mortuary activity and the existence of burial reentry as a means to alter the contract between the living and the dead. These patterns are consistent both with theoretical discussions of the significance of contemporary and historic mortuary activity and with discussions of double funerals and the liminal aspects of death ritual (Hertz 1960; Metcalf and Huntington 1991). The Caracol data confirm the symbolic importance of ancient mortuary ritual in codifying the liminal aspects of death, connecting the living and the dead, and maintaining linkages among members of the living and ancestral community. This analysis suggests that variations in mortuary ritual reflect the dynamics of ancient sociopolitical relationships as well as altered relationships between the living and the dead.

Caracol, Belize

The archaeological site of Caracol, located in the Vaca Plateau of western Belize, has been the locus of annual investigations by the Caracol Archaeological Project since January 1985 (www.caracol.org). Caracol Archaeological Project excavations have focused both on the site epicenter and on the settlement in the surrounding core. The focus of research has varied over the course of the project. While there has always been a consideration of the relationship between Maya hieroglyphic history and archaeology, research also has focused extensively on warfare, status differences, settlement boundaries, field systems, urban development, and, in some cases, simply salvage excavation. Over the course of 24 years, most epicentral structures have been investigated, and approximately 115 residential groups have been sampled.

Archaeological remains indicate that Caracol was first occupied at approximately 600 BC and continued to be occupied through AD 950. However, the majority of the site's occupation dates to the Late Classic period (AD 550–780). Caracol also has a hieroglyphic history, with named rulers and key dynastic events occurring on its carved stone monuments and stucco-adorned buildings. Texts indicate that the site's dynasty was founded in AD 331 and that its latest recorded date is AD 859 (A. Chase et al. 1991). These texts describe Caracol's prowess in war through defeats of neighboring sites, such as Tikal, Naranjo, and Ucanal (D. Chase and A. Chase 2002, 2003b). Caracol reached its maximum size by AD 650, covering an area of approximately 177 square kilometers that contained a population of more than 115,000 people (A. Chase and D. Chase 1994a:5). The site administrative and residential areas were conjoined by a series of causeways that radiated from the epicenter to outlying areas (A. Chase 1988; A. Chase and D. Chase 2001a), presumably connecting markets within a centrally administered economic system (A. Chase and D. Chase 2004). Agricultural terraces were located throughout the core area between residential plazuelas (A. Chase and D. Chase 1998, 2007).

The prosperity of the site's occupants is indicated by the widespread use of tombs (fig. 4.1; see A. Chase 1992; D. Chase 1994) and in the distribution of artifacts ranging from obsidian to marine shell to polychrome pottery throughout the site (D. Chase 1998). Status differentiation among the members of the population is apparent in stable isotope assessment of diet using ancient bone. These studies suggest that the elite living in Caracol's palaces consumed high-maize and high-protein diets and that a support population living immediately adjacent to the site epicenter consumed the least amount of maize and protein; intermediate diets were consumed by the inhabitants of the surrounding settlement core (A. Chase and D. Chase 2001b; A. Chase et al. 2001).

Late Classic Caracol is also characterized by a shared identity (A. Chase and D. Chase 1996; D. Chase and A. Chase 2004a). A key aspect of this identity was Caracol mortuary ritual that centered on symbolic, as opposed to actual, egalitarianism (e.g., A. Chase and D. Chase 2009;). Basic mortuary practices were the same throughout greater Caracol (A. Chase and D. Chase 1994b; D. Chase and A. Chase 2004b). Mortuary activity in elite as well as in nonelite contexts throughout Late Classic Caracol centered on the placement of caches and burials in association with the eastern structure of residential plazas (fig. 4.2). The caches generally consisted of specially made ceramic containers (A. Chase 1994), sometimes accompanied by obsidian eccentrics or human finger bones (D. Chase and A. Chase 1998). Burials in eastern buildings also usually included at least one tomb as well as multiple individual interments. These interments also contained a large number of individuals with

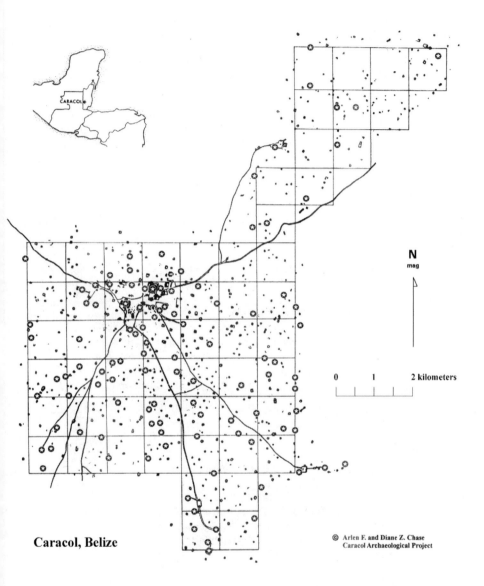

Caracol, Belize

© Arlen F. and Diane Z. Chase
Caracol Archaeological Project

FIGURE 4.1. Map of Caracol, Belize, showing the distribution of known tombs relative to mapped residential groups. Each square measures 500 m on each side; north is to the top of the page.

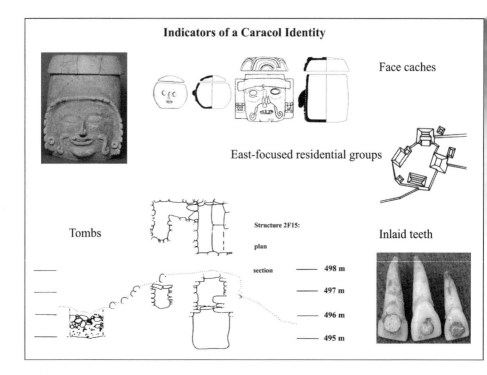

FIGURE 4.2. The establishment of a "Caracol identity" is based largely on common ritual and mortuary activities at Caracol, Belize, that focused on eastern buildings in residential groups, interments with multiple individuals, the use of formal tombs, offerings in special-function cache vessels, and a high percentage of individuals with inlaid teeth.

modified teeth; some 33 percent of Caracol's burials exhibit teeth that are either filed or inlaid with jadeite and hematite (D. Chase 1998).

Investigations at Caracol have uncovered 282 formal interments from the site epicenter and core areas. While Caracol's inhabitants were frequently interred within formal tombs (109 chambers have been investigated), over 60 percent of Caracol's interments were simple burials placed directly in the fill of structures or plazas, in cists that had a formal grave outline but no stone lining, or in small stone-lined crypts. However, in the majority (ca. 80%) of investigated residential groups, at least one tomb was located. Nearly half of the interments at Caracol (46%) contain more than one individual (D. Chase 1998). Many of these burials are indicative of secondary or compound burial events (D. Chase 1994; D. Chase and A. Chase 2003a). Most of these multiple individual interments were the result of a single deposition event, with an articulated individual being placed at the same time as additional bundled and/or partial individuals. However, other interments represent multiple entries, with new placements, disruptions, and removals of human material over time. The fact that interments are often not immediate or primary has been interpreted to suggest the likely existence of double funerals—a two-stage process that entailed a final burial event occurring a considerable period of time after an individual's death (D. Chase and A. Chase 1996:76–77). This research builds upon earlier work by Hertz (1960) and Metcalf and Huntington (1991). However, at least some of these events may also have been episodic—occurring at specific temporal intervals—rather than timed relative to the death of specific individuals. An archaeological consideration of interment history in several of Caracol's mortuary constructions reveals that the sequential burials in many of the site's residential groups were separated by temporal intervals on the order of 40 to 50 years (D. Chase and A. Chase 2004b). These archaeologically dated intervals are consistent with the other data pertaining to the ancient Maya that indicate their timing of events correlates with temporal cycles (e.g., A. Chase 1991; A. Chase and D. Chase 2006). The tightly sequenced archaeological data from Caracol strongly suggest that residential burials in eastern buildings may have been timed to occur with temporal cycles relating to the passage of two *k'atuns* (40 years) or of one calendar round (52 years).

Linking the Dead and the Living: The "Social Compact"

The tie between the living and ancestral Maya is most clearly seen in the colocation of ancient Maya mortuary and household activity within residential plazuela groups (see also McAnany 1995, 1998). Despite statements made by Bishop Landa (Tozzer 1941:130) that Maya residences might have been abandoned once interments were made, this does not appear to have been actual practice. Archaeological evidence demonstrates the consistent conjunction of household and mortuary activity within the same residential plaza, often over an extended period of time.

However, distinct spaces appear to have been reserved for specific residential and mortuary activities.

Interments at Late Classic Caracol were generally located within and in front of identifiable mortuary buildings located on the eastern sides of residential plazuela groups. This correlation between burials and the eastern buildings was recognized early in the research undertaken by the Caracol Archaeological Project (A. Chase and D. Chase 1987:54–57) and built on earlier work by Marshall Becker (1971, 1982, 1992, 2003; Becker and Jones 1999) at Tikal, Guatemala, that dealt with spatial patterning in Maya residential groups. Becker (1971, 1982:120, 2003:259) had demonstrated that the eastern buildings in 14–15 percent of Tikal's residential groups were special-function mortuary structures. At Caracol, our research has shown that this pattern is even more widespread than at Tikal; some 85 percent of eastern constructions tested appropriately at Caracol contained burials or caches (D. Chase 1998:17). It is further apparent that human remains at Caracol were interred in a specific sequence relative to a single edifice: first placed would be a tomb in the core of the building; next, a burial, cist, or crypt would be deposited at the front of the stair; then, a tomb, crypt, or cist was secreted within the stair itself (D. Chase and A. Chase 2004b). Even later burials could then be placed far into the plaza to the front of the building. While the majority of Caracol's interments have been found in or associated with eastern mortuary structures, some burials in residential groups also were located in northern structures (one of the traditional locations for ancestors; see Ashmore 1991).

Caches, consisting either of lidded urns with modeled ceramic faces or of small dishes placed lip-to-lip, were commonly located in association with the same eastern constructions, either above and/or to the sides of interments during the Late Classic period. While the face caches were generally devoid of contents, indicating that they probably had held perishable items, they were sometimes associated with obsidian eccentrics. The smaller lip-to-lip caches were found either empty or containing the remains of human fingers. These fingers were primarily from adults but also included children. As few as a single disarticulated phalange to over 30 articulated fingers have been recovered in a single cache—presumably as a sacrifice to the dead within the building (D. Chase and A. Chase 1998). Other evidence of ritual activity within residential groups includes the placement of complete incense burners both within tombs and on (or under) the steps of eastern buildings (A. Chase and D. Chase 1994b) — and of broken *incensarios* within the fill of cist burials. The conjunction of interments and caches in living spaces indicates the strong ritual connection between the living and the dead. It has also been interpreted as an indication of ancestor veneration by the ancient Maya (McAnany 1995).

During the full temporal occupation of Caracol, plazuela groups continued to be built, lived in, used, and rebuilt as human remains were deposited. A clear and conspicuous proximity existed between the dead and the living that must have reinforced the relationship between the dead ancestors and their living descendants. The continuing nature of this relationship is symbolized by the existence of entranceways (for reentry) into chambers (to place additional dead and/or to remove bone relics). It is further reinforced by the presence of multiple individuals within a chamber (placed contemporaneously and over time).

The Social Bond: Accidental and Purposeful Reentries of Interments

Caracol's interments are directly reflective of the society that inhabited the ancient city. The placement of multiple individuals within a chamber reduced the focus on the individual, reinforced the unity of the residential group, and confirmed the social compact between the living and the dead (see also Bloch 1981:139; Bloch and Parry 1982:34; Gillespie 2001; and Humphreys 1981:6). The ultimate disarticulation of human remains through both double funerals and reentry activities further served to commingle the individualities of the dead. However, there were different types of reentry, and it is argued that these varied reentry activities served social purposes (D. Chase and A. Chase 2003a). Tomb reentry has been identified by researchers such as Bloch (1971), who studied the Merina of Madagascar. Thus, the concept of tomb reentry is not new or unique. However, patterns of ancient Maya tomb reentry at Caracol suggest that the significance of any given tomb was multifaceted, going beyond ancestor veneration, beyond the final placement of an important ancestor, and beyond the establishment and reinforcement of social identity.

Many of Caracol's tombs had formal entryways, meaning that they could be easily accessed and reopened. In some cases chambers were reentered and bodies were removed after the passage of a certain amount of time. In other cases, chambers may have been constructed and initially left empty in anticipation of housing a specific individual but ultimately were occupied and formally sealed. For the purpose of this chapter, the term *reentry* is reserved for situations in which an already occupied and sealed tomb was reopened and new activity ensued.

Two distinct types of burial reentry can be identified in the archaeological record at Caracol. Initially identified only for tomb chambers, these reentries have been subdivided into the categories "accidental" and "purposeful"; purposeful reentries can be further subdivided into the categories "traditional" and "transformational" (fig. 4.3). Archaeological signatures exist for each of these reentry types, and each also has different potential cultural implications. While reentry types may be most easily distinguishable in tombs, similar reentries may be defined and identified for other kinds of interments.

The archaeological signature for accidental reentry is a chamber whose contents are largely intact but is filled entirely with earth and rubble (and whose roof is often difficult to distinguish from the material comprising the engulfing fill). The implication is either that these chambers had their roofing stones collapse unexpectedly (exposing the open-air chamber) or that they were found during the modification of an existing construction (meaning that these interments were outside of any social memory). These tombs were then infilled and hidden during rebuilding efforts. Often, what is presumed to be a sacrificial victim (perhaps representing reconsecration) was placed within the overlying fill. The overall disruption to the original interment is relatively minimal, the burial contents being disturbed only by the laying down of the new fill. Several examples of this kind of reentry have been found in residential groups at Caracol (D. Chase and A. Chase 2003a:271–72); all consist of what were once open-air chambers that have had their roofs largely removed and the chambers completely infilled with dirt and rubble that rests directly on the original interment (in some cases clearly smashing ceramic vessels and upending in situ bone); in at least two cases, this infilling was accompanied by the placement of flexed bodies that were centered in the fill at roof level prior to a structural addition being constructed on the eastern building. A similar kind of reentry may occur in other interment types but is more difficult to detect archaeologically because of even less disruption of the original interment. The clear

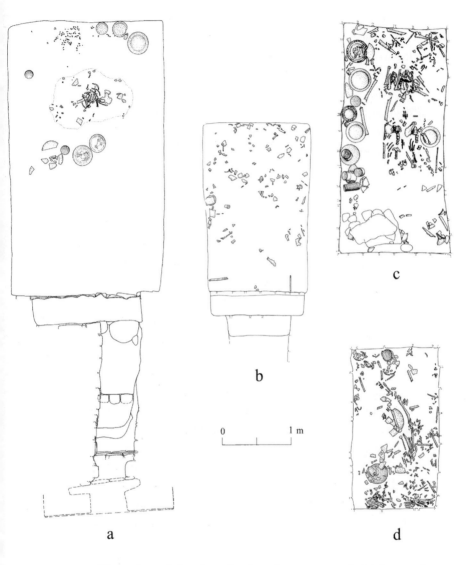

FIGURE 4.3. Floor plans of chambers that have been reentered: (*a*) "reentry" of preconstructed chamber to place bundled burial and associated items; (*b*) purposeful and transformational reentry, showing the patchwork of materials left on the chamber's floor; (*c*) purposeful and traditional reentry, showing largely intact vessels and some articulation; (*d*) accidental reentry, showing the disturbance of an intact burial due to infilling of the chamber.

attempt at not overly disrupting the previously placed burials and their contents, but rather simply reobscuring them, suggests that this kind of reentry likely did not indicate any changes in the sociopolitical order or in the social compact between the dead and the living.

The archaeological signature for a purposeful, but traditional, reentry is an open-air chamber (or other interment) whose human remains and artifacts show signs of some disturbance and suggest the addition and/ or removal of contents. Often, covering capstones are replaced askew, or sealed floors are pierced by circular entry holes. Rationales for these reentries likely varied substantially. Some incorporated additional individuals and artifacts, usually many years or cycles past the initial interment date (see D. Chase and A. Chase 1996). Other chambers may have been entered to remove relics (see Fitzsimmons 1998 and Grube and Schele 1993 for comparative statements). These kinds of reentries are particularly recognizable in the archaeological record through floor patches that permitted chamber reentry (assuming the lack of a formal entryway) or through contextual analysis that indicates either sequent events separated by a substantial period of time or the addition of ritual objects like cache vessels or *incensarios* into a chamber. While primary individuals in interments may have changed and/or some ritual items may have been removed and others added, the chamber remained open-air without added debris, and the interment is largely intact and without major disruption. Thus, it is argued that the social compact between the dead and the living likely remained intact.

The archaeological signature for a transformational reentry (which is also "purposeful") is an interment whose contents are completely disturbed, often having been broken and burnt and then redeposited. If the interment is in a chamber, the chamber is often partially infilled with earth and rubble, and the subsequent roof closure may be fairly crude in its construction standards; however, the chamber roofs are still present, and there is usually some open-air quality preserved in the chamber. Skeletal remains and offerings alike are generally fragmentary. Burning is fairly ubiquitous. Even in the rare instances in which bodies are partially articulated, they are still burnt; jadeite beads are usually shattered and burnt; ceramic vessels are often partial, with heavy burning on some sherds but not others. A fairly wide range of behaviors entered into these transformational deposits, and they are also usually located in architecturally prominent locations and places. The implication is that these transformational reentries are intentional disturbances of both the interment and the social compact between the dead and the living. At Caracol, transformational reentries are known from two time horizons. The first occurs in elite tombs dating to the beginning of the Late Classic era, precisely when Caracol announced its independence from Tikal. The second occurrence of transformational reentries can be dated to the Terminal Classic period, another time of dynastic change at the site. Thus, transformational reentries also potentially served political purposes and may be indicative of sociopolitical transition. Bodies and chambers were treated symbolically to effect change. A similar use of human remains for political purposes has been documented for the royal houses of Europe (Weiss-Krejci 2001).

The Timing and Placement of Maya Interments

We have argued previously that the east-focused mortuary activity within residential plazuela groups represented a strong focus on ancestor veneration (A. Chase and D. Chase 1994b, 1996) and was thus the basis for a social compact between the living and the dead. However, we also have shown that the timing of placement of these household interments was periodic and may have been undertaken in accord with ritual cycles rather than with the death events of specific individuals (D. Chase and A. Chase 2004b). Two specific lines of evidence support this interpretation. First, a dramatically smaller number of burials were made within residential groups than can be expected when based on the projected number of household occupants that would have existed in these groups; only some 10 percent of the total household population that once resided in a residential group can be archaeologically documented as having been buried there (D. Chase 1997). Second, the materials included within many of the burials recovered in a residential group permit the fairly precise dating of these interments (e.g., A. Chase 1994) and suggest that a sizeable temporal span existed between inhumations. Detailed stratigraphic and contextual review of interments recovered from eastern buildings in a series of Caracol's residential groups (and tightly dated by associated ceramic assemblages) suggested that this interval may have been approximately 40 to 50 years, perhaps even having been timed to coincide with a calendar round or 52-year cycle (D. Chase and A. Chase

2004b:table 1). Pru Rice (2004) has argued recently that the entire Classic period Maya sociopolitical order was timed to coincide with the *may*, or 256-year, ritual cycle. Archaeologically, it can also be argued that certain building assemblages, ranging from E Groups (A. Chase and D. Chase 2006) to radial structures (Schele and Mathews 1998:175–196), were erected or rebuilt to commemorate *b'ak'tun* (or 400-year) cycles. Jones (1996:91) has demonstrated that plaza plans of a very specific form were erected to celebrate 20-year *k'atun* intervals at Tikal, Guatemala, in the Late Classic era. We have previously argued that certain Maya caching patterns were reflective of calendric ritual and that some incense burners may have served as *k'atun* idols, further marking the passage of time (D. Chase 1985a, 1985b, 1988; D. Chase and A. Chase 1988, 2008). We would argue that such overriding concerns with temporal cycles also were manifest in Caracol residential plazas in the episodic placement of burials relative to the site's eastern buildings. Thus, household interment events appear to have been conjoined with community-wide ritual activities that not only bolstered ties between direct ancestors and their living descendants but also emphasized the wider connection between the dead and the living in the broader sociopolitical environment of "greater Caracol."

Liminality in Death Ritual and Maya Concepts of Death

Life and death were not absolute opposites for the ancient Maya. Just as the Maya did not abandon their living areas after placing the dead within them, the archaeological record also suggests that Landa's (Tozzer 1941:129) statement that the Maya had "a great and excessive fear of death" does not mirror the Classic period situation. Much theoretical discussion has focused on the transition of the corpse (and essence or soul of the deceased) in death ritual and on the use of symbols to represent both transition and regeneration (Metcalf and Huntington 1991:32–33; Turner 1969; Van Gennep 1960). We would argue not only that there were liminal phases and symbolism in mortuary ritual, but that the ancient Maya dead during the Classic period were conceived of as being liminal or transitional beings, only partially separated from the living. The dead could reappear in the present world; the living (at least dwarfs [A. Chase and D. Chase 1994b]) could access the places of the dead by reentering their tombs. Interactions between the dead and the living were possible and necessary in that the living were obliged to venerate their ancestors. At Caracol, the interactions took several forms. Some dead may have been literally housed in the superstructures of the eastern buildings in the residential groups, which likely functioned as mausoleums. Offerings associated with these eastern buildings are fairly common in the archaeological record and consist of ceramic cache vessels as well as vestiges of other perishable objects, indicating a potentially proactive form of intercession on the part of the living. These offerings can be taken as evidence that ancestors also could intercede (positively and negatively) in the affairs of their descendants. The continued relationship among the living and the dead was facilitated at Caracol by the colocation of mortuary activity with household occupation. Veneration was therefore possible on a day-to-day basis. Furthermore, mortuary ritual was not a single, one-time event correlated with the death of an individual. Compound burial processes suggest the existence of double funerals that took place over an extended period of time. Each household may also have engaged in episodic mortuary activities conducted at key intervals, probably associated with calendric cycles. Formal entranceways into chambers encouraged reentries; however, interments without entranceways were also reaccessed. Reentries into interments added or removed remains and offerings over time, implying the continuous nature of the social contract between the dead and the living.

While the living could visit the resting places of their dead ancestors with relative ease due to their proximity to day-to-day activities within the household, the dead and the living were predominantly situated in different places—the living were above ground, and the dead (for the most part) were underground in the underworld. Separating the worlds of the living and the dead was a surface that could be penetrated, often depicted iconographically as the surface of water with fantastic underworld creatures below and more mundane contemporary worldly creatures above (Coe 1978; Schele and Miller 1986). Beings that could penetrate this surface and exist simultaneously in both worlds were liminal, like the ancestors themselves (D. Chase and A. Chase 2009). Such creatures included dwarfs as well as sharks, turtles, alligators, snakes, and water lilies. Viewing one world from the other was possible with the aid of reflective devices such as mirrors or mercury (D. Chase and A. Chase 1998).

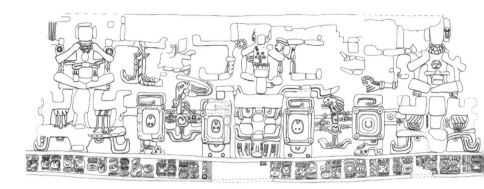

FIGURE 4.4. Examples of ancestral portraits on a Late Classic building facade from Caracol, Belize.

Transition to the underworld for the dead was also a process, the journey likely comparable to the timing of the second funeral. Even artwork suggests that this transition was not instantaneous. Incised bone from a Tikal tomb shows a boat with the dead individual surrounded by personified animals about to sink into the depths of the watery underworld, implying a journey that ends in submersion. Hieroglyphic texts also hint that a substantial period of time was involved (see the discussion in McAnany 1998:289 of *muknal* activities extending to 24 years, and in Fitzsimmons 1998 of mortuary anniversaries). Ancestors continued to exist even after being transferred into the underworld and often were iconographically portrayed in the world of the living in locations such as building facades; at Caracol these ancestral portraits on monumental architecture (fig. 4.4) depicted them in association with underworld creatures (such as fish eating transitional water lilies). The liminal aspects of death and mortuary ritual, in conjunction with the ongoing relationships among the dead and the living, led to reentries into interments and necessitated rectifying the relationships among the dead and the living through transformational reentries.

Conclusions

The dead were clearly important to the ancient Maya. Yet Maya interments were not simply placed to coincide with the death of an individual or with the commemoration of such an event. Some researchers have argued that interments placed in monumental architecture were dedicatory to building construction (see W. Coe 1990 and discussion in D. Chase 1988), essentially serving as elaborated offerings or caches (Becker 1992). Others have suggested that these buildings instead served as funerary monuments for great rulers (see M. Coe 1956, 1988). Most interments, however, are not located within monumental site architecture, but rather within residential plazuelas (as indicated above). While abundant, there are not nearly as many individuals recovered from residential burials as there were proposed inhabitants of specific residential groups. Even in the largest samples of well-excavated residential compounds, there are far too few interments to indicate the existence of a sustained population over time. This is evident in residential groups not only at Caracol (D. Chase 1997) but also in the neighboring and well-excavated central Petén site of Tikal (A. Chase et al. 2002; Haviland 1988; Haviland et al. 1985). Analysis of interment placement and sequence at Caracol has been facilitated by the existence of hieroglyphically dated tomb contexts, substantial contextually recovered ceramic inventories, and radiocarbon dates. While it is possible that the deceased were cremated or were placed elsewhere, a review of the interments at Caracol suggests yet a different situation—that tombs were sometimes a temporary, as opposed to a final, resting place (A. Chase and D. Chase 1994b; D. Chase and A. Chase 1996) and that the timing and placement of interments was more likely related to larger community-wide cycles than to specific life and death events of particular individuals (D. Chase and A. Chase 2004b). The recent proposal by Pru Rice (2004) to relate regional sociopolitical events to the adherence of a *may*, or 256-year cycle, may be viewed as the logical extension of cyclically timed household interment ceremonies and calendric caching rituals (D. Chase 1985a, 1988). The existence of periodic or episodic community-wide mortuary ritual, while not generally proffered or referenced for the ancient Maya, was a key component of such patterns among a number of native North American groups (Hickerson 1960; Ubelaker 1989:40) and thus makes sense in the Maya archaeological context.

The conjunction of mortuary ritual with contemporary household activity, the temporal sequence of burial events within households, and the iconographic portrayals of ancestors all demonstrate the strong ties between the dead and the living among the ancient Maya. Eastern mortuary constructions constituted mausoleums and ritual loci that were used both for ancestor veneration and to establish a broader social identity for the group's inhabitants through the placement of multiple individuals in a single grave. The eastern buildings not only contained burials but also had cached offerings. Burials could be reaccessed over time to add or remove bones and offerings. Tombs with multiple individuals and disarticulated and bundled bones served to commingle remains, thus symbolizing the unity of the group as opposed to the veneration of individual ancestors. However, the relationship between the dead and the living was not limited to a single family. The episodic patterning of burial deposits suggests regular cycles of interment that were community-wide. Thus, while ancestors of a family might be more likely to intervene in the affairs of their living descendants, death ritual formed a unifying factor for the entire community. Reentries into chambers generally occurred within these larger interment cycles; however, some reentries were distinctive in disturbing and destroying remains. These reentry contexts are called "transformational"; they disrupted and/or destroyed the individuality of interred individuals as well as of any burial offerings associated with them, ritually and symbolically cleansing the locale of past social and political meaning. These transformational reentries were limited in number and coincide with political transitions at the site. Thus, the transformational reentries that are associated with the interments at the base of Structure B19 on the summit of Caracol's tallest building complex, Caana, are coeval with the shift from a known dynastic line with identified rulers to a period with unclear historic and dynastic connections (see D. Chase and A. Chase 2003a). Transformational reentries not only destroyed the individuality of tomb occupants but also signaled the end of a particular dynastic tradition, representing either the end of a cycle or a political change—or both.

Archaeological investigations at Caracol have demonstrated the importance of mortuary remains in maintaining family continuity and in unifying the wider community. These data further suggest that the Maya viewed the dead as conjoined with the living. While liminal aspects of death ritual symbolism often are noted as a key phase in the transition of the corpse, the continued connection between the dead and the living and the possibility that liminality may be a state of being associated with deceased individuals have not been as thoroughly explored. The Caracol Maya (and probably other groups) practiced episodic interment events on a community-wide basis. Most initial mortuary contexts and reentries into interments were consistent with the continuation of a social contract between the dead and the living; however, burial contexts could also redefine the relationships between the dead and the living and reflect changes in the social and political order. In sum, ancient Maya mortuary remains from Late Classic Caracol, Belize, give insight into the larger Maya worldview. These data confirm the intimate and continuing relationship between deceased ancestors and their living descendants and underscore the value of analyzing mortuary contexts to analyze broader cultural and sociopolitical change.

Acknowledgments

The research reported on here has been funded by a variety of sources. The work at Caracol, Belize, has been funded by the Ahau Foundation, the Alphawood Foundation, the Dart Foundation, the Geraldine and Emory Ford Foundation, the Government of Belize, the Foundation for the Advancement of Mesoamerican Studies, Inc., the Harry Frank Guggenheim Foundation, the Institute of Maya Studies, the J. I. Kislak Foundation, the National Aeronautics and Space Agency (NNX-08AM11G), the National Science Foundation (BNS-8619996, SBR-9311773, SBR-9708637, DBI-0115837), the Stans Foundation, the United States Agency for International Development, the University of New Mexico Research Foundation, and the University of Central Florida Trevor Colbourn Endowment. Many articles published on Caracol may be found as PDF files at http://www .caracol.org.

Works Cited

Ashmore, Wendy
1991   Site Planning Principles and Concepts of Directionality Among the Classic Maya. *Latin American Antiquity* 2(3):199–226.
Becker, Marshall J.
1971   The Identification of a Second Plaza Plan at Tikal, Guatemala, and Its Implications for Ancient Maya Social Complexity. Ph.D. dissertation, Department of Anthropology, University of Pennsylvania.
1982   Ancient Maya Houses and Their Identification: An Evaluation of Architectural Groups at Tikal and Inferences Regarding Their Function. *Revista Española de Antropología Americana* 12:111–129.
1992   Burials as Caches: Caches as Burials: A New Interpretation of the Meaning of Ritual Deposits Among the Classic Lowland Maya. In *New Theories on the*

> *Ancient Maya*, edited by Elin C. Danien and Robert J. Sharer, pp. 185–196. University Museum Monograph 77. University of Pennsylvania, Philadelphia.

2003   Plaza Plans at Tikal: A Research Strategy for Inferring Social Organization and Processes of Culture Change at Lowland Maya Sites. In *Tikal: Dynasties, Foreigners, and Affairs of State*, edited by Jeremy A. Sabloff, pp. 253–280. School of American Research Press, Santa Fe.

Becker, Marshall J., and Christopher Jones

1999   *Excavations in Residential Areas of Tikal: Groups with Shrines: Tikal Report 21.* University Museum Monograph 104. University of Pennsylvania, Philadelphia.

Beetz, Carl P., and Linton Sattherthwaite

1981   *Monuments and Inscriptions of Caracol, Belize.* Monograph 44. University of Pennsylvania, University Museum, Philadelphia.

Bloch, Maurice

1971   *Placing the Dead: Tombs, Ancestral Villages, and Kinship Organization in Madagascar.* Waveland Press, Prospect Heights, Ill.

1981   Tombs and States. In *Mortality and Immortality: The Anthropology and Archaeology of Death*, edited by S. C. Humphreys and Helen King, pp. 137–147. Academic Press, New York.

Bloch, Maurice, and Jonathan Parry

1982   *Death and the Regeneration of Life.* Cambridge University Press, Cambridge.

Chase, Arlen F.

1988   Jungle Surveying: Mapping the Archaeological Site of Caracol, Belize. *P.O.B. (Point of Beginning)* 13(3):10–12, 14, 16, 18, 22, 24.

1991   Cycles of Time: Caracol in the Maya Realm. In *Sixth Palenque Round Table, 1986*, vol. 8, edited by Merle Greene Robertson, pp. 32–42. University of Oklahoma Press, Norman.

1992   Elites and the Changing Organization of Classic Maya Society. In *Mesoamerican Elites: An Archaeological Assessment*, edited by Diane Z. Chase and Arlen F. Chase, pp. 30–49. University of Oklahoma Press, Norman.

1994   A Contextual Approach to the Ceramics of Caracol, Belize. In *Studies in the Archaeology of Caracol, Belize*, edited by Diane Z. Chase and Arlen Chase, pp. 157–182. Monograph 7. Pre-Columbian Art Research Institute, San Francisco.

Chase, Arlen F., and Diane Z. Chase

1987   *Investigations at the Classic Maya City of Caracol, Belize: 1985–1987.* Monograph 3. Pre-Columbian Art Research Institute, San Francisco.

1994a   Details in the Archaeology of Caracol, Belize: An Introduction. in *Studies in the Archaeology of Caracol, Belize*, edited by Diane Z. Chase and Arlen F. Chase, pp. 1–11. Monograph 7. Pre-Columbian Art Research Institute, San Francisco.

1994b   Maya Veneration of the Dead at Caracol, Belize. In *Seventh Palenque Round Table, 1989*, edited by Merle Greene Robertson, pp. 55–62. Pre-Columbian Art Research Institute, San Francisco.

1996   A Mighty Maya Nation: How Caracol Built an Empire by Cultivating Its "Middle Class." *Archaeology* 49(5):66–72.

1998   Scale and Intensity in Classic Period Maya Agriculture: Terracing and Settlement at the "Garden City" of Caracol, Belize. *Culture and Agriculture* 20(2):60–77.

2001a   Ancient Maya Causeways and Site Organization at Caracol, Belize. *Ancient Mesoamerica* 12(2):1–9.

2001b   The Royal Court of Caracol, Belize: Its Palaces and People. In *Royal Courts of the Ancient Maya:2: Data and Case Studies*, edited by Takeshi Inomata and Stephen D. Houston, pp. 102–137. Westview Press, Boulder, Col.

2004   Exploring Ancient Economic Relationships at Caracol, Belize. *Research Reports in Belizean Archaeology* 1:115–127.

2006   Before the Boom: Caracol's Preclassic Era. *Research Reports in Belizean Archaeology* 3:41–67.

2007   Ancient Maya Urban Development: Insights from the Archaeology of Caracol, Belize. *Journal of Belizean Studies* 29(2):60–71.

2009   Symbolic Egalitarianism and Homogenized Distributions in the Archaeological Record at Caracol, Belize: Method, Theory, and Complexity. *Research Reports in Belizean Archaeology* 6:15–24.

Chase, Arlen F., Diane Z. Chase, and William A. Haviland

2002   Maya Social Organization from a "Big Site" Perspective: Classic Period Caracol, Belize and Tikal, Guatemala. In *Organizacion social entre los mayas: Memoria de la Tercera Mesa Redonda de Palenque*, vol. 1, edited by Vera Tiesler, Rafael Cobos, and Merle Greene Robertson, pp. 251–276. Conaculta–Instituto Nacional de Arqueología e Historia, Mexico.

Chase, Arlen F., Diane Z. Chase, and Christine White

2001   El paisaje urbano maya: La integración de los espacios construidos y la estructura social en Caracol, Belice. In *Reconstruyendo la ciudad maya: El urbanismo en las sociedades antiguas*, edited by A. Ciudad Ruiz, María Josefa Iglesias Ponce de Léon, and Maria del Carmen Martinez, pp. 95–122. Sociedad Española de Estudios Mayas, Madrid.

Chase, Arlen F., Nikolai Grube, and Diane Z. Chase

1991   Three Terminal Classic Monuments from Caracol, Belize. *Research Reports on Ancient Maya Writing* 36:1–18.

Chase, Diane Z.

1985a   Between Earth and Sky: Idols, Images, and Postclassic Cosmology. In *Fifth Palenque Round Table, 1983*, vol. 7, pp. 223–233, edited by Merle Greene Robertson and Virginia M. Fields. Pre-Columbian Art Research Institute, San Francisco.

1985b   Ganned But Not Forgotten: Late Postclassic Archaeology and Ritual at Santa Rita Corozal, Belize. In *The Lowland Maya Postclassic*, edited by Arlen Chase and Prudence Rice, pp. 104–125. University of Texas Press, Austin.

1988   Caches and Censerwares: Meaning from Maya Pottery. In *A Pot for All Reasons: Ceramic Ecology Revisited*, edited by Charles Kolb and Louana Lackey, pp. 81–104. Laboratory of Anthropology, Temple University, Philadelphia.

1994   Human Osteology, Pathology, and Demography as Represented in the Burials of Caracol, Belize. In *Studies in the Archaeology of Caracol, Belize*, edited by

Diane Z. Chase and Arlen F. Chase, pp. 123–138. Monograph 7. Pre-Columbian Art Research Institute, San Francisco.

1997   Southern Lowland Maya Archaeology and Human Skeletal Remains: Interpretations from Caracol (Belize), Santa Rita Corozal (Belize), and Tayasal (Guatemala). In *Bones of the Maya: Studies of Ancient Skeletons*, edited by Stephen C. Whittington and David M. Reed, pp. 15–27. Smithsonian Institution Press, Washington, D.C.

1998   Albergando a los muertos en Caracol, Belice. *Los investigadores de la cultura maya* 6(1):9–25. Universidad Autonoma de Campeche, Campeche.

Chase, Diane Z., and Arlen F. Chase

1988   *A Postclassic Perspective: Excavations at the Maya Site of Santa Rita Corozal, Belize*. Monograph 4. Pre-Columbian Art Research Institute, San Francisco.

1996   Maya Multiples: Individuals, Entries, and Tombs in Structure A34 of Caracol, Belize. *Latin American Antiquity* 7(1):61–79.

1998   The Architectural Context of Caches, Burials, and Other Ritual Activities for the Classic Period Maya (as Reflected at Caracol, Belize). In *Function and Meaning in Classic Maya Architecture*, edited by Stephen D. Houston, pp. 299–332. Dumbarton Oaks, Washington, D.C.

2000   Inferences About Abandonment: Maya Household Archaeology and Caracol, Belize. *Mayab* 13:67–77.

2002   Classic Maya Warfare and Settlement Archaeology at Caracol, Belize. *Estudios de Cultura Maya* 22:33–51.

2003a   Secular, sagrado, y revisitado: La profanacion, alteracion, y reconsagracion de los antiguos entierros mayas. In *Antropología de la eternidad: La muerte en la cultura maya*, edited by A. Ciudad Ruiz, Mario Humberto Ruz Sosa, and María Josefa Iglesias Ponce de Léon, pp. 255–277. Publicación 7. Sociedad de los Estudios Mayas, Madrid.

2003b   Texts and Contexts in Classic Maya Warfare: A Brief Consideration of Epigraphy and Archaeology at Caracol, Belize. In *Ancient Mesoamerican Warfare*, edited by M. Kathryn Brown and Travis W. Stanton, pp. 171–188. Alta Mira Press, Walnut Creek, Calif.

2004a   Archaeological Perspectives on Classic Maya Social Organization from Caracol, Belize. *Ancient Mesoamerica* 15:111–119.

2004b   Patrones de enterramiento y cíclos residenciales en Caracol, Belice. In *Culto funerario en la sociedad maya: Memoria de la Cuarta Mesa Redonda de Palenque*, edited by Rafael Cobos, pp. 203–230. Instituto Nacional de Antropología e Historia, Mexico, DF.

2006   Framing the Maya Collapse: Continuity, Discontinuity, Method, and Practice in the Classic to Postclassic Southern Maya Lowlands. In *After the Collapse: The Regeneration of Complex Societies*, edited by Glenn Schwartz and John Nichols, pp. 168–187. University of Arizona Press, Tucson.

2008   Late Postclassic Ritual at Santa Rita Corozal, Belize: Understanding the Archaeology of a Maya Capital City. *Research Reports in Belizean Archaeology* 5:79–92.

2009   Changes in Maya Religious Worldview: Liminality and the Archaeological Record. In *Maya Worldviews at Conquest*, edited by Timothy W. Pugh and Leslie G. Cecil, 219–238. University of Colorado Press, Boulder.

Ciudad Ruiz, Andrés, Mario Humberto Ruz Sosa, María Josefa Iglesias Ponce de Léon (editors)

2003   *Antropología de la eternidad: La muerte en la cultura maya*. Publicación 7. Sociedad Española de Estudios Mayas, Madrid.

Cobos, Rafael (editor)

2004   *Culto funerario en la sociedad maya: Memoria de la Cuarta Mesa Redonda de Palenque*. Instituto Nacional de Antropología e Historia, Mexico, DF.

Coe, Michael D.

1956   The Funerary Temple Among the Classic Maya. *Southwestern Journal of Anthropology* 12(4):387–394.

1978   *Lords of the Underworld: Masterpieces of Classic Maya Ceramics*. Princeton University Press, Princeton.

1988   Ideology of the Maya Tomb. In *Maya Iconography*, edited by Elizabeth P. Benson and Gillett G. Griffin, pp. 222–235. Princeton University Press, Princeton.

Coe, William R.

1990   *Excavations in the Great Plaza, North Terrace, and North Acropolis of Tikal: Tikal Report 14*. 6 vols. Monograph 61. University of Pennsylvania Museum, Philadelphia.

Fitzsimmons, James

1998   Classic Maya Mortuary Anniversaries at Piedras Negras, Guatemala. *Ancient Mesoamerica* 9(2):271–278.

Gillespie, Susan

2001   Personhood, Agency, and Mortuary Ritual: A Case Study from the Ancient Maya. *Journal of Anthropological Archaeology* 20:73–112.

Grube, Nikolai, and Linda Schele

1993   *Naranjo Altar 1 and Rituals of Death and Burials*. Texas Notes on Precolumbian Art, Writing, and Culture 54. Center of the History and Art of Ancient American Culture, University of Texas, Austin.

Haviland, William A.

1988   Musical Hammocks at Tikal: Problems in Reconstructing Household Composition. In *House and Household in the Mesoamerican Past*, edited by Richard Wilk and Wendy Ashmore, pp. 121–134. University of New Mexico Press, Albuquerque.

Haviland, William A., with Marshall J. Becker, Anne Chowning, Keith A. Dixon, and Karl Heider

1985   *Excavations in Small Residential Groups of Tikal: Groups 4F-1 and 4F-2: Tikal Reports 19*. 6 vols. University Museum, University of Pennsylvania, Philadelphia.

Hertz, Robert

1960   A Contribution to the Study of the Collective Representation of Death. In *Death and the Right Hand*, translated by Rodney Needham and Claudia Needham. Free Press, New York.

Hickerson, Harold
1960   The Feast of the Dead among the Seventeenth-Century Algonkians of the Upper Great Lakes. *American Anthropologist* 62:81–107.

Humphreys, S. C.
1981   Introduction: Comparative Perspectives on Death. In *Mortality and Immortality: The Anthropology and Archaeology of Death*, edited by S. C. Humphreys and Helen King. Academic Press, New York.

Jones, Christopher
1996   *Excavations in the East Plaza of Tikal*. Tikal Reports No. 16. University Museum Monograph 92. University of Pennsylvania Museum, Philadelphia.

McAnany, Patricia A.
1995   *Living with the Ancestors: Kinship and Kingship in Ancient Maya Society*. University of Texas Press, Austin.
1998   Ancestors and the Classic Maya Built Environment. In *Function and Meaning in Classic Maya Architecture*, edited by Stephen D. Houston, pp. 271–298. Dumbarton Oaks, Washington, D.C.

Metcalf, Peter, and Richard Huntington
1991   *Celebrations of Death: The Anthropology of Mortuary Ritual*. Cambridge University Press, New York.

Rice, Prudence M.
2004   *Maya Political Science: Time, Astronomy, and the Cosmos*. University of Texas Press, Austin.

Schele, Linda, and Peter Mathews
1998   *The Code of Kings: The Language of Seven Sacred Maya Temples and Tombs*. Scribner, New York.

Schele, Linda, and Mary E. Miller
1986   *The Blood of Kings: Dynasty and Ritual in Maya Art*. Kimball Art Museum, Fort Worth.

Tiesler, Vera, and Andrea Cucina
2007   *New Perspectives on Human Sacrifice and Ritual Body Treatment in Ancient Maya Society*. Springer, New York.

Tozzer, Alfred M. (editor and translator)
1941   *Landa's Relacion de las Cosas de Yucatan*. Papers of the Peabody Museum of Harvard 18. Harvard University, Cambridge.

Turner, Victor
1969   *The Ritual Process*. Aldine, Chicago.

Ubelaker, Douglas H.
1989   *Human Skeletal Remains: Excavation, Analysis, Interpretation*. 2nd ed. Taraxacum, Washington, D.C.

Van Gennep, Arnold
1960/   *The Rites of Passage*. Translated by Monika Vizdom and Gabrielle L. Caffee.
[1909] University of Chicago Press, Chicago.

Weiss-Krejci, Estella

2001   Restless Corpses: "Secondary Burial" in the Babenberg and Habsburg Dynasties. *Antiquity* 75:769–780.

Welsh, W.B.M.

1988   *An Analysis of Classic Lowland Maya Burials*. BAR International Series 409. BAR, Oxford.

Wright, Lori E.

2004   Osteological Investigations of Ancient Maya Lives. In *Continuities and Changes in Maya Archaeology: Perspectives at the Millennium*, edited by Charles W. Golden and Greg Borgstede, pp. 201–215. Routledge, New York.

CHAPTER 5

Bodies, Bones, and Burials

Corporeal Constructs and Enduring Relationships in Oaxaca, Mexico

JEFFREY P. BLOMSTER

BRIGHTLY COLORED AND GLOWING SKULLS, made of sugar, flash through the nights during the Day of the Dead throughout Oaxaca state, a powerful visual reminder of the ongoing social relationships that continue between the living and the dead both in the prehispanic past and among contemporary Oaxacan residents. It is a time when all members of a household—living and dead—are together (Monaghan 1996). Small skeleton sculptures abound in stores and depict the full range of activities that the dead continue to enjoy—marriage, drinking, even performing music. People from all walks of life in Oaxaca today plan parties and feasts to celebrate the return of the spirits of their loved ones, recognizing the importance of death in their everyday lives and the performative ways in which it is experienced (Norget 2006). Class and economic issues impact Day of the Dead and other death rituals in Oaxaca today, just as deceased ancestors in the past played important roles in the ongoing social negotiations of elites and commoners.

While death may be universal, the treatment of the corpse and its relation to the living vary. Even the conception of a corpse as a non-living object, as opposed to a transforming body that still contains vital life essences, shows remarkable cross-cultural variability. After death, the body may be burned, buried (in a variety of positions), preserved through smoking or embalming, or eaten; offerings and sacrifices may or may not be presented (Metcalf and Huntington 1991:24). These tactics, as well as others, serve to remove the dead from the domain of the living or demarcate them as dead or somehow different from living members of society (Parker Pearson 1999); mortuary practices transform the deceased and reintegrate them into society as something else. The American way of treatment of the dead is one of the most exotic and costly, with the corpse removed from the space of the living family to be ensconced at a funeral home, where it is embalmed and transformed into what Jessica Mitford (1963:54) called a "Beautiful Memory Picture." It is common for the corpse to be displayed and visited; most of the familiar funeral rituals of the United States developed between 1830 and 1920 (Farrell 1980).

Anthropologists focus especially on the significance of mortuary ritual and how death and ritual affect social life and the negotiation of social roles, as well as the relationship between ritual and emotion, with death and burial as part a long transformative process. Durkheim (1938) incorporated mortuary rites into his assertion that religion expressed the moral cohesion of society. Funeral rites bring together a spectrum of different social agents within a society and represent a liminal moment when social boundaries may be reconstituted or challenged through a series of stages in this rite of passage involving the articulation between the living and the dead (van Gennep 1960). The deceased may actually be viewed as between death and life during mortuary practices, which vary greatly in their duration (Hertz 1960). The nature of the mortuary practices and specific symbols and rites deployed are both polyvalent and ambiguous, referencing a larger societal context, ideology, and cosmology (Turner 1967).

While death may be the ultimate leveler, the effort invested in the treatment of the dead and attendant mortuary rituals can reinforce social status, although efforts to correlate offerings with social ranking ignore often contradictory agendas of different social actors (Ucko 1969). The placement and treatment of the dead reflect more about negotiations of social relations among the living. As with the case of the similarly outfitted dead New England Puritans, who were anything but egalitarian in life, the living may use the treatment of the dead as an attempt to construct a social order that never existed. Mortuary practices serve to create lasting relationships between the living and the dead, with tombs created for the active negotiation of the living as much as a repository for the dead (Dillehay 1995). Although numerous factors are involved, generally one's identity and position in life affect burial, with different ways of representing identity in the symbols and execution of the funerary rites. The social identity and status of both the deceased and the mourners are actively negotiated and manipulated during mortuary practices (Binford 1971; Parker Pearson 1999; Saxe 1970).

Throughout Mesoamerica, death both continued and transformed social relationships and memories. A diachronic perspective on interaction between the living and the dead throughout Oaxaca, Mexico, reveals the contingent nature and complexity of these enduring relationships. Corpses materialize social space and identities and transform relationships; corporeal constructs in prehispanic Oaxaca included households established on the bones of ancestors and claims to legitimacy through the curation and display of bodies and parts. I provide a brief overview of changes in treatment of the dead and utilization of the body and its components through three major epochs in prehispanic Oaxaca, drawing upon literature from the three best-documented regions in the modern state—the Mixteca Alta, the Valley of Oaxaca, and the coast/Río Verde region. As summaries of burial practices have appeared (Martínez López et al. 1995;Winter 2002; Winter et al. 1995), I focus on changing patterns in treatment of the dead, and especially interaction between the dead and the living.

Bodies, Bones, and Personhood

Throughout this essay I employ concepts encompassing bodies and burials, exploring diachronic variation in body treatment and its manipulation in death. Anthropologists focus on how bodies are produced through cultural practices, through patterns of action and interaction among social agents. The body tracks and is a medium of social processes and political change (Bourdieu 1977; Butler 1993). As objects constructed through cultural practices, they are monitored by society, although the degree and extent of the impact of this monitoring remains a source of debate. The term *body* itself can be ambiguous, as it refers to different things, including a physical/natural entity (the individual body) and also a social or representative body (Douglas 1970; Van Wolputte 2004). An additional third body—the body politic, a tool of domestication—is also referred to by some scholars (Scheper-Hughes and Lock 1987). At any one time, the body can be any or all of these things. Critical in these various conceptualizations of the body is the idea that this very physical entity is also a medium of expression, closely linked to the social system in which it is contextualized. I focus on the physical body, as well as on its constituent parts, as a site of representation and identity by different social agents, living and dead, operating and negotiating within society. This view both accepts the real existence of the body and acknowledges the social construction of bodies. Social meaning is inscribed on the body, which has led to its being referred to as text, something that is performed (Butler 1993; Douglas 1970; Joyce 1998). A body is both symbol and agent and is a primary site for the construction and performance of gender identities (Reischer and Koo 2004).

In thinking of bodies as social constructs, there are also issues about what bodies represent, and what body parts signify—the relationships among bodies, personhood, and identities. While western notions of the body closely link it with individuals and individuality (the idea of a bounded, nondivisible person), Chris Fowler (2004:3) focuses on concepts of personhood linked with identities "that were highly contextual, and relational to specific events and interactions." Just as bodies are social constructs, so are identities and persons constituted through different social practices, interactions, and contexts (in both life and death). Fowler (2004:9) contrasts individuality with dividuality, whereby a person is composite and multiauthored. These concepts are not mutually exclusive; there is a tension between individual and dividual in all persons (ibid.:36). Indeed, even in Western society, with its focus on individuals, living bodies and their parts may be treated as divisible objects that can be sold, stolen, and purchased, as seen with the commercial trafficking of human organs (Scheper-Hughes 2001).

In terms of bodies and their parts, the concept of dividual persons proves extremely relevant. The bodies of dividual persons can be seen as evincing partibility, whereby a person's parts/substances can be extracted and given as part of a social debt, either in life or death, or permeability, in which a person's component parts are seen as flows of substances, rather than as objects (Fowler 2004). Thus, there are very different responses to death and the treatment of the body (in life and death) based on the nature of personhood. In the death of the western individual, the intact body is often memorialized; while the deceased's possessions are transferred or inherited, bodily parts and substances/essences are not passed on. Fowler (ibid.:96) contrasts the death of individuals with the passing of dividuals: with the partible deceased, the body, its essences, and associated items of the deceased's social identity are socially circulated, while with permeable persons' bodies, because they draw in creative elements and permeate the universe generally, body parts are not kept as specific objects.

Given the distinctions between individual and dividual, and noting the nonexclusivity of such concepts in any one person, the Oaxacan bodies discussed below can be seen as partible in both life and death. During life, autosacrifice constitutes a continual primordial debt repayment, with blood and essences fed to the earth, as well as recognizing societal debts and community well-being. After or during death, the body serves as the ultimate debt repayment; while the body is offered, its parts may be further utilized and actively manipulated to signify various relationships and meanings among the living.

Bones represent in a very tangible way the presence of the dead among the living and may signify the person from which they came—they are a durable signifier of the person and an important referent in the construction and performance of social memory (see also Connerton 1989). The treatment and significance of individual bones vary along with specific mortuary practices. While bones my be maintained to reference and venerate the specific deceased person, in Tibetan Buddhist mortuary practices—geared toward casting off the old body so the deceased's soul will be guided to rebirth—bones are sometime retained to be used in rituals (such as drums, drinking vessels), but are viewed as powerful ritual objects for contacting supernaturals rather than referencing the deceased individual from whom they came (Malville 2005). As inalienable objects extracted after death, bones may substitute for the relationships connecting people and be deployed in relations between people either through partible relations or exchange between permeable bodies (Fowler 2004:114). The use of bones as referents for people and relationships signals continuity in the face of the ruptures usually associated with death.

Regions of Oaxaca

At least 16 distinct ethnic and linguistic groups have occupied Oaxaca state (Winter 1989), the vast majority of which remain poorly known and studied. Some cultures associated with Oaxaca did not follow modern state boundaries, making recent investigations in eastern Guerrero— adjacent to Oaxaca—of great interest (Gutierrez 2008). Three regions of Oaxaca have been well studied and form the focus of this study: the Valley of Oaxaca, the Mixteca Alta, and Lower Río Verde region on the Pacific Coast (see fig. 5.1). I also briefly discuss data from two other regions, the Isthmus of Tehuantepec and the Cañada. I draw upon data from three major epochs: the Early/Middle Formative period of villages

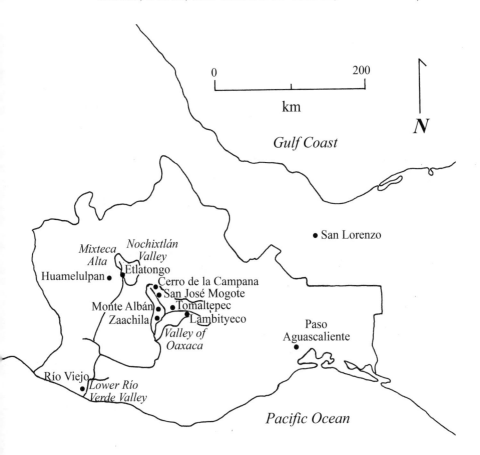

FIGURE 5.1. Map of Oaxaca state, showing select sites mentioned in the text.

(1500–500 BCE, uncalibrated), the Late Formative/Classic period of large, centralized states (500 BCE–CE 600), and the Late Classic/Post-classic period of city-states (CE 600–1521).

The Valley of Oaxaca

Covering 2,500 km², the Valley of Oaxaca is one of the largest regions for productive farming in southern Mexico and is situated at approximately 1,500 m above sea level. Systematic archaeological investigations in the Valley of Oaxaca began with the pioneering efforts of Alfonso Caso and his associates in 1931; since that time, substantial surveys and excavations have taken place throughout the three sub-branches of the Oaxaca Valley. One of the first urban centers in Mesoamerica emerged around 500 BCE at Monte Albán, on a series of hills in the center of where the three subvalleys of the Oaxaca Valley converge. Monte Albán became the head of a Zapotec state after 200 BCE. This state integrated much of the Valley of Oaxaca; its control over adjacent regions remains debated (Marcus and Flannery 1996; Winter 1989; Zeitlin and Joyce 1999). At its Classic period height, the city probably covered 6.5 km^2 (Blanton 1978). After its collapse by CE 800, numerous competing city-states, many of which initially challenged Monte Albán, became the dominant political paradigm in Oaxaca until the arrival of the Spanish (Blomster 2008). Alliances proved crucial in the fortunes of different royal dynasties, including relationships with groups—specifically the Mixtec—that had traditionally been outside the boundaries of the Valley of Oaxaca.

Mixteca Alta

The various Mixtec regions cover approximately 50,000 km^2 of rugged terrain. The largest of these regions, the Mixteca Alta, features mountains that surround small, irregular valleys, which account for only 20 percent of the land mass (Smith 1976:24). Much of the archaeological research in the Mixteca Alta centers on the largest valley, the Nochixtlán, which was systematically surveyed by Ronald Spores in the 1960s (Spores 1972) and was the setting for the large Classic urban center of Yucuñudahui. Other areas of the Mixteca Alta produced important centers after 500 BCE, such as Monte Negro and Huamelulpan. The relationships between Classic Mixtec centers in adjacent valleys remain unclear. The impact of Monte Albán's demise on Mixtec states varied, as ongoing archaeological research demonstrates their multiplicity of external relations that went beyond the Zapotec state, including connections with the major urban center—Cerro de las Minas—in the Mixteca Baja to the northwest.

The Lower Río Verde Valley

Beginning with research in the late 1980s (Joyce 1994), a long-term project in the lower Río Verde Valley, a hot, coastal plain along the western Pacific Oaxaca coast, has provided independent cultural sequences that challenge Valley of Oaxaca–centric interpretations about the spread of complex society throughout modern Oaxaca state. A combined program of survey and excavation has shown that trends in political centralization culminated during the Terminal Formative (150 BCE–CE 250) in the emergence of a state centered at Río Viejo. Rather than interpretations that focus on Zapotec conquest (Marcus and Flannery 1996), research suggests a complex indigenous development, marked by periods of political collapse and centralization, with political and economic ties that distinguish this region from the Valley of Oaxaca (Joyce 2008). The prehispanic sequence culminated in the massive city-state of Tututepec, associated with the Mixtec cultural hero Lord 8 Deer.

The Dead and the Living in Oaxaca

From the earliest part of the prehispanic sequence in Oaxaca, the initial engagement and interaction with the body of the deceased focused on mortuary ritual and burial; through time, increasingly elaborate rites and ideology developed that encompassed shared beliefs and practices of both commoners and elites. Death is a process that continues and transforms relationships and identities. Following the work of Arnold van Gennep (1960), burial ceremonies represent a transformation from one state to another, with a series of basic stages that have unique cultural configurations: separation, a liminal transition stage, and reincorporation/acceptance of new status. Victor Turner (1967) focused on the liminal phase, which he saw as an autonomous stage in the death process, where the deceased lay between normal social roles. The placement in the ground represented a transformation, with the burial place a charged site through both mortuary practices and presence of the physical remains of the deceased. Through both practice and material manifestations, the living transformed the social identity of the dead and inscribed them into social memory and strategies of social negotiation.

The veneration of certain dead individuals as ancestors, so well attested in the chronicles of the early Spanish invaders during the sixteenth century, appears to extend back to early villages in Oaxaca (Marcus and Flannery 1996). The transformation of the deceased into an ancestor, as sociopolitical complexity increased, both unified society with collective beliefs (both commoner and elite ancestors were venerated) and reflected the basic socioeconomic divisions within society (Joyce and Winter 1996). Powerful ancestors—both through imagery and actual body parts—were deployed by elites to strengthen their legitimacy and materialize their connection to supernatural forces. Ancestors were reintegrated into society as important intermediaries with divine forces and could be invoked for oracular purposes. The materiality provided by their bones and bodies served as a powerful referent in displays and physical performances linked with the community and social memory.

Bones of important, higher-status individuals became important symbols of authority and legitimacy. As noted above, bones may reference the specific person from whom they came, but there are also examples where they represent a more anonymous power that can be used to contact supernaturals (Malville 2005). I believe Oaxaca bones fused both of these concepts—signifying both specific important partible personages and the access such powerful individuals could grant to other realms. Bones served as a medium for both social relations and conceptions of the world, and access to them could be both highly spiritual and political (Fowler 2004:99). The stiff, preserved bones may have been seen as life-giving or as a way of invoking such forces through their roles in ritual performances. Just as Classic Maya iconography focused on the life cycle of the maize plant as a metaphor for human life, death, and rebirth, in the Andes, dried parts of plants are still seen as potentially life-giving, but they must be ritually nourished to sustain humans (Allen 1988; Salomon 1995). Just as freeze-dried potatoes can be stored for many years and reconstituted by soaking in water, so bones are conceived of as seedlike, capable of providing for the future.

Through time in the three regions of Oaxaca on which I focus there was an increase in the manipulation of body parts, shown by the presence of bones apart from burials. The curation and preservation of skeletal materials, at least of select individuals, proved an important part of mortuary and postmortuary practices in Oaxaca. Indeed, such was the inviolate nature of bones in Oaxaca that rarely does the archaeological record show evidence of cremation as in other parts of Mesoamerica. Even when a large hearth was discovered near a coastal cemetery, no charred human remains were found (Barber and Joyce 2007:226). Two possible cremations, one highly disturbed by modern plowing, have recently been reported from Tayata, in the Mixteca Alta (Duncan et al. 2008). In addition

FIGURE 5.2. Detail of *Codex Nuttall* 20, showing the smoking, but not actually burning, mortuary bundles of two brothers (detail modified from Anders et al. 1992:pl. 20).

to the problem of the bones not being carbonized and their close proximity to modern ground surface, the dating of these burials is problematic, as a figurine associated with this occupation is at least 300 years more recent (probably dating to between 700 and 500 BCE) than the reported AMS date (Duncan et al. 2008:fig. 5). The investigators attempt to link these supposed cremations from Tayata with a long tradition of the burning of high-status individuals in Oaxaca. Such a connection seems unlikely, given the importance of bones and bodies in Oaxaca, and is not supported by the rich documentation of Mixtec life and death provided by the Postclassic and Colonial painted books or codices (see below). Indeed, several scenes in the codices (see fig. 5.2) interpreted by Duncan et al. (2008) as the cremation of corpses (depicted as mummy bundles) may actually show the bundles only smoking (Byron Hamann 2009, personal communication), perhaps indicating their power/sacred heat and invoking (through offerings) some of their life-giving properties, as discussed above for Andean dried seeds and bones. The smoking may also be part of the preparation of the corpse as a mummy bundle (see below).

Exceptions in treatment of bones may have been made when the bodies were not being interred, but perhaps consumed. Throughout the Classic period in the Mixteca Alta urban centers of Yucuita, Huam-elulpan, and Yucuñudahui, concentrations of bones, with signs of burn-ing and cut marks, have been interpreted by Ronald Spores (1984:35–36) as evidence of cannibalism. Additional research is needed to corroborate this observation.

While burials in Oaxaca served as the resting places for the deceased, and became highly charged through both mortuary practice and the presence of skeletal remains, burials could also be revisited, with tombs particularly showing evidence of reentry and the placement of additional offerings. Tomb reentry could also involve either secondary burial of isolated bones (also potentially placed as offerings) or the interment of relatively intact individuals. Isolated bones—particularly the skull and long bones—could be removed from burials and curated to access the deceased's spiritual presence. In addition to bones, important ances-tors in Oaxaca were represented by sacred bundles that contained their remains, as shown in the scene of mummy bundles from the *Codex Nuttall* (fig. 5.2). All of these presentations of the dead suggest the long-term emphasis on the important role of the deceased and their skeletal remains in ancient Oaxaca sociopolitical life.

Death and Ancestors: Early Villages in Oaxaca (1500–500 BCE)

Fortunately for archaeologists, the treatment of the dead in prehispanic Oaxaca provides material referents, with actual excavated burials as well as depictions of bodies and ancestors in various media. Just as bodies are social constructions, so are their placement in burials and additional manipulation of bodies and their parts. As populations throughout Oax-aca became sedentary with the advent of and ultimate dependence on agriculture, the early villages that developed after 1500 BCE shared an important feature with many other villages across the world associated with full-time agriculture, such as Natufian villages in the Near East: the concentration of burials within and under the settlements, as ideas of community and territory became more developed (Parker Pearson 1999:158). In some places, burials have been linked to claims over stra-tegic resources and land (McAnany 1995), with postfunerary rites trans-forming the deceased into sources of authority and inspiration (Dillehay

1995:283). It is problematic, however, to look for universal links among mortuary practice, social organization, and affirmation of corporate rights over restricted resources (Charles 2005).

In both the Mixteca Alta and the Valley of Oaxaca, the earliest villagers established the long-standing practice of burying their dead under or close to the house. Although physically separated from the activities of daily life, the dead continued to share the general living space with their descendants. Rather than being placed far from the household, they remained close to the family, and their presence intimates their ongoing relationship with the living, who continued to care for them (Miller 1995; Winter 2002). Boundaries between the living and the dead appear fluid. Just as modern artists in Oaxaca depict the dead engaged in normal activities of the living (perhaps also evoking the similarity of the afterlife world with our own), with skeletons shown in marriage ceremonies, dancing, and, ironically, at the doctor's office, Early Formative artists created objects that showed the union between the living and the dead or the fluidity between these states, as well as the duality of nature. Primarily known from Central Mexican villages such as Tlatilco (Ochoa Castillo and Orueta Cañada 1994:pl. 158), clay heads and masks show half of the face skeletalized, while the other half appears covered with flesh. Such images also appeared later in Oaxaca (see below).

There was also a rapid change in burial treatment by early villagers. While the earliest burials demonstrate little attention to sumptuary goods or standardized burial positions, changes and greater consistency in mortuary practices began after 1200 BCE. In burials at villages such as Tierras Largas and San José Mogote, the corpse was placed in an extended position; this position, similar to a sleeping individual, is common in many cultures throughout the world (Parker Pearson 1999:54). Other burials may have been seated, flexed, or in other positions to accommodate a more confined burial chamber, as in abandoned bell-shaped storage pits often reused for interments. Some offerings were placed with the burials, although status differences, which remained along a continuum rather than as disjunctive categories, appear to be primarily based on age of the interred.

In contrast to primarily extended burials, several burials of adult men in the Valley of Oaxaca were placed in seated positions. As these burials were not confined by a small space, the choice of this position has been interpreted as indicative of high status, based primarily on comparisons with elite burials 2,000 years later from Panama (Marcus and Flannery 1996:84–85). Marcus Winter (2005:49), however, contests this interpretation, noting that some burials interpreted as "seated" may actually be flexed, with very different connotations. Seated burials excavated from Late Formative commoner contexts at Etlatongo (see below) directly contradict the idea that such a position invariably invokes high status.

Paired burials of individuals linked in life also began in the Early Formative, with examples of probable conjugal pairs dating to after 1200 BCE at San José Mogote and Santo Domingo Tomaltepec in the Valley of Oaxaca (Marcus and Flannery 1996; Whalen 1981). Such burials demonstrate that new social identities—that of conjugal pairs or marriage partners—were considered important during this crucial time of societal change and transformation. Differential treatment of the male and female is visible in these paired burials, with the male interments at San José Mogote surrounded and covered by limestone slabs, and the adjacent females without any slabs (Marcus and Flannery 1996:67, 98). Such paired burials increase markedly after 800 BCE (ibid.:117).

As many scholars have noted (cf. Goldstein 1981; Saxe 1970), burial practices indicate the links between people and places, as well as rights to tangible and intangible resources. At the preceramic Wawakiki cemetery in Peru, portions of ancestors were displayed as a visual reminder of interregional relationships (Buikstra 1995:239). Especially in Oaxaca, where ancestor veneration constitutes an important part of both ancient and contemporary indigenous cultures across the entire social spectrum, the placement of at least some of the deceased among the household indicates the desire to maintain close physical proximity and is part of the transformation of the deceased into an ancestor, a process that is often enacted through funerary rites (Parker Pearson 1999:27). Not all burials were placed within the sphere of the physical house, suggesting some selectivity in who was destined for ancestor veneration. Ancestors and their activities may also have been easier to manipulate by attendant factions; the dead would have been more pliable and amenable to the needs of the living corporate group.

While the deceased in Formative Oaxaca were usually associated with households, archaeologists have discovered, however, several examples of formal disposal areas, or "cemeteries." A large cemetery, dating to 1150–850 BCE, was recovered at Tomaltepec. Nearly 80 individuals, mostly in an extended face-down position, oriented west to east, were exposed in the cemetery at the village's outskirts. Some individuals were flexed, which has been problematically linked with representing leadership positions in life (Marcus and Flannery 1996:97; see above). Males and females were both well represented; it was primarily age that impacted inclusion in the cemetery, with only one child interred (Whalen 1981:48–50). Indeed, most Tomaltepec adults were buried in the cemetery, while children were placed near domestic structures.

Of great interest at Tomaltepec is the presence of several secondary burials, represented by loose long bones or skulls. Most commonly associated with flexed primary burials, secondary burials provide evidence of interaction with the bones of the deceased. In some cases, skulls were arranged around the head and upper body of the primary interment (Whalen 1981:57). Some secondary burials may represent accidentally disturbed and/or relocated burials that may not directly relate to the "primary" burial with which archaeologists associate them. While the secondary interments, when possible to sex, could be either male or female, they mostly occurred with male primary interments. Many of the secondary burials probably represent individuals who had died at an earlier date and were then reburied with their spouses (Marcus and Flannery 1996:96). A contemporaneous but smaller group burial area, referred to as a barrio cemetery (Flannery and Marcus 1983:55), occurred at the west edge of San José Mogote and is similar in composition to that from Tomaltepec, although the criteria for classifying this as a group cemetery have not been clearly demonstrated.

Formal disposal areas are often linked with the existence of corporate groups and the control of resources through descent from buried ancestors (Goldstein 1981; Parker Pearson 1999; Saxe 1970). While the Formative Oaxacan cemetery at Tomaltepec may represent an effort by corporate groups to mark their rights over scarce resources—as expressions of hereditary rights (Marcus and Flannery 1996:84)—such interpretations have been critiqued as too functional (Hodder 1982; Morris 1991). Instead, such formal burial areas may represent part of a larger strategy of a group's symbolic connection with the land and ancestors; funerals and subsequent commemorative rituals may have materialized social relationships between the living and the dead and among the living.

Colonial documents reveal that the buried dead formed part of the sacred landscape envisioned by indigenous peoples (see below).

After 800 BCE, the Tomaltepec cemetery was abandoned, and adults were buried within their household. Compared with the great uniformity of burials in the Early Formative cemetery at Tomaltepec, these subsequent burials show great variety in mortuary treatment; burials were more standardized within household units than between them (Whalen 1988:261).

Other than the regrouping of bones for secondary burials, there is little additional Early Formative evidence for direct interaction and manipulation of the deceased's bones. A rare early example of human bone reutilization comes from San José Mogote. The House 16/17 dooryard trash pit contained a shallow saucer made from a human cranium; as Flannery and Marcus (2005:358) correctly note, the purpose of this unique find, and whether it signifies an ancestral relic or trophy from an enemy, cannot be determined.

From the earliest villages in Oaxaca, an additional line of evidence reveals the great interest these people had in bodies—their fabrication in clay as figurines. While there is much debate about the function of figurines, clearly these mimetic representations served a multiplicity of uses (Blomster 2009). The fact that they are commonly found around domestic areas suggests that all members of society could have accessed them, and they may have been deployed in negotiations of social identity. Throughout the Early Formative period, figurines largely depicted biological females, with male depictions largely absent until after 1200 BCE, after which they remained less common than female depictions.

Etlatongo figurines show a pattern similar to those in the Valley of Oaxaca, where the earliest ones, prior to 1200 BCE, depict relatively naturalistic images of the body, with much individuality in hairstyle and facial features (fig. 5.3). Creators of these figurines rarely focused on depicting primarily sexual characteristics, forcing archaeologists to attempt to assign sex based on secondary sexual characteristics, leading to many figurine fragments that can best be described as "ambiguous" in terms of sex. After 1200 BCE, figurine bodies became less naturalistic and can be divided into several types, in which breasts, bellies (often of pregnant women), and thighs were greatly exaggerated, although generally not all on the same body (fig. 5.4). In the Mazatán region of Soconusco,

FIGURE 5.3. Early Formative clay figurine head from Etlatongo. Stylistically, this head dates to before 1200 BCE and shows great attention paid to the face and hairdo.

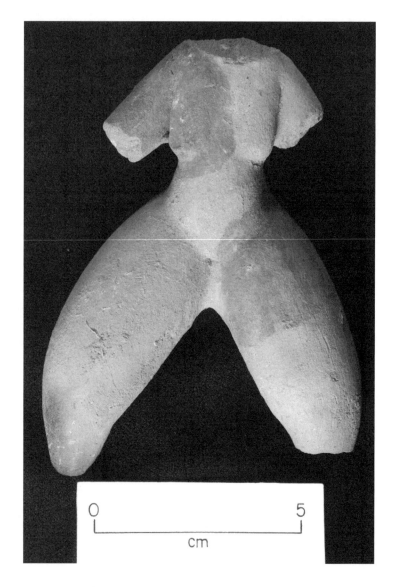

FIGURE 5.4. Early Formative clay figurine body from Etlatongo, from between 1150 and 900 BCE. This female body features exaggerated thighs and a relatively slim waist; pigment has been applied in distinct zones, perhaps representing actual body paint.

the early preponderance of what appears to be young female figurine bodies, made without arms, has been interpreted as showing the control of the more senior members of the village over the identities and labor of the more junior members, especially females (Lesure 1997). Whether figurines depicted dead ancestors, stereotypical social roles, living villagers, or something else, they represent an early effort through mimesis at using the body to inscribe changing social relations and identities.

Status, Ancestors, and Trophies: Late Formative to Classic (500 BCE–CE 600)

Sociopolitical complexity increased after 500 BCE throughout Oaxaca, marked in the Valley of Oaxaca by the first urban center at Monte Albán, with smaller urban centers ultimately emerging in both the Mixteca Alta (Huamelulpan, Monte Negro, Yucuita, Etlatongo) and the Lower Río Verde region (Río Viejo). Along with these political and social transformations were important changes in the treatment of the dead and the manipulation of body parts of the deceased.

The basic burial placement (close to the house) continued, as did the most common body position—supine and extended. While flexed burials existed, these often were of fetuses/neonates, whose bodies were placed inside ceramic pots or other constraining features (Martínez López et al. 1995:239). In the Valley of Oaxaca, burials appeared nearly exclusively associated with residential areas. One possible example of a cemetery (dating from CE 200–350), represented by at least 22 individuals, comes from Terrace C at Yagul (Urcid 2005:29). Additional Middle to Late Formative burial concentrations have been encountered at the Valley of Oaxaca sites of Fábrica San José (Drennan 1976:129) and Tierras Largas (Winter 1972:244–245), but both appear to represent burial space for household members. Some exceptional deposits of human remains have been found later in this epoch, such as the 18 child skulls found in a pit on Monte Albán's North Platform, dating to before CE 500 (Martínez López et al. 1995:151–175).

Several examples of mass burials, however, have been documented in the Lower Verde region. Dating from 400 to 150 BCE, a burial of 48 individuals was encountered at Cerro de la Cruz (Joyce 1994). These individuals were located along the interior and exterior of the foundation walls of a two-room structure; none of the individuals had offerings. Just as with the earlier cemetery at Tomaltepec, only adults were included. As later burials disturbed earlier ones, these individuals were deposited over several generations and probably represent a specialized communal mortuary practice (Joyce 1994:158).

An additional group burial area occurred east of Río Viejo, at the coastal village of Yugüe (Barber 2005). Several hundred years later (CE 100–250) than the group burial at Cerro de la Cruz, the largest and most elaborate building at this small site was used as a community burial area, where at least 42 individuals, ranging from neonate to elderly adult, were concentrated in an area less than 7 m². Indeed, much of the summit of Yugüe was essentially a necropolis. The individuals had been stacked atop one another, each in an extended position, with more recent burials disturbing earlier ones. Unlike the other cemeteries, the Yugüe cemetery included the full range of ages of the ancient villagers, although differentiation occurred in terms of orientation between adults and juveniles (Barber 2005; Barber and Joyce 2007). Also, in an era when status differences were increasingly marked, at least one possible high-ranking individual was buried here—a subadult interred with an inscribed deer-bone flute, although this item could signify more about social role than status of this individual. At Yugüe, individual bodies were subordinated to a larger collective meaning; villagers used bodies to consecrate the central, public part of their village, making a statement about identities and relationships that involved the full spectrum of ages and socioeconomic classes, from commoner to elite. For hundreds of years on the coast, both commoners and elites were involved in materialization of meaningful social groups and designation of space and local community in a way that deemphasized status inequality (Barber and Joyce 2007:233).

Burials, Bodies, and Houses at Etlatongo

Burials manifest connections among bodies, ancestors, and houses. I briefly present data on burials dating to around 500 BCE at Etlatongo, in the Nochixtlán Valley (Blomster 2004). Excavations of this area, explored as Excavation Area 1, or EA-1, exposed an area of 14 m² (Blomster 2004). Ceramic offerings from the well-defined EA-1 mortuary contexts, as well as associated midden and house deposits, contribute to the definition of a new ceramic phase for the Nochixtlán Valley—the Yucuita phase, from 500 to 300 BCE (Blomster 2004). While the full presentation of data and interpretations is beyond the scope of this chapter, these burials evince the importance of bodies as physical entities that are also representations, as both mediums and operators of social processes (Bourdieu 1977; Douglas 1970).

The earliest occupation exposed by EA-1 exhibited a well-constructed clay-loam surface (Floor 7) placed over bedrock, with features including four burials that contained six individuals. The earliest interment was placed in a shallow pit in the northwest section of EA-1; the floor of this area was then resurfaced. No clear offerings were included with this individual. Three additional interments were placed at the base of a bell-shaped pit (Feature 7) excavated into bedrock from Floor 7. While two of the individuals had their legs at least partially flexed or bound, the third did not receive such preparation. Although ten probable offerings were recovered from Feature 7, only two of these can be associated with a particular individual (Blomster 2004).

I argue that the final two burials (Burials 1 and 2) associated with this household, both of which lay in parallel extended positions on Floor 7 (fig. 5.5), were deposited together. One represents a primary burial, the other a secondary burial. While Burial 1 lay in a slab-lined chamber covered by four roughly rectangular roofstones, Burial 2, half a meter to the east and parallel to Burial 1, had large slabs covering only the lower portion of the body. Both burials contained adults but were poorly preserved, making more specific sex and age identifications difficult. Burial 1 lay face up, and all bones appeared present and in proper anatomical position. Most of the bones above the legs of Burial 2, however, were absent; the few upper body bones present did not appear to have been in proper anatomical orientation, as is the case with some of the lower bones as well. I believe this individual died—and had been interred elsewhere—prior to Burial 1, the death of which led to Burial 2 being exhumed and reburied. A similar pattern of burial involving conjugal pairs was noted above in the Valley of Oaxaca.

As with the paired burials from the Valley of Oaxaca, I believe Burials 1 and 2 represent a conjugal pair. After their interment on—not under— Floor 7, occupation of this first house ceased. The abandonment of a structure due to a prominent household member's death has been ethnographically documented across the world from as far away as the Luo

FIGURE 5.5. Paired burials, dating to about 500 BCE, from Etlatongo. The individual in Burial 1 has already been removed, while the roofstones, covering only the lower portion of Burial 2, are about to be excavated. Scale at top is 30 cm; arrow points north.

of western Kenya (Herbich and Dietler 1993). The descendants shifted occupation to the west in EA-1, where we encountered a house elevated above the Floor 7 house and dating to the same phase. Indeed, numerous generations of this family abandoned and created new houses in the typical "corkscrew" fashion in which early villages grew (Blomster 2004; Marcus and Flannery 1996). In the process of constructing what I interpret as the second house in EA-1, the builders covered the house represented by Floor 7, and its burials, with fill, which elevated their new house on a layer of platform fill. They also created a feature to maintain access to some of the ancestors buried in that first house, fashioning a cylindrical stone-lined chamber, Feature 4, directly over the entry to the storage pit (Feature 7) filled with the bodies of three individuals. Feature 4 would have provided both actual and symbolic access to those individuals and could have served as a place for rituals and offerings. The connection through a cylindrical shaft to a storage pit with burials also materializes the storage relationship between actors and the landscape they create and inhabit (Bourdieu 1977; Hendon 2000). The location of these burials and access to them inscribed relationships and identities on the landscape and the social memory of the occupants, and through the materialized presence of ancestors created a genealogy of place that linked descendants to land and ancestors and legitimized the rights and holdings of the household (McAnany 1995:65, 94).

Tombs: Houses for the Dead and the Living

A major change in burials occurred concurrent with the rise of Monte Albán—the appearance of the tomb. Showing a greater concern with permanence, tombs consist of a formal masonry chamber (or chambers) where the deceased could be placed and revisited, offerings made, and counsel provided. Formal masonry tombs represented an important innovation in the ongoing status negotiations of emergent elites. Unlike commoners, whose bones were buried—and consumed—by the earth, elite bones rested on masonry floors, inviolate. These elite bones remained to be celebrated and consulted (Barber and Joyce 2007:222), as befits the remains of sacred ancestors.

While this mortuary innovation is largely linked with the rise of the first urban center at Monte Albán, a possible pre–500 BCE example of a tomb has been presented from San José Mogote. Tomb 10, divided into a main chamber and antechamber, contained no human remains, possibly signifying that any bones and offerings were removed as the residents abandoned the associated house at San José Mogote (Marcus and Flannery 1996:133). Based on both artifacts and architecture associated with the Tomb 10 residence, Winter (2009, personal communication) disputes the early dating of this tomb, preferring a post–500 BCE date, which better tracks with other contemporaneous mortuary data.

As an urban center, Monte Albán incorporated many unrelated individuals occupying the same place on a different scale than previously.

Great continuity in domestic rituals retained some traditional links for early households at this center, with continuity in burials—although more varied and complex—a key feature (Winter 2002:67). Most adults continued to be buried beneath or adjacent to the house in an extended position; children and the aged did not receive such careful treatment (ibid.:70). While burials were primarily in domestic contexts, they have also been documented in public and/or sacred contexts, such as at the architectural construct referred to as "Temple-Plaza-Adoratory," where they constituted sacrificial and/or dedicatory offerings (Urcid 2005:30–31; Winter 1989).

Tombs occurred at Monte Albán from its earliest occupation and continued until its demise. Tombs were important components of residences, usually with access (sometimes in the form of a stairway) to the tomb from the patio around which the different rooms of the house were arranged. Usually tombs contained one or two skeletons in an extended position, as well as disarticulated bones of other individuals. These unmodified dried bones may represent either prior occupants of the tomb or, in some cases, human offerings. The remains in tombs consist primarily of adults of both sexes (Urcid 2005:33). Tombs exhibit a great range in size and quality; the size of tombs and nature of offerings at Monte Albán correlate with residence size (Winter 2002; Winter et al. 1995). Tombs, then, were important expressions of economic inequality at the center of the Zapotec state. Variety in burials is also evident at Monte Negro, a site in the Mixteca Alta contemporaneous to the first few hundred years of Monte Albán. Based on offerings and location, differences in tombs and burials lay along a continuum rather than the marked differences seen at Monte Albán (Acosta and Romero 1992).

Shortly after the emergence of Monte Albán, a diagnostic artifact of Zapotec civilization appeared, often found in tombs: the grayware urn or effigy vessel, spanning the entire time spectrum of this important city (until its circa CE 800 demise). While often called funerary urns, these vessels are more accurately referred to as effigy vessels, as the Zapotecs did not cremate their dead, and these vessels did not contain human ashes, nor have they been found solely in funerary contexts (Sellen 2007:27). These effigy vessels, which probably depicted elite ancestors bedecked in motifs indicating they personified deities, possibly related to the calendar (ibid.:124), may have been used in rites to invoke such ancestors, who served as intermediaries between the living and the supernatural realm.

Sacrifice and Skulls: Ancestors and Trophies

Throughout Mesoamerica, human bodies constitute the ultimate sacrificial offering, ensuring community well-being. Clear iconographic evidence for this can be found for the first time in Oaxaca around 500 BCE at San José Mogote. While the dating of Monument 3 from that important village remains controversial, with ranges provided from 600 BCE (Marcus and Flannery 1996:129) to 300 BCE (Winter 1989:118), it clearly shows a victim of human sacrifice. The bas-relief human figure lies splayed on the stone, eyes closed, with a trilobal heart glyph emerging from the torso—perhaps the locus of sacrifice—with the circle and triangle "blood motif" flowing over one side of the stone. The victim's calendric name is provided between the legs: Glyph 1L (1 Eye) in Alfonso Caso's system (Urcid 2005; Winter 1989).

In addition to the human body, there was a focus on body parts starting in the Late Formative and into the Classic periods in the Valley of Oaxaca and the Mixteca Alta, where representation, manipulation, and modification were focused on the head and, later, the long bones—especially the femur. The importance of certain body parts is seen throughout the vast span of time in Mesoamerica. Given the nature of the dividual and partible person in Mesoamerica, specific body parts probably had distinct associations as well as serving as discrete portions of the self or personhood (Fitzsimmons 2009:168; Fowler 2004). Shortly after 1200 BCE, the Olmec at San Lorenzo (and later La Venta) focused on heads, with the multi-ton colossal heads representing early Gulf Coast leaders. For the Classic Maya, the head—actual or metaphorical—served to identify an individual as part of a particular category of person, with the headdress often exhibiting name glyphs (Houston et al. 2006:62). In royal burials from Uaxactun and Tikal, the deceased's head—and occasionally femur—may be missing, suggesting that certain skeletal elements were viewed as more powerful or useful in postmortuary religious and political contexts (Fitzsimmons 2009:168). Similar to the Classic Maya, the Postclassic Mixtec placed personal names in codical figures' headdresses (Smith 1973:27), while in Aztec concepts of the body, the head was the locus of consciousness, reason, and values; it distilled one's individual qualities (López Austin 1988). Similarly, in the Andes, the head is viewed at the key site of human spirituality and sensibility, and is the body part curated from ancestors and/or taken as a trophy from an enemy (Arnold and Hastorf 2008:108).

It is important to distinguish modifications of the skull done in life versus those in death. Modifications during life include reshaping the skull from an early age (often through cradle boards), dental inlay and mutilation, and trephination, in which holes were made through the skull by scraping, linear cutting, circular grooving, drilling, and boring (Verano 2003). In these examples, the body serves as a stage for different aesthetic and surgical performances; trephination may have both medical and ritual purposes. Examples of trephined skulls have been recovered at Monte Albán, Monte Negro, and Huamelulpan (Christensen and Winter 1997).

Huamelulpan and Monte Albán also feature skulls that have been modified after death by perforations. Three skulls were found at the Altar of the Skulls at Huamelulpan (Gaxiola González 1984), each with two holes through the frontal bone that probably served as places for cords for suspension and possibly also to hold the skulls together, enabling their display long after all soft tissue had disappeared, through exhumation or boiling (Christensen and Winter 1997:470–471). These skulls may have represented venerated ancestors or defeated enemies and may have been displayed at public ceremonies or rituals. Indeed, a femur found near the Altar of the Skulls at Huamelulpan is suggestive of later displays (see below) of elite long bones deployed for legitimization. A modified left maxilla bone from Cerro Tilcajete, a Valley of Oaxaca site dominated by Monte Albán and occupied from 100 BCE to CE 200, suggests that even a small part of the skull could materialize important ancestral or triumphal meanings. Unfortunately, the bone was a surface find, perhaps from a looted burial, making its ultimate interpretation problematic (Duncan et al. 2009).

In addition to actual crania, representations of skulls also marked architectural spaces at Huamelulpan. In addition to two roughly life-sized limestone skulls, stylistically dated to the Late Formative but whose original context has long since been lost, four larger-than-life stone skull sculptures, with tenons to project from a wall, may have been incorporated into a public building (Structure B) during the Classic period. While only one skull sculpture was found in situ, two others have been moved nearby; their projected placement on the facade of Structure B leaves space for a fourth stone skull, with two on each side of the central staircase (Winter 2009, personal communication). The focus on skull imagery at Huamelulpan suggests that perhaps certain structures were associated with ancestor or death-related rituals, similar to representations in later Mixtec codices of skull temples or other oracular sites (such as caves) marked by skulls. Another possibility is that such skull imagery distinguished Huamelulpan as a political and territorial entity, similar to later places, such as the Mixtec city of Chalcatongo (see below), identified in Postclassic codices by a place glyph incorporating skulls.

While some skulls were displayed as representing venerated ancestors, other perforated skulls have a connection with warfare. The practice of taking trophy heads is well documented in Mesoamerica. The Classic Maya wore war captives' bones as trophies and also wore the heads of ancestors (or representations of them) as belt ornaments (Fitzsimmons 2009). Although the distinction between the heads of enemies and those of dead friends and ancestors is important (Bloch and Parry 1982), examples from Peru and Bolivia, where head taking (both actual and symbolic) is still practiced, provide valuable ethnographic concepts of the importance of heads and show the blurring that can occur between the categories of captured enemy trophies and venerated ancestral heads (Arnold and Hastorf 2008). Contemporary disputes in Bolivia over land include head taking and the curation of enemy heads, with the belief that captured heads will lead to the regeneration and fecundity of the victorious group (ibid.:37). While the power of ancestral heads is considered benign, captured trophy heads can be "tamed" and domesticated through a series of wrapping and unwrappings, with the heads considered potential seeds (ibid.:61). It is unclear whether the power of enemy heads in Oaxaca was considered dangerous and underwent transformations into a more useful, benevolent force.

In Oaxaca, examples of male crania found at Monte Albán, Cerro de las Minas, Monte Negro, and Yucuita have cervical vertebrae attached or associated, which is clear evidence of decapitation of living men (Christensen and Winter 1997:table 2). Such skulls may have perforations for display as trophies. A series of poorly preserved skull fragments excavated at the site of La Coyotera, in the Cuicatlán Cañada region north of the Valley of Oaxaca, have been interpreted (Spencer 1982:236–239) as representing a *tzompantli*, or skull rack, that dates to 100 BCE to CE 200, evidence of an early conquest by the Zapotecs of Monte Albán, who are known from Spanish chronicles to have displayed skulls to terrorize and dominate their enemies. The evidence for this skull rack is problematic, and it is nearly 1,000 years earlier than any other Mesoamerican skull rack, leading some (Braniff and Hers 1998:66) to question the presence of an actual skull rack as well as its dating.

Of the 61 skulls/skull fragments, only three have any possible evidence of perforations necessary for being mounted on a skull rack, while several partially complete skulls clearly show the absence of perforations (Wilkinson 1997:table B.1). The skull (Skull 22) with the best evidence for display, in the form of two perforations in the parietals, exhibits holes of only 10 mm, suggesting that the skull was suspended on a cord—as a trophy head—rather than on a skull rack (Wilkinson 1997:619). Most of the skulls that can be identified are of adults; of the 18 that could be sexed, there was an even split between male and female. This pattern does not accord with the Mesoamerican trope of displaying trophy heads from male warriors, as shown in various media and documented by the Spanish invaders. Several skulls were burned and skulls varied in how much flesh would have been present (ibid.). Clearly these remains represent an important feature that could have related to the display of heads and/or skulls, but the conflation of this feature with the kind of *tzompantli* known from Postclassic groups is not the most parsimonious interpretation.

Decapitated heads clearly could serve as trophies during this period of early urbanism; their importance was graphically displayed on the so-called Danzantes of Monte Albán's Building L. Begun shortly after the 500 BCE founding of Monte Albán, the Danzantes represent the first sculptural program at this Zapotec urban center. While interpretations of the nature of the human bodies portrayed on the Danzantes vary, generally scholars focus on a martial reading, with sacrificed war captives (Coe 1962:95–96) or different members and tiers of a victorious warrior sodality (Urcid n.d.:33) depicted. The images were probably multivalent, representing both sacrificial victims and heroic ancestors central to the creation of Monte Albán. The depiction of bodies—both living and dead—commemorated an important event in the founding of this city (fig. 5.6).

As symbols of violence and conquest, this sculptural program included four images that solely exhibit isolated heads—what are clearly decapitated heads (Scott 1978:figs. D-96, D-123, J-112, 7V-3). Three of these reliefs have a blood scroll (see fig. 5.7a) issuing from below the head, where the neck should be, indicating these heads were severed from living victims. Javier Urcid (n.d.:fig. 21A) has reconstructed a blood glyph for the fourth head, 7V-3. Such a graphic detail is absent on the generally gorier gallery of decapitated heads and other severed body parts (juxtaposed with images of prowling warriors) at the site of Cerro Sechin, approximately 700 years earlier than the Danzantes program and on the Peruvian coast near Casma, although some heads clearly show the cut marks utilized in severing them from the neck (fig. 5.7b). As with the ethnographic Andean skulls discussed above, these Danzante heads remained animated by forces, as shown by the speech scroll on J-112— perhaps a reference to the oracular power of the dead depicted in later Postclassic codical imagery. Urcid (2007, personal communication) suggests, based on the legible inscriptions on these stones depicting severed heads, that only one specific individual may be named.

Bodies and their parts proved crucial in conveying meaning in pictorial narratives as well as texts at Monte Albán. The entire corpus of Danzante sculptures may have been assembled to form a pictorial narrative, with the sculptors focused on depicting elements of the human body and associated paraphernalia (and limited glyphic texts) that emphasized both social identity and the message to be conveyed by the corporeal image; bodies and their placement proved crucial in conveying intended narrative(s). An upside-down, probably decapitated, head is also important as part of the glyphic representation of places in the subsequent "Conquest Slab" program of Building J at Monte Albán. While it seems clear that the inverted head with closed eyes carries the semantic value of "dead," it may be incorrect to assume that the heads represent rulers conquered by Monte Albán. Urcid (n.d.) suggests an equally plausible reading: Building J commemorated Zapotec war heroes.

The importance of body parts in representing information in the Zapotec writing system probably dates to the inception of that script by 500 BCE, with feet/footprints, hands, and the upper and lower torso (the seated version

FIGURE 5.6. Danzantes, ca. 500 BCE, in situ at Building L, Monte Albán.

a

b

FIGURE 5.7. (*a*) Danzante that depicts a severed head, complete with blood scroll issuing from where the missing neck should be, with a partially preserved glyph on top. Redrawn from Scott 1978:fig. D-123. (*b*) Severed head from sculptural program at Cerro Sechin, Casma, Peru. Note closed eye, flowing hair (perhaps for ease in grasping as a trophy head?), and cut marks at the neck.

of which is probably related to accession rituals) appearing in some of the earliest texts at Monte Albán. It is generally agreed that glyph compounds with hands are verbs and signified action (Urcid 2001:392).

Bodies and Bundles

An additional development in body imagery and ideology that occurred after the rise of states throughout Oaxaca is the depiction of deceased rulers as compact bundles—a practice well documented from the final centuries of prehispanic Oaxaca (see below).

Although physical evidence of funeral bundles—or mummy bundles—does not occur until the Postclassic in Oaxaca, imagery suggestive of an early inauguration of this practice comes from circa CE 350–450 at Monte Albán. Recovered from the massive South Platform, a series of large stelae were relocated to the corners of the platform after initially forming a unified compositional scene, as documented by Urcid (2001, 2005). Stela SP-1 (see fig. 5.8) illustrates an enthroned ruler, wearing a jaguar suit, reviewing a series of possibly six costumed prisoners; the figure in SP-1 is the most important personage in this larger scene, which spanned five additional monoliths (Urcid 2001:334–337). In addition to the rich costume and elaborate paraphernalia of the SP-1 figure, I note especially that the spear he holds appears to have at its apex the proximal portion of a femur, although oriented upside down. The presence of this femur may be related to practices better documented in later contexts involving ancestral long bones displayed as legitimizing symbols, although not enough detail is visible to be confident that a human femur is depicted.

Stela SP-1 preserves two columns of glyphs. The second glyph in the right-hand column exhibits a locative glyph, atop of which appears an object with a face (see Urcid 2001 for a discussion of the structure of this text). Upon closer inspection, this appears to be a bundle with a human face or mask, complete with headdress (see fig. 5.9). Much of the figure is obscured by the locative glyph, but there is a bundle-shaped body under the head, the eyes of which are closed. Such depictions of funerary bundles of important rulers and ancestors, topped by the individual's actual head or a mask, appear frequently in the Mixtec codices (see below and fig. 5.2). It appears that by the creation of Stela SP-1 between CE 350 and 450, deceased rulers may already have been depicted as sacred

FIGURE 5.8. Stela SP-1, Monte Albán, circa CE 400. Note the jaguar-costumed seated figure, who holds a staff topped by a bone, indicated by the arrow. The photograph is of the cast of SP-1 in situ in the northeast corner of the South Platform; the original, in the site museum, is extremely eroded.

bundles, to be displayed and venerated. As noted above, elite ancestors were already displayed seated and often bundlelike—with most of their corporeal features obscured by costume—in Zapotec effigy vessels.

Support for the idea of Classic period bundlelike funerary images comes from an offering roughly contemporaneous with SP-1. Alfonso

FIGURE 5.9. Close-up of the second glyph in the second column of SP-1, Monte Albán. The figure above the locative glyph appears to be a mummy bundle. Photographed from the cast of SP-1.

Caso (1939:figs. 18 and 19) explored Tomb 103, on Monte Albán's North Platform, in the late 1930s. In the patio atop the tomb, Caso documented a scene illustrating a mortuary or ancestral cult comprised of 16 ceramic figures, representing musicians, priests, and other participants, arranged around a larger stone object, which appears to be a mortuary bundle. While all the other figures surrounding the stone figure have very three-dimensional and humanlike faces, the stone figure has a removable flat head that appears to be a mask (as is placed atop bundles during the Postclassic; see below). In addition to materializing the deceased as a bundle, with few corporeal features shown, this scene may have depicted the kinds of rituals that went on in the tomb below.

With the ascendance of Monte Albán after 500 BCE, bodies—or their parts—became important symbols and were highly visible subjects of monumental art. The convention of depicting deceased rulers as sacred bundles may have begun by CE 400. In addition to public displays on sculptural programs, bodies and their parts were also abstracted onto portable ceramic pieces. Contemporaneous to the Conquest Slabs of Building J are several ceramic vessels in the shape of human spinal columns, one example of which is connected to pelvic bone effigies at the base of the vessel, all of which was painted white with red highlights providing additional anatomical details (Caso et al. 1967:pl. XIb; Winter 1994:pl. 40). At least one served as a vessel stand and has only a shallow bowl atop to hold liquid, allowing only a token amount of liquid to be consumed. One example, however, on display in the Museo de las Culturas de Oaxaca, forms a vessel with the shallow bowl atop extending down into the chamber of the spinal column; in this case, a substantial amount of liquid could be drunk. Thus, users of these vessels would appear to be drinking or pouring liquids from spinal columns, as if imbibing or dispensing precious bodily and life fluids. The practice could have been similar to that observed for the Inka, who fashioned vessels for drinking maize beer from the trophy heads of enemy leaders. Indeed, to imbibe the vital force contained in the head, the brains were apparently sucked out of the cranium through a straw (Arnold and Hastorf 2008). Using the head-vessel mimetically referenced the consumption of this force, and a similar phenomenon may have been signified by the spinal column vessels from Monte Albán. Vessels made from actual human bone are also known from Oaxaca; in addition to the Early Formative bone saucer noted above, a shallow bowl made from a human skull was found on the chest of a Late Formative burial of an adult male (Burial 25) at Tomaltepec, along with the skull and long bones of a secondary burial (Whalen 1981:153–154).

Display and Curation of Bodies: Late Classic through Postclassic (CE 600–1521)

This final prehispanic period spans the final 200 years (600–800) of the florescence of Zapotec Monte Albán, as well as the nearly 700 years after its collapse, after which competing city-states filled the vacuum formed by the demise of large urban centers throughout Oaxaca (Blomster 2008). Some of the most famous tombs from Oaxaca, filled with paintings and inscriptions, derive from these final 200 years of the Monte Albán state. As Arthur Miller (1995:4) notes, the dead were represented in paint, and their bones were painted as well—often with the same paint (Urcid 2005:37). During this time, Oaxacans increasingly used and manipulated bodies and their components, as skulls and long bones served as symbols of power and legitimization.

Throughout this era of changing politics, there was great continuity in treatment of the body in burial, especially among commoners, whose houses also showed great stability. For example, a house at Macuilxóchitl, dating to CE 600–800, served as the setting for a nearly identical house in terms of construction and orientation when the site was substantially reoccupied 300 years later (Markens et al. 2008). Burials remained close to residences, although sometimes associated with temples and other public contexts. In the Mixteca Alta, burials were seated and continued unchanged during this period of transition. Even in the most elaborate Zapotec tomb, the interment was still generally placed in an extended dorsal position, with the head pointed toward the east. There may be, however, different mortuary treatments within a single household, with some individuals (probably lineage or household heads) placed inside elaborate subterranean tombs, while others were deposited within simple graves, sometimes lined with slabs. Marcus Winter (2002:79) defines three types of standardized houses from CE 600–800; tomb size increased with house size, with palaces associated with elaborate tombs such as Monte Albán's Tomb 104. While tomb design changed in the final 400 years of the prehispanic sequence, and important burials were sometimes placed under public structures, as at Mitla (see below), the importance of the ancestors, and their legitimating force, remained constant.

Tombs, as liminal spaces occupied by the dead, served as dynamic arenas of interaction between the living and the dead, constantly receiving new interments and offerings, and served as stages for ongoing ancestral and mortuary rituals (see above). The ongoing use of tombs to receive additional burials, as well as offerings to previous interments, makes it difficult to distinguish between primary and secondary burials, as some bones were removed to accommodate new skeletal material (Middleton et al. 1998). To reinforce the concept of tombs as houses for the dead, the elaborate Tomb 5 at Cerro de la Campana or Huijazoo, which dates to CE 700, was designed as a miniature palace, with a patio surrounded by rooms. By the Late Postclassic, tombs became family ossuaries, with less emphasis placed on age and rank (Caso 1969:59; Winter 2002:82). The physical interaction with bones in tombs reflected ongoing spiritual connections with ancestors, through which they could be venerated, invoked, and consulted. The complex of tomb and elite residence/palace formed an important component of Zapotec leadership (Winter 2002:84), with supplications to ancestors made for the benefit of Zapotec leaders and the community at large. Members of the community from all statuses petitioned ancestors for guidance and intervention. Additionally, some elaborate Postclassic tombs, such as Monte Albán Tomb 7, have been hypothesized as dedicated to the cults of particular oracles (McCafferty and McCafferty 1994).

The practice of depicting important rulers and ancestors as bundles expanded after CE 600: shrouded or decorated corpses were exhibited in latticework boxes before being interred (Urcid 2005:93). This practice, known throughout Mesoamerica around the time of the conquest, is well documented in the paintings from Tomb 5 at Cerro de Campana. Along the back wall of the main chamber, bodies, with elaborate masks and headdresses, are shown seated in latticework boxes. In the West Room of Tomb 5, the upper register shows two bodies, possibly in boxes (too much damage has occurred to this portion of the mural to be certain; see Miller 1995:fig. 77 and Urcid 2005:fig. 5.30). While there is little detail invested in the anatomy of these bundlelike bodies, one appears to be female, while the other is probably male. A detail indicated on the body of the male appears to be a skeletalized leg. Both figures probably hold incense burners, and they may be celebrating the bundle of an even more distant ancestor placed between them (Urcid 2005:84). Rulers were also shown in funeral boxes outside of the Valley of Oaxaca. One example contemporaneous with Cerro de la Campana Tomb 5 was fashioned on the Oaxacan coast, where Stela 1 from Río Grande depicts a ruler bedecked in a jaguar costume and with arms folded over the chest, placed inside a box (Urcid 2005:fig. 2.1).

Additionally, a deceased individual may simply be shown as a bundle and not in a box. The north wall murals from Tomb 3 at Xoxocatlán (Urcid 2008:fig. 15.1), roughly contemporaneous with those from Cerro de la Campana, depict a series of bundlelike seated individuals, perhaps interspersing the living and the dead. In one of the earliest (circa

CE 400) tombs known at Monte Albán, Tomb 112 (Lombardo de Ruíz 2008:fig. 4.9), the north mural shows a bundlelike individual seated on a small decorated platform, looking remarkably similar to contemporaneous Zapotec ceramic effigy vessels, which also depicted ancestors (see above). Differences between showing humanlike ancestors and more reified supernaturals (or more distant ancestors) are clearly visible in the mural on the interior of Monte Albán's Tomb 104, dating to about CE 500 (Díaz Castro 2008:fig. 14.4). On both of the long axes of the tomb, humanlike figures lead a procession to the rear of the tomb, where a disembodied head emerges from a central offering niche in the wall.

In addition to mortuary murals that depict ancestral bundles, graphic displays of the transient division between life and death also occurred on clay and stone images of the human face. In a practice that extends back to the Early Formative in the Valley of Mexico (see above), artists at Classic and Late Classic sites such as Cerro de las Minas in the Mixteca Baja and Soyaltepec in the Valley of Oaxaca (Caso and Bernal 1952:fig. 522) depicted faces that are half skeletalized and half fleshed. A clay figurine recovered at Etlatongo, probably Postclassic, combines features of life and death in the same face (fig. 5.10). While the face, especially the nose, appears skeletalized, there is flesh on the cheeks and hair atop the head (hair—real or a wig—may also be depicted in funerary bundles in the Mixtec codices). Large, closed eyes bulge in their sockets. An unusual feature—for a figurine—is the careful delineation of the teeth, typical in other media for depicting a skull.

Sacred and Legitimizing Bones

One result of frequent interaction with ancestral bodies was the removal, curation, and manipulation of sacred bones, which served as important symbols of power and legitimization. Three important sources of information document these practices: actual burial inventories, depictions in Terminal Classic and Postclassic stone public art, and Mixtec codices. These sources confirm that most of the focus remained on long bones, especially the femur, and the skull. These bones appear to have abstracted and summarized the entire divisible body. Skulls in particular were not only displayed, but also modified, and served as the canvas for elaborate art. Some skulls were decorated with mosaics of turquoise and

FIGURE 5.10. Clay figurine head from Etlatongo, probably Postclassic. The head shows both fleshy and skeletalized features, with teeth and hair carefully indicated.

other stones and minerals, such as one from Monte Albán Tomb 7 (Caso 1969:63–64). Ethnohistoric documents for the Aztecs reveal that a captive warrior, chosen for the physical perfection of his body, served as the *ixiptla* (vessel/image) of Tezcatlipoca for one year; upon his sacrifice, his head was defleshed, with the skull covered in mosaics in the deity's image (Carrasco 1999). It is difficult to determine whether the Tomb 7 mosaic skull represented a revered ancestor or a war/sacrificial trophy, such as the thousands of skulls that would have been displayed at any given time on the *tzompantli* at Tenochtitlan and large cities throughout Postclassic Mesoamerica.

In addition to the mosaic skull, Tomb 7 provides other evidence of interaction and manipulation of body parts. Five mandibles were found in Tomb 7, all of which were painted red and perforated with holes in the ascending ramus for suspension (Caso 1969:60); codical images demonstrate that mandibles served as masks placed in front of the mouths of oracles, supplicants, and living representations of deities (ibid.:61). Unlike a mandible from the site of Eloxochitlán in the Mazatec region of Oaxaca, with Zapotec Glyph D inscribed on it (Winter and Urcid 1990), no designs appear on the Tomb 7 mandibles. A carved mandible, from the Terminal Classic, has recently been found at the Valley of Oaxaca site of Macuilxóchitl (Marcus Winter 2007, personal communication), while two carved mandibles (one from a juvenile/young man, the other from an unsexed juvenile) were included as offerings for the burial of a young man (Burial 2004-23) at the site of Paso Aguascalientes, near Jalapa del Marqués in the Isthmus of Tehuantepec; both mandibles had been drilled for suspension (Cortés Vilchis and Herrera Muzgo T. 2009). Other noncranial bones were also incised, such as a human long bone from Xaagá (near Mitla) with a Late Postclassic codex-style image of a figure in a jaguar costume (Robert Markens 2009, personal communication).

In addition, the proximal portions of three femora, cut just above the middle of the shaft, were found in Monte Albán's Tomb 7, all of which had traces of red pigment placed on them; two of them probably came from the same individual (Caso 1969:61). The cut femora may derive from a ceremony similar to that on the twentieth day of the Aztecs' Tlacaxipeualiztli, or the Feast of the Flaying of Men, where after dancing in the skins of a captive, portions of whom had been butchered and consumed, the captor planted the sacrificed warrior's femur (usually with a mask and feather attached) at his house as evidence that he had flayed a captive (Carrasco 1999:160). While these Tomb 7 proximal femora may derive from venerated ancestors or captives, they contained such power that they were included as important offerings along with exquisite objects made from gold, silver, rock crystal, and other precious materials. Proximal femora, such as those found in Tomb 7, were also displayed attached to staffs, as suggested above from the earlier Stela SP-1 at Monte Albán, or held as legitimating devices.

It appears that throughout Late Classic and Postclassic Oaxaca, the bodies of dead elites and rulers were transformed into symbols of authority, materialized by the curation and performative display of their corpses and component parts, and referencing the continuity between the living and the dead. In the Valley of Oaxaca, the lower south and north plaster friezes from an "altar complex" associated with Mound 195 Sub, Tomb 6 at Lambityeco, in the Valley of Oaxaca, graphically illustrates this deployment of elite body parts in performances of social memory. Carbonized corn cobs from Tomb 6 yielded an uncalibrated date of CE 690 (Rabin 1970:15), or CE 610–990 calibrated at the two-sigma level (Markens et al. 2010: table A1.2). A series of stucco friezes covered the bases and tops of the walls of the altar complex, although only fragments of the upper panels were recovered (Rabin 1970:7) These images depict four generations of *coquis* (great lords) and their wives. On the fully preserved lower friezes, two elite males, Lord 4 "Glyph Ñ" (correlated with the fourth day name in the Zapotec calendar, Lachi, or Ball Court) and Lord 8 Owl (Lind and Urcid 2010:159–160), both wearing loincloths and named by glyphs that occur next to their faces, grasp a human femur in one hand (fig. 5.11). While the men are shown as complete profile figures in the lower friezes, their marriage partners (Lady 10 Monkey and Lady 3 Earthquake) are depicted only from the waist up and do not hold femora. In the proposed reconstruction of the upper friezes, the women are shown from head to toe in full profile, while the men are truncated, and one wears an armband made of a human mandible; none of the figures in the upper friezes hold femora (Lind and Urcid 2010:160–161). These sculpted lords and ladies, depicted as aged, represent the ruling lineage and were probably the grandparents and great-grandparents of the ruling couple Lord 1 Glyph Ñ and Lady 10 Corn, who occupied the associated final house constructed on Mound 195 Sub (Structure 195-3) and were the final royal couple interred in Tomb 6, where they were commemorated on its facade by slightly larger-than-life plaster portrait heads. Tomb 6 was first constructed with the earlier Structure 195-5 and modified as subsequent married couples were interred in it (see Lind and Urcid 2010). While Lord 8 Owl was also

FIGURE 5.11. Lower panel frieze from Lambityeco showing Lord 8 Owl holding a human femur.

probably buried in Tomb 6, the great-grandfather—Lord 4 Glyph Ñ— was probably interred in Tomb 5 (ibid.).

As an affirmation of their sacred lineage and symbol of their legitimacy to rule, Lords 4 Glyph Ñ and 8 Owl were depicted holding the femora of their ancestors, buried in the adjacent tombs. The completely preserved plaster femur held by Lord 8 Owl in the south frieze reveals that the proximal portion of this bone was not modified into an awl or spatula; the condyle is clearly depicted (Rabin 1970:4). The distal portion has been cut off, resembling the long bones found in Tomb 7 at Monte Albán. Alternatively, the absence of the distal portion may have been due to space limitations for the sculpture in the entablature (Urcid 2007, personal communication).

Supporting the removal of ancestral bones as heirlooms for display is the actual Tomb 6 inventory, which reveals the removal of long bones— especially femora—from generations of the corpses of *coquis* (Lind and Urcid 1983, 2010). These bones may have actively been held by descendants, a practice engaged in by Lords 4 Glyph Ñ and 8 Owl on the Lambityeco friezes, or they may have been worn on certain occasions, as is shown in the roughly contemporaneous murals of Cacaxtla (in Tlaxcala), where a battling warrior wears a femur, covered with red spots. The importance of bones and body parts brought into battle is well attested for Aztec warriors, who were especially interested in body parts of women who died in childbirth, whose bodies were infused with supernatural energy. In the Cacaxtla example, the bone may also represent part of a glyph for the warrior's name (Urcid 2007, personal communication). The Lambityeco lower friezes show two pairs of married ruling couples, but in both cases it is the male who holds the femur. The "altar" or mausoleum upon which these friezes occur at Lambityeco was probably a throne or dais upon which the ruler sat and conducted business, with the actual bones of his ancestors below him and perhaps held by him, and also depicted in the friezes under him—an extremely visual reminder of the power of bones, bodies, and lineage.

The imagery of the Lambityeco panels includes another detail on the use and display of human bones. As noted above, one of the males in the preserved fragments of the central upper frieze wears a mandible on his lower arm (Winter and Urcid 1990:fig.7). The mandible itself was probably decorated, such as the few examples found in Oaxaca (see above). A recent archaeological discovery dating to several hundred years after the Lambityeco panels comes from the Isthmus of Tehuantepec and documents the actual application of this practice. At the site of Paso Aguascalientes, the skeleton (Burial 2004-24) of a mature adult male was discovered with a human mandible, used as a bracelet, on his left humerus (Cortés Vilchis and Herrera Muzgo T. 2009). It would be interesting to know whether such mandibles came from the skulls of captives or ancestors.

During the Late Classic, Valley of Oaxaca images abound in which ancestors intercede for supplicants in the supernatural realm. In what are referred to as genealogical registers (usually comprising ruling couples receiving divine intercession), ancestral figures descend from the sky to provide a ruling conjugal pair with badges of office and legitimacy (Marcus and Flannery 1996; Urcid 2005). In an example from the important political center of Zaachila (Stone 13, see fig. 5.12), four figures are incised in the corners of the stone (in addition to a central descending figure), in contrast to the sculpted central male/female pair. Compared to the more active and articulated central male, who clearly sits cross-legged (the central female is probably deceased), the four corner figures are depicted as bundlelike (fig. 5.13), with arms/hands relatively close to the body and not actively engaged in the central scene, which takes place in a mortuary context (Urcid 1995:19). The four corner figures gesture at

FIGURE 5.12. Stone 13 from Zaachila, Museum of Natural History, Smithsonian Institution, currently at the Museum Support Center, Suitland, Maryland, catalog number 215210 (drawing by Javier Urcid).

the central scene and represent ancestors of the central pair—the figures in the top corners are male, while those in the bottom are female.

The legitimating power of ancestors—and their material correlates—remained important during the political changes from the Late Classic to the Postclassic in the Mixteca Alta as well (Blomster 2008). Skeletalized figures, including representations of death gods, became increasingly common in various media, including painted Mixtec codices, painted stucco sculptures of figures with human bodies but skulls as heads (with clawlike hands but fleshed feet) in Tomb 1 at Zaachila, and a tripod vessel with an attached skeleton from Tomb 2 at Zaachila (Gallegos Ruiz 1978). The Mixtec codices illustrate abundant examples of skulls (often demarcating important structures, such as temples), bones, and skeletalized figures, and further document the importance of the ruler's body for the legitimate accession of heirs. Both mummy bundles and skulls appear frequently in the codices; indeed, the location of one of the most important oracles in the codices, Lady 9 Grass, invariably shown wearing a mandible as a buccal mask, had a major shrine at Chalcatongo, the original Mixtec name of which was Nuundaya—which means "death"

FIGURE 5.13. Detail of lower left figure, Lady 8 Serpent, in Zaachila Stone 13 (photograph by Jeffrey P. Blomster of catalog number 215210, Department of Anthropology, Smithsonian Institution).

or "skull temple/skull place" (Pohl 1994:75). In the Postclassic, Mixtec mummy bundles served as physical proof of the royal line upon which social order was defined, with the corporeal remains of the royal ancestors carefully curated, sometimes stored in caves (Spores 1984). These mummies were hidden from the Spanish, whose ethnohistoric accounts refer to the conservation and veneration of dead rulers' remains (Christensen and Winter 1997:474). Ignacio Bernal (1949) recovered examples of actual mummy bundles at Coixtlahuaca; of the 39 documented tombs, he found two examples of individuals wrapped in *petates*, or mats, and tied up in seated positions. The reconstruction of one of these burials in the Museo Nacional de Antropología e Historia in Mexico City includes a ceramic mask atop the bundle.

The prehispanic *Codex Nuttall* is particularly vivid with scenes depicting bundles. Considering the frequent depictions of mortuary bundles, the lack of flames and burning appears noteworthy and follows the long-standing interest in curating physical remains of ancestors in Oaxaca. Images of mortuary bundles are illustrated on *Nuttall* 4 and 20 as smoking, but not actually in flames (fig. 5.2). These curls of smoke may indicate the power/sacred heat that emanates from such bundles, as well as smoke/cloud conjuring that is so critical in Mixtec ceremonies (Hamann 2009, personal communication). Offerings made to these bundles include a decapitated quail and a flowery song.

One of the few codical narratives clearly showing flames associated with an elite body is on *Nuttall* 81–82, pages that follow the assassination of Lord 12 Motion, half-brother of Lord 8 Deer "Jaguar Claw" (an assassination Lord 8 Deer seems to have ordered). Following Lord 12 Motion's murder in a sweatbath, his bundled body is displayed in a wooden rack (see fig. 5.14), very similar to the latticework boxes (in which bodies were displayed before being interred) depicted in Zapotec art nearly 800 years prior to the creation of this codex (see above). Flames are indicated below his bundle, and a priest holds a flaming torch to the body, followed by other men bringing additional offerings. Rather than an actual cremation, this scene dealing with the named body of Lord 12 Motion has been interpreted as showing the drying and smoking of the body to prepare it as a mortuary bundle (Anders et al. 1992:237). Indeed, on the following page (82), a turquoise-masked bundled body is shown displayed (but not named). Later on *Nuttall* 82, a torch is being

FIGURE 5.14. Detail from *Codex Nuttall* 81, showing the corpse of Lord 12 Motion displayed in a wooden rack or box while receiving offerings (such as the quail offered by the priest, 9 Motion, to his right). A priest to his left holds a torch close to the body, with flames also shown below the body. Note what is probably a painted skull below the wooden rack (detail modified from Anders et al. 1992:pl. 81).

placed on a bundle of painted bones (a skull and femur are depicted); a similar image occurs on the unfinished *Nuttall* 84. The scenes on *Nuttall* 82 and 84, however, are not technically a cremation, as the flesh is not being burned from the body—the artist depicted painted bones, none of which are blackened. Presumably, on *Nuttall* 82 these are the bones of Lord 12 Motion, but they are not named as such, and the whole *Nuttall* 81–84 sequence—assassination and various funerary displays and subsequent vengeance—remains difficult to understand (Byron Hamann 2009, personal communication). Given the paucity of name glyphs and the complex political-familial context of Lord 12 Motion's murder and its aftermath, these scenes should not be assumed to demonstrate a "tradition" of elite cremation among the Mixtecs.

An additional scene that depicts two mortuary bundles above flames occurs on *Codex Bodley* 30 and 29 (see below). The bundles, descendants of the important Lord 4 Wind, are on a rack, with flames below—not actually on—the bundles, which once again could indicate either a stage in the drying of the body in preparing it as a mummy bundle or offerings to these mortuary bundles.

The above interpretations do not preclude the possibility of burning and destruction of the royal corpse. I argue, however, that such acts do not honor powerful elites, but rather represent violence against the body and associated royal house, whose ancestors could no longer be physically venerated. In the scene from the *Bodley* noted above, a reading of the image as narrating a torching of bundles signifies the destruction of Lord 4 Wind's dynasty by the burning of his descendants around CE 1173 (Byland and Pohl 1994:171). The *Nuttall* scenes also occur in a context that includes Lord 8 Deer's vengeance against enemies. If ancestors could be seen as supernatural protectors of their city and region, burning their remains would remove these bones from ongoing negotiations of political power and status. Unlike the display of body parts, and the powerful authoritative claims and social memory thus invoked, cremation of bodies and bones leaves nothing to venerate or to legitimate. For example, the mummy bundles of Lord 4 Wind's descendants, possibly being destroyed in the *Bodley,* are named as representatives of the deities 1 Eagle and 1 Grass, supernatural patrons of the westerly direction of Lord 4 Wind's realm (Byland and Pohl 1994:172–175). Rather than elite mortuary practices (Duncan et al. 2008), burning of elite bodies represents the destruction of sacred ancestors and their supernatural patrons.

Sacred bundles (without a clear body indicated) are also shown in the codices as crucial legitimizing objects. While not as explicit as mortuary/mummy bundles, sacred bundles also represented deified founding ancestors (Oudijk 2002), and probably contained some bones of royal ancestors, perhaps from damaged/disintegrated mummy bundles. In addition to actual bones, sacred bundles also may have contained *penates,* small greenstone images, perforated on the back for suspension/attachment, of what appear to be humans with their hands folded over their stomachs. Found in Late Postclassic burials and offerings in both the Valley of Oaxaca and the Mixteca Alta, *penates* probably depict sacred ancestors, perhaps ones so distant that they no longer were remembered as specific people. Small stone *caritas,* or heads, that depict similar facial features as those on *penates,* but in a mimetic pattern extending back to the Olmec, represent the corporeal essence through the head. The importance of sacred bundles is shown in the codices by the four priests who carry them (Pohl 1994), as they represented the sacred charter of rulership, as well as containing the actual essence of royal ancestors. In addition to being used as oracular bundles, these have been interpreted as serving as "battle standards" (ibid.); the destruction of such a sacred bundle removed the power base of the associated lineage.

Thus, the importance of bones in establishing legitimacy remained until the Spanish conquest and beyond, as bodies were an important source of evidence for the 1540s Inquisitorial investigation of three Mixtec rulers of Yanhuitlán. The practice of burying the dead under houses (as well as sacrifice and other elements of the interment procedure) was considered part of the paganism of indigenous religions that the Spanish were attempting to eradicate; investigators in the Yanhuitlán idolatry trial excavated the house of one Mixtec elite to look for bodies (Hamann 2007). Indeed, the sixteenth-century Mixtec landscape was filled with sacrificed bodies, which imbued sacrality to places throughout the region. The Spanish clergy connected the concern with dead ancestors to idolatry, and throughout the sixteenth century the church issued documents that discouraged feasts and dancing at funerals (Lomnitz 2005:139). In an effort to understand what he refers to as the "nationalization" of death in Mexico, Claudio Lomnitz (2005) traces the changing attitudes about death from Colonial Mexico—the hesitant introduction of purgatory and the use of fearful death imagery in an attempt to inculcate a fear of one's death—to the ironic intimacy with death that characterizes twenty-first-century attitudes in Mexico (see also Norget 2006).

Conclusion

While western attitudes associate skulls and skeletalized figures with death, in ancient Oaxaca bones represented the creative and legitimizing force of ancestors. Bones were deployed as symbols of status and power for individuals, as well as marking important structures and temples. Personhood in Oaxaca can be characterized as dividual rather than individual, with partible bodies from which nurturing essences were drawn in both life and death. As Jill Furst (1982:207) suggests, skeletalized deities in Mixtec codices often had generative and life-sustaining functions. Just as in the Maya narrative the *Popol Vuh* (Tedlock 1985), where the skull of Hun Hunahpu (one of the first set of Hero Twins) impregnated Blood Woman, thus becoming the father of the Hero Twins who are the focus of that narrative, pairs of historical/ancestral and supernatural Mixtec figures, either wearing a skeletal mask or completely skeletalized, engaged in generative acts. In an example from the *Codex Vienna*, a pair wearing the skeletalized jaw, headdress, and mask of Lord 9 Wind (related to the Central Mexican deity/cultural hero Ehecatl/Queztalcoatl), are shown with almost 50 offspring. Such beings are also shown creating or personifying stones, pulque, and the milpa (Furst 1982:209–214). Throughout Mesoamerica, bones are associated with new life. A famous part of the creation of the Aztecs' Fifth Sun centers on Quetzalcoatl's journey to the underworld to rescue the bones of ancestors from a previous creation; grinding these bones formed the substance for new humans (Leon-Portilla 1963).

The importance of bodies and bones in Mesoamerica also refers back to the original blood debt between humans and the deities, which can only be satisfied by the blood and body of humans. Davíd Carrasco (1999) notes that for the Aztecs, bodies were charged—animated by supernatural forces. The energy and charisma of Aztec warriors, for example, was especially powerful in their skin and body parts—thus, the importance of displaying objects such as a defleshed femur.

Early villagers in Oaxaca utilized the bodies of ancestors—as did many other early agricultural villages across the world—to socially transform the landscape. Kent Flannery (1972:29) notes: "In a world without written deeds, the presence of the ancestors frequently serves as a group's best evidence that the land has been theirs 'since time began.'" Bodies, bones, and ancestors, however, were invoked in a myriad of ways beyond claims to land. Placement of bodies near the houses of their living descendants became increasingly important and reflected social identities focused more on corporate groups and factions than on the entire village, while more communal identification is suggested by the Early Formative Tomaltepec cemetery. Ancestral bones materialized lineal ties and descent. The corpses of ancestors remained important referents in ongoing social negotiations and performances of social memory among the living. Just as modern Oaxacans eat skulls made of sugar and also feed their departed relatives, prehispanic consumption, display, and interaction with bodies transferred charisma and the essence of the deceased. A diachronic perspective on bodies and bones from Oaxaca illustrates their increasing importance through time in materializing the ancestors to represent and reinforce social identities.

The founding of Monte Albán around 500 BCE coincided with increasingly elaborate burials for some individuals, materializing the increasing social distinctions between commoners and elites. Masonry tombs served to curate elite bones rather than having them consumed by the earth, the fate awaiting commoners' bones. The treatment of elite bones in Oaxaca focused on conservation rather than being destroyed through cremation. Some Late Postclassic tombs—such as at Mitla in the eastern Valley of Oaxaca—served as ossuaries for numerous individuals, rather than a select few royals (Robles García and Molina Vargas 1998). While contemporary Oaxacans deploy skeletalized images of the dead to enact passages and transformations in their own lives, from marriages to drunkenness, ancient Oaxacans manipulated images of the dead, in a variety of media, as well as actual bodies and parts. Through time, invoking ancestors involved more actual physical remains of them, from long bones and skulls to the mummy bundles of the Postclassic Mixtec. The past served as an important source of power in the present, from the creation of households to the display of ancestral bones as symbols of power.

Acknowledgments

The research reported here was made possible by permits and support of the Consejo de Arqueología and both national and state-level branches of the Instituto Nacional de Antropología e Historia, while funding came primarily from a Fulbright (IIE) Fellowship. I thank all past and current directors and members of the various agencies that have been so helpful, especially the Centro INAH Oaxaca, as well as the many field assistants from Etlatongo. The human remains from Etlatongo were analyzed by Pedro Antonio Juarez and Alec Christensen. I also wish to thank several scholars who have graciously provided feedback on this chapter and/or have provided me with additional data, both published and unpublished: Catherine Allen, Byron Hamann, Alicia Herrera Muzgo T., George Lau, Michael Lind, Robert Markens, Barbara Miller, Javier Urcid, Marcus Winter, and two anonymous reviewers. I also thank James Fitzsimmons for his invitation to contribute to this volume, and his encouragement throughout the writing process. Any errors remain my own.

Works Cited

Acosta, Jorge R., and Javier Romero

1992   *Exploraciones en Monte Negro, Oaxaca.* Instituto Nacional de Antropología e Historia, Mexico City.

Allen, Catherine J.
1988   *The Hold Life Has: Coca and Cultural Identity in an Andean Community.* Smithsonian Institution Press, Washington, D.C.
Anders, Ferdinand, Maarten Jansen, and Gabina Aurora Pérez Jiménez
1992   *Crónica mixteca: El rey 8 venado "Garra de Jaguar" y la dinastía de Teozacualco-Zaachila. Libro explicativo del llamado Códice Zouche-Nuttall.* ADEVA/Fondo de Cultura Económica, Mexico City.
Arnold, Denise Y., and Christine A. Hastorf
2008   *Heads of State: Icons, Power, and Politics in the Ancient and Modern Andes.* Left Coast Press, Walnut Creek, California.
Barber, Sarah B.
2005   Identity, Tradition, and Complexity: Negotiating Status and Authority in Pacific Coastal Oaxaca. Unpublished Ph.D. dissertation, Department of Anthropology, University of Colorado, Boulder.
Barber, Sarah B., and Arthur A. Joyce
2007   Polity Produced and Community Consumed: Negotiating Political Centralization through Ritual in the Lower Río Verde Valley, Oaxaca. In *Mesoamerican Ritual Economy: Archaeological and Ethnological Perspectives,* edited by E. Christian Wells and Karla L. Davis-Salazar, pp. 221–244. University Press of Colorado, Boulder.
Bernal, Ignacio
1949   Exploraciones en Coixtlahuaca, Oaxaca. *Revista Mexicana de Estudios Antropológicos* 10:5–76.
Binford, Lewis R.
1971   Mortuary Practices: Their Study and Their Potential. In *Approaches to the Social Dimensions of Mortuary Practices,* edited by James A. Brown, pp. 6–29. Memoir 25. Society for American Archaeology, Washington, D.C.
Blanton, Richard E.
1978   *Monte Albán: Settlement Patterns at the Ancient Zapotec Capital.* Academic Press, New York.
Bloch, Maurice, and Jonathan Parry
1982   Introduction: Death and the Regeneration of Life. In *Death and the Regeneration of Life,* edited by Maurice Bloch and Jonathan Parry, pp. 1–44. Cambridge University Press, New York.
Blomster, Jeffrey P.
2004   *Etlatongo: Social Complexity, Interaction, and Village Life in the Mixteca Alta of Oaxaca, Mexico.* Wadsworth, Belmont, Calif.
2008   Changing Cloud Formations: The Socio-Politics of Oaxaca in Late Classic/Postclassic Mesoamerica. In *After Monte Albán: Transformation and Negotiation in Late Classic/Postclassic Oaxaca, Mexico,* edited by Jeffrey Blomster, pp. 3–46. University Press of Colorado, Boulder.
2009   Identity, Gender, and Power: Representational Juxtapositions in Early Formative Figurines from Oaxaca, Mexico. In *Mesoamerican Figurines: Small-Scale*

Indices of Large-Scale Phenomena, edited by Cristina Halperin, Katherine Faust, Rhonda Taube, and Aurora Giguet, pp. 119–148. University Press of Florida, Gainesville.

Bourdieu, Pierre

1977   *Outline of a Theory of Practice.* Cambridge University Press, New York.

Braniff, Beatriz, and Marie-Areti Hers

1998   Herencias chichimecas. *Arqueología* 19:55–80.

Buikstra, Jane

1995   Tombs for the Living . . . or . . . for the Dead: The Osmore Ancestors. In *Tombs for the Living: Andean Mortuary Practices*, edited by Tom Dillehay, pp. 229–280. Dumbarton Oaks Research Library and Collection, Washington, D.C.

Butler, Judith

1993   *Bodies That Matter: On the Discursive Limits of "Sex."* Routledge, New York.

Byland, Bruce E., and John M. D. Pohl

1994   *In the Realm of 8 Deer: The Archaeology of the Mixtec Codices.* University of Oklahoma Press, Norman.

Carrasco, Davíd

1999   *City of Sacrifice: The Aztec Empire and the Role of Violence in Civilization.* Beacon Press, Boston.

Caso, Alfonso

1939   Resumen del informe de las exploraciones en Oaxaca, durante la 7ª y la 8ª temporadas 1937–1938 y 1938–1939. *XXVII Congreso Internacional de Americanistas*, Vol. II, pp. 159–187. Instituto Nacional de Antropología e Historia, Mexico City.

1969   *El tesoro de Monte Albán.* Memorias No. 3. Instituto Nacional de Antropología e Historia, Mexico City.

Caso, Alfonso, and Ignacio Bernal

1952   *Urnas de Oaxaca.* Memorias No. 2. Instituto Nacional de Antropología e Historia, Mexico City.

Caso, Alfonso, Ignacio Bernal, and Jorge R. Acosta

1967   *La cerámica de Monte Albán.* Memorias No. 13. Instituto Nacional de Antropología e Historia, Mexico City.

Charles, Douglas K.

2005   The Archaeology of Death as Anthropology. In *Interacting with the Dead: Perspectives on Mortuary Archaeology for the New Millennium*, edited by Gordon Rakita, Jane Buikstra, Lane Beck, and Sloan Williams, pp. 15–24. University Press of Florida, Gainesville.

Christensen, Alexander F., and Marcus Winter

1997   Culturally Modified Skeletal Remains from the Site of Huamelulpan, Oaxaca, Mexico. *International Journal of Osteoarchaeology* 7:467–480.

Coe, Michael D.

1962   *Mexico.* Frederick A. Praeger, New York.

Connerton, Paul

1989   *How Societies Remember.* Cambridge University Press, New York.

Cortés Vilchis, Marisol Yadira, and Alicia Herrera Muzgo T.

2009   Exploraciones en el Edificio J de Paso Aguascalientes. In *Proyecto Salvamento Arqueológico Carretera Oaxaca-Istmo 2004–2005: Tramo Jalapa del Marqués Km 190–210*, edited by Marcus Winter. Final report submitted to Instituto Nacional de Antropología e Historia. Centro INAH Oaxaca, Oaxaca.

Díaz Castro, Susana

2008   Representaciones de glifos de espacio en la pintura mural de Oaxaca. In *La pintura mural prehispánica en México III: Oaxaca*, vol. 4, edited by Beatriz de la Fuente, pp. 469–511. Universidad Nacional Autónoma de México, Mexico City.

Dillehay, Tom D.

1995   Mounds of Social Death: Araucanian Funerary Rites and Political Succession. In *Tombs for the Living: Andean Mortuary Practices*, edited by Tom Dillehay, pp. 281–313. Dumbarton Oaks Research Library and Collection, Washington, D.C.

Douglas, Mary

1970   *Natural Symbols: Explorations in Cosmology*. Praeger, New York.

Drennan, Robert D.

1976   *Fábrica San José and Middle Formative Society in the Valley of Oaxaca, Mexico*. Memoirs of the University of Michigan Museum of Anthropology No. 8. University of Michigan, Ann Arbor.

Duncan, William N., Andrew K. Balkansky, Kimberly Crawford, Heather A. Lapham, and Nathan J. Meissner

2008   Human Cremation in Mexico 3,000 Years Ago. *Proceedings of the National Academy of Science* 105(14):5315–5320.

Duncan, William N., Christina Elson, Charles S. Spencer, and Elsa M. Redmond

2009   A Human Maxilla Trophy from Cerro Tilcajete, Oaxaca, Mexico. *Mexicon* 31:108–113.

Durkheim, Emile

1938/   *The Rules of Sociological Method*. Translated from the French by Sarah A. Solovay
[1895]   and John H. Mueller. Free Press, New York.

Farrell, James J.

1980   *Inventing the American Way of Death, 1830–1920*. Temple University Press, Philadelphia.

Fitzsimmons, James L.

2009   *Death and the Classic Maya Kings*. University of Texas Press, Austin.

Flannery, Kent V.

1972   The Origins of the Villages as a Settlement Type in Mesoamerica and the Near East: A Comparative Study. In *Man, Settlement, and Urbanism*, edited by Peter Ucko, Ruth Tringham, and G. W. Dimbleby, pp. 23–53. Duckworth, Hertfordshire.

Flannery, Kent V., and Joyce Marcus

1983   The Growth of Site Hierarchies in the Valley of Oaxaca: Part I. In *The Cloud People*, edited by Kent V. Flannery and Joyce Marcus, pp. 53–64. Academic Press, New York.

2005   *Excavations at San José Mogote I: The Household Archaeology*. Memoirs of the Museum of Anthropology No. 40. University of Michigan, Ann Arbor.

Fowler, Chris

2004   *The Archaeology of Personhood: An Anthropological Approach.* Routledge, New York.

Furst, Jill L.

1982   Skeletonization in Mixtec Art: A Re-evaluation. In *The Art and Iconography of Late Post-Classic Central Mexico,* edited by E. Boone, pp. 207–225. Dumbarton Oaks Research Library and Collection, Washington, D.C.

Gallegos Ruiz, Roberto

1978   *El señor 9 flor en Zaachila.* Universidad Nacional Autónoma de México, Mexico City.

Gaxiola González, Margarita

1984   *Huamelulpan: Un centro urbano de la Mixteca Alta.* Colección Científica 114. Instituto Nacional de Antropología e Historia, Mexico City.

Goldstein, Lynn G.

1981   One-Dimensional Archaeology and Multidimensional People: Spatial Organization and Mortuary Analysis. In *The Archaeology of Death,* edited by Robert Chapman, Ian Kinnes, and Klavs Randsbourg, pp. 53–69. Cambridge University Press, New York.

Gutierrez, Gerardo

2008   Classic and Postclassic Archaeological Features of the Mixteca-Tlapaneca-Nahua Region of Guerrero: Why Didn't Anyone Tell Me the Classic Period Was Over? In *After Monte Albán: Transformation and Negotiation in Late Classic/ Postclassic Oaxaca, Mexico,* edited by Jeffrey Blomster, pp. 367–392. University Press of Colorado, Boulder.

Hamann, Byron E.

2007   Landscapes of Divinity and Landscapes of Idolatry. Paper presented at Dumbarton Oaks, Washington, D.C.

Hendon, Julia A.

2000   Having and Holding: Storage, Memory, Knowledge, and Social Relations. *American Anthropologist* 102(1):42–53.

Herbich, Ingrid, and Michael Dietler

1993   Space, Time and Symbolic Structure in the Luo Homestead: An Ethnoarchaeological Study of "Settlement Biography" in Africa. In *Actes du XIIe Congrès International des Sciences Préhistoriques et Protohistoriques, Bratislava, Czechoslovakia (September 1–7, 1991),* Vol. 1, pp. 26–32.

Hertz, Robert

1960/   *Death and the Right Hand.* Translated by Rodney Needham and Claudia Needham.
[1907]   Cohen and West, London.

Hodder, Ian

1982   *Symbols in Action: Ethnoarchaeological Studies of Material Culture.* Cambridge University Press, New York.

Houston, Stephen D., Karl A. Taube, and David Stuart

2006   *The Memory of Bones: Body, Being and Experience Among the Classic Maya.* University of Texas Press, Austin.

Joyce, Arthur A.

1994   Late Formative Community Organization and Social Complexity on the Oaxaca Coast. *Journal of Field Archaeology* 21(2):147–168.

2008   Domination, Negotiation, and Collapse: A History of Centralized Authority on the Oaxaca Coast Before the Late Postclassic. In *After Monte Albán: Transformation and Negotiation in Late Classic/Postclassic Oaxaca, Mexico*, edited by Jeffrey Blomster, pp. 219–254. University Press of Colorado, Boulder.

Joyce, Arthur A., and Marcus Winter

1996   Ideology, Power, and Urban Society in Pre-Hispanic Oaxaca. *Current Anthropology* 37(1):33–47, 70–73.

Joyce, Rosemary A.

1998   Performing the Body in Pre-Hispanic Central America. *RES: Anthropology and Aesthetics* 33 (Spring):147–165.

Leon-Portilla, Miguel

1963   *Aztec Thought and Culture: A Study of the Ancient Nahuatl Mind.* Translated by Jack Emory Davis. University of Oklahoma Press, Norman.

Lesure, Richard G.

1997   Figurines and Social Identities in Early Sedentary Societies of Coastal Chiapas, Mexico. In *Women in Prehistory: North America and Mesoamerica*, edited by Cheryl Claassen and Rosemary Joyce, pp. 227–248. University of Pennsylvania Press, Philadelphia.

Lind, Michael, and Javier Urcid

1983   The Lords of Lambityeco and Their Nearest Neighbors. *Notas Mesoamericanas* 9:76–111.

2010   *The Lords of Lambityeco: Political Evolution in the Valley of Oaxaca.* University Press of Colorado, Boulder.

Lombardo de Ruiz, Sonia

2008   Los estilos en la pintura mural de Oaxaca. In *La pintura mural prehispánica en México III: Oaxaca*, vol. 3, edited by Beatriz de la Fuente, pp. 89–175. Universidad Nacional Autónoma de México, Mexico City.

Lomnitz, Claudio

2005   *Death and the Idea of Mexico.* Zone Books, New York.

López Austin, Alfredo

1988   *Human Body and Ideology.* 2 vols. Translated by Thelma Ortiz de Montellano and Bernard R. Ortiz de Montellano. University of Utah Press, Salt Lake City.

Malville, Nancy J.

2005   Mortuary Practices and Ritual Use of Human Bone in Tibet. In *Interacting with the Dead: Perspectives on Mortuary Archaeology for the New Millennium*, edited by Gordon Rakita, Jane Buikstra, Lane Beck, and Sloan Williams, pp. 190–204. University Press of Florida, Gainesville.

Marcus, Joyce, and Kent V. Flannery

1996   *Zapotec Civilization: How Urban Society Evolved in Mexico's Oaxaca Valley.* Thames and Hudson, New York.

Markens, Robert, Marcus Winter, and Cira Martínez López

2008   Ethnohistory, Oral History and Archaeology at Macuilxóchitl: Perspectives on the Postclassic Period (C.E. 800–1521) in the Valley of Oaxaca. In *After Monte Albán: Transformation and Negotiation in Late Classic/Postclassic Oaxaca, Mexico*, edited by Jeffrey Blomster, pp. 193–215. University Press of Colorado, Boulder.

2010   Appendix 1: Calibrated Radiocarbon Dates for the Late Classic and Postclassic Periods in the Valley of Oaxaca, Mexico. In *The Lords of Lambityeco: Political Evolution in the Valley of Oaxaca*, Michael Lind and Javier Urcid, pp. 345–363. University Press of Colorado, Boulder.

Martínez López, Cira, Marcus Winter, and Pedro Antonio Juárez

1995   Entierros humanos del Proyecto Especial Monte Albán 1992–1994. In *Entierros humanos de Monte Albán: Dos estudios*, edited by Marcus Winter, pp. 79–244. Proyecto Especial Monte Alban 1992–1994, Contribución No. 7. Centro INAH Oaxaca, Oaxaca.

McAnany, Patricia

1995   *Living with the Ancestors: Kinship and Kingship in Ancient Maya Society.* University of Texas Press, Austin.

McCafferty, Sharisse D., and Geoffrey G. McCafferty

1994   Engendering Tomb 7 at Monte Albán: Respinning an Old Yarn. *Current Anthropology* 35(2):143–166.

Metcalf, Peter, and Richard Huntington

1991   *Celebrations of Death: The Anthropology of Mortuary Ritual.* 2nd ed. Cambridge University Press, New York.

Middleton, William D., Gary M. Feinman, and Guillermo Molina Villegas

1998   Tomb Use and Reuse in Oaxaca, Mexico. *Ancient Mesoamerica* 9(2):297–307.

Miller, Arthur G.

1995   *The Painted Tombs of Oaxaca, Mexico: Living with the Dead.* Cambridge University Press, New York.

Mitford, Jessica

1963   *The American Way of Death.* Simon and Schuster, New York.

Monaghan, John

1996   The Mesoamerican Community as a "Great House." *Ethnology* 35(3):181–194.

Morris, Ian

1991   The Archaeology of Ancestors: The Saxe-Goldstein Hypothesis Revisited. *Cambridge Archaeological Journal* 1(2):147–169.

Norget, Kristin

2006   *Days of Death, Days of Life: Ritual in the Popular Culture of Oaxaca.* Columbia University Press, New York.

Ochoa Castillo, Patricia, and Óscar Orueta Cañada

1994   *La sala del Preclásico del Altiplano.* Colección Catálogos. Instituto Nacional de Antropología e Historia, Mexico City.

Oudijk, Michel R.

2002   The Zapotec City-State. In *A Comparative Study of Six City-State Cultures: An Investigation Conducted by the Copenhagen Polis Centre*, edited by Mogens

Herman Hansen, pp. 73–90. Royal Danish Academy of Sciences and Letters, Copenhagen.

Parker Pearson, Mike

1999   *The Archaeology of Death and Burial.* Texas A&M University Press, College Station.

Pohl, John M. D.

1994   *The Politics of Symbolism in the Mixtec Codices.* Publications in Anthropology No. 46. Vanderbilt University, Nashville.

Rabin, Emily

1970   *The Lambityeco Friezes: Notes on Their Content with an Appendix on C14 Dates.* Boletín de Estudios Oaxaqueños No. 33. Museo Frissel, Mitla, Oaxaca.

Reischer, Erica, and Kathryn S. Koo

2004   The Body Beautiful: Symbolism and Agency in the Social World. *Annual Review of Anthropology* 33:297–317.

Robles García, Nelly, and Guillermo Molina Vargas

1998   Exploración de una tumba prehispánica en el sitio Llaadzie en la comunidad de Mitla, Oaxaca. *Cuadernos del Sur* 12:21–52.

Salomon, Frank

1995   "The Beautiful Grandparents": Andean Ancestor Shrines and Mortuary Rituals as Seen Through Colonial Records. In *Tombs for the Living: Andean Mortuary Practices,* edited by Tom Dillehay, pp. 315–353. Dumbarton Oaks Research Library and Collection, Washington, D.C.

Saxe, Arthur A.

1970   Social Dimensions of Mortuary Practices. Unpublished Ph.D. dissertation, Department of Anthropology, University of Michigan, Ann Arbor.

Scheper-Hughes, Nancy

2001   Bodies for Sale—Whole or in Parts. *Body and Society* 7(2–3):1–8.

Scheper-Hughes, Nancy, and Margaret M. Lock

1987   The Mindful Body: A Prolegomenon to Future Work in Medical Anthropology. *Medical Anthropology Quarterly* 1(1):6–41.

Scott, John F.

1978   *The Danzantes of Monte Albán: Part II. Catalogue.* Studies in Pre-Columbian Art and Archaeology No. 19. Dumbarton Oaks Research Library and Collection, Washington, D.C.

Sellen, Adam T.

2007   *El cielo compartido: Deidades y ancestros en las vasijas efigie zapotecas.* Universidad Nacional Autónoma de México, Mérida.

Smith, C. Earle Jr.

1976   *Modern Vegetation and Ancient Plant Remains of the Nochixtlán Valley, Oaxaca.* Publications in Anthropology No. 16. Vanderbilt University, Nashville.

Smith, Mary Elizabeth

1973   *Picture Writing from Ancient Southern Mexico: Mixtec Place Signs and Maps.* University of Oklahoma Press, Norman.

Spencer, Charles S.

1982   *The Cuicatlán Cañada and Monte Albán: A Study of Primary State Formation.*
        Academic Press, New York.

Spores, Ronald A.

1972   *An Archaeological Settlement Survey of the Nochixtlán Valley, Oaxaca.* Publica-
        tions in Anthropology No. 1. Vanderbilt University, Nashville.

1984   *The Mixtecs in Ancient and Colonial Times.* University of Oklahoma Press,
        Norman.

Tedlock, Dennis

1985   *Popol Vuh.* Simon and Schuster, New York.

Turner, Victor

1967   *The Forest of Symbols: Aspects of Ndembu Ritual.* Cornell University Press,
        Ithaca, NY.

Ucko, Peter J.

1969   Ethnography and the Archaeological Interpretation of Funerary Remains. *World
        Archaeology* 1:262–290.

Urcid, Javier

1995   Comentarios a una lápida zapoteca en el Museo Nacional de Historia Natural,
        Smithsonian Institution, Washington, D.C. *Cuadernos del Sur* 3(8–9):8–27.

2001   *Zapotec Hieroglyphic Writing.* Studies in Pre-Columbian Art and Archaeology
        No. 34. Dumbarton Oaks Research Library and Collection, Washington, D.C.

2005   Zapotec Writing: Knowledge, Power, and Memory in Ancient Oaxaca. Founda-
        tion for the Advancement of Mesoamerican Studies, Inc., Coral Gables, Fla.
        Electronic document, http://www.famsi.org/zapotecwriting/, accessed August 1,
        2008.

2008   El arte de pintar las tumbas: Sociedad e ideología zapotecas (400–800 d.C.).
        In *La pintura mural prehispánica en México III: Oaxaca,* vol. 4, edited by Bea-
        triz de la Fuente, pp. 513–627. Universidad Nacional Autónoma de México,
        Mexico City.

n.d.   Oracles and Warfare: The Role of Pictorial Narratives in the Early Development
        of Monte Albán (500 B.C.E.–200 A.C.E.). Manuscript on file, Department of
        Anthropology, Brandeis University, Waltham, Mass.

van Gennep, Arnold

1960/   *The Rites of Passage.* Translated by Monika Vizdom and Gabrielle L. Caffee.
[1909] University of Chicago Press, Chicago.

Van Wolputte, Steven

2004   Hang on to Your Selves: Of Bodies, Embodiment, and Selves. *Annual Review of
        Anthropology* 33:251–269.

Verano, John W.

2003   Trepanation in Prehistoric South America: Geographic and Temporal Trends
        over 2,000 Years. In *Trepanation: Discovery, History, Theory,* edited by Robert
        Arnott, Stanley Finger, and C.U.M. Smith, pp. 223–236. Swets and Zeitlinger
        B.V., Lisse.

Whalen, Michael E.

1981   *Excavations at Santo Domingo Tomaltepec: Evolution of a Formative Community in the Valley of Oaxaca, Mexico*. Memoirs of the University of Michigan Museum of Anthropology No. 12. University of Michigan, Ann Arbor.

1988   House and Household in Formative Oaxaca. In *Household and Community in the Mesoamerican Past*, edited by Richard Wilk and Wendy Ashmore, pp. 249–272. University of New Mexico Press, Albuquerque.

Wilkinson, Richard G.

1997   Appendix B. Human Skeletal Remains from La Coyotera. In *Archaeology of the Cañada de Cuicatlán, Oaxaca*, edited by Charles Spencer and Elsa Redmond, pp. 614–620. Anthropological Papers No. 80. American Museum of Natural History, New York.

Winter, Marcus

1972   Tierras Largas: A Formative Community in the Valley of Oaxaca. Unpublished Ph.D. dissertation, Department of Anthropology, University of Arizona, Tucson.

1989   *Oaxaca: The Archaeological Record*. Minutiae Mexicana, Mexico City.

1994   *Tesoros del Museo Regional de Oaxaca*. Honorable Ayuntamiento de Oaxaca, Oaxaca.

2002   Monte Albán: Mortuary Practices as Domestic Ritual and Their Relation to Community Religion. *Domestic Ritual in Ancient Mesoamerica*, edited by Patricia Plunket, pp. 67–82. Costen Institute of Archaeology, UCLA.

2005   Producción y uso de figurillas tempranas en el Valle de Oaxaca. *Acervos* 29:37–54.

Winter, Marcus, and Javier Urcid

1990   Una mandibula humana grabada de la Sierra Mazateca, Oaxaca. *Notas Mesoamericanas* 12:39–49.

Winter, Marcus, William O. Autry, Jr., Richard G. Wilkinson, and Cira Martínez López

1995   Entierros humanos en una area residencial de Monte Albán: Temporadas 1972–1973. In *Entierros humanos de Monte Albán: Dos estudios*, edited by Marcus Winter, pp. 11–78. Proyecto Especial Monte Alban 1992–1994, Contribución No. 7. Centro INAH Oaxaca, Oaxaca.

Zeitlin, Robert N., and Arthur A. Joyce

1999   The Zapotec-Imperialism Argument: Insights from the Oaxaca Coast. *Current Anthropology* 40(3):383–392.

CHAPTER 6

Interactions between the Living and the Dead at Major Monuments in Teotihuacan

SABURO SUGIYAMA

IT IS WELL DOCUMENTED ethnohistorically that Mesoamerican people shared a unique worldview; they conceived natural phenomena and living beings, including the life and death of humans, as continuous segments of a cyclically changing world. Natural and social events, interrelated in the eyes of Mesoamericans, were recorded by sophisticated calendar systems in relation to the cycles of celestial objects and were often explained in terms of the sacred forces or gods who were sacrificed or who practiced autosacrifice. Thanks to these gods, people could live in the present world and therefore they must repay their debt with their own sacrifices, preferably of significant people (Nicholson 1971; Sahagún 1950–1982). This particular worldview seems to have persisted as a fundamental principle for millennia among Mesoamerican societies, with numerous related versions having significant differences in terms of conceptualizations of world divisions, related mythologies, associated gods and animals, and the methods employed for sacrificial rituals (Sahagún 1950–1982).

Intensive archaeological research in Mesoamerica for more than a century has confirmed that ancient cities developed as sacred centers where people interacted with the gods through ritual. Archaeological and iconographic information indicate that the interactions with the gods, the dead, and other sacred forces took place especially through mortuary rituals, including human sacrifice at sacred monuments. The Aztec believed that Teotihuacan, the "place of the gods," was a legendary spot where the sun, the moon, and other natural entities, including humans, were created by autosacrifice on the part of the gods (Codex

Chimalpopoca 1992). We do not know how far back this Postclassic myth can be traced. Archaeologically, we had been insufficiently informed regarding how Teotihuacan was first founded, its early development, and what kind of worldview inspired these events during the Late Formative–Early Classic periods. Recent explorations have provided important new information relevant to these issues. Although our reconstruction of Teotihuacan beliefs lacks a sufficient understanding of Teotihuacan's symbolism and writing system, new excavation data from major monuments, particularly burials uncovered inside of them, allow us to interpret how the Teotihuacanos interacted with their gods or natural forces through mortuary rituals.

In this paper, I describe both sacrificial and elite graves found to date at the major monuments in Teotihuacan, reanalyzing previously reported excavation contexts, and presenting new ideas developed with new data. I discuss burials explored in the 1980s at the Feathered Serpent Pyramid (FSP) (Cabrera Castro et al. 1991; Sugiyama 2005), sacrificial/elite graves explored recently at the Moon Pyramid (Sugiyama and Cabrera Castro 2007; Sugiyama and López Luján 2007), and burials uncovered at the Sun Pyramid (Batres 1906). I also discuss a possible royal grave in a tunnel found under the Sun Pyramid (Heyden 1975) that we mapped three-dimensionally in 2007. Additionally, I will give a brief overview of elite graves found at Mounds A and B, and Teotihuacan-style platforms at Kaminaljuyú, Guatemala, as comparative data, because they share analogous characteristics with elites' graves in Teotihuacan.

At the three major monuments in Teotihuacan, sacrificial victims were buried during episodic construction events at different levels, including at subsoil, on upper floors, and in their geometric centers. No burials were reused for secondary interments; instead, destructive manipulations of interments and associated symbolic items often took place in later periods. As the monumental constructions were evidently carried out by the ruling groups of the city, the contents of the mortuary assemblages discussed here seem to have reflected politico-religious organizations at the state level. It is argued that the major monuments functioned as the central places where ruling entities repeatedly performed mortuary rituals with sacrificial victims and deceased elites and buried them with symbolic offerings of exceptionally high quality and quantity to express their worldview. The dead and grave items were often placed purposefully in groups composed of calendrically and cosmologically significant numbers (marked in italics in this chapter) to articulate Mesoamerican concepts of time and space. The living rulers thus manipulated events of state by interacting with the dead to proclaim their divine rulership at Teotihuacan.

Sacrificial Burials in Teotihuacan

Teotihuacanos did not make cemeteries; rather, they typically kept their dead under the floors of their living spaces. More than 1,400 skeletons (Manzanilla and Serrano Sánchez 1999; Rattray 1992; Rodríguez García 1992; Sempowski and Spence 1994) have been excavated to date from the ancient city. The majority of these were individually buried in pits excavated into *tepetate* (the local indurated subsoil) within rooms, porticos, temples, altars, plazas, corridors, and other domestic areas. It can be said that the city was a place both for the living and for the dead who remained under the floors, presumably in the same residences where they used to live, perhaps to interact with their descendants from the underworld. Most individuals in burials are thought to have died natural deaths, as they were usually buried with more utilitarian items than symbolic objects, without clear indications on bones of sacrifice or other intentional trauma. There are, however, several instances that apparently resulted from sacrificial rituals. They include the remains of dismemberments, decapitations, and infanticides performed in residential areas (Jarquín Pacheco and Martínez Vargas 1991; Gómez Chávez 2000, 2002; González Miranda 1993; González Miranda and Fuentes 1982; Martínez Vargas and González Miranda 1991; Rattray 1992:12; Rodríguez García 1992; Serrano Sánchez and Lagunas 1975; see also Sugiyama 2005:201–206, for a summary). There are other possible sacrificial burials as well, though the reports are not of sufficient clarity (e.g., Almaráz 1865; Armillas 1950; Bastien 1946; Mogor 1966). Close examination of cut marks on bones, particularly from salvage excavations, may significantly increase the number of sacrificial burials that have been found in living spaces. These data demonstrate that highly varied sacrificial burials also took place in residential zones, particularly in relation to the new construction of temples, altars, or other communal buildings. They could have been linked with the sacrificial burials at the major monuments described below or may have been district or sector versions of foundation rituals conducted at a smaller scale.

The sacrificial graves found in residential compounds contrast significantly with those discovered at Oztoyahualco, the Sun Pyramid, the FSP, and at the Moon Pyramid in terms of complexity, scale, materials included, and, perhaps, ritual meanings and sociopolitical implications. Rattray (1992:6) suggests that several three-temple complexes, constructed during early periods, might also have contained sacrificial burials in this category.

Cook de Leonard (1957b, 1971:191) excavated "Plaza One," a "three-temple" complex in Oztoyahualco, by means of a tunnel dug into the central mound (1B:N5W2 in Millon et al. 1973). Inside, 12 adult burials were unearthed, in flexed positions, and many associated with Tlaloc vessels. They were wrapped mummy-style in cotton cloth and, in one instance, placed on the steps of the substructure. Although excavation contexts in the reports are brief, they do not exclude the possibility that the dead may have been either elites or sacrificial victims buried in association with the monument. Rattray (1992) dates them to the Tzacualli phase (AD 0–150), an early time approximately contemporaneous with the Sun Pyramid, the earliest substructures (Buildings 1 and 2) found in the Moon Pyramid, and early constructions at the FSP. Cook de Leonard (1957a:1) found an infant burial in a low platform of Plaza One at Oztoyahualco, which she interpreted as a possible sacrifice made in dedication to the structure (Cook de Leonard 1957a:1, 1957b; Millon 1957). This seems to have been another case of an early dedication burial associated with a monumental construction.

Feathered Serpent Pyramid (FSP)

The Ciudadela (Citadel) was the largest ceremonial precinct in the city. The most important structure in this precinct was the Feathered Serpent Pyramid, constructed to face its entrance on its central axis. Because the Feathered Serpent was a symbol of political authority until Aztec times, the Ciudadela may be assumed to have been a politico-religious headquarters of the state (Carrasco 1982:123; Cowgill 1983). Some researchers believe that rulers lived in the twin residential complexes called "Palaces," located at both sides of the main pyramid (Millon 1973).

Because of a discovery of multiple sacrificial burials on the southern side of the pyramid in 1983 (Sugiyama 1989), the interior and exterior of the Feathered Serpent Pyramid were extensively and systematically explored in 1988–1989. The rest of an earlier construction prior to the Feathered Serpent Pyramid was uncovered with a sacrificial burial (Grave 12). The second level, corresponding to the Ciudadela and the Feathered Serpent Pyramid, was one of the most monumental construction programs in the city and was dated to around AD 200–250 (the end of Miccaotli phase). The Adosada platform was the third construction level, occurring around AD 350, at this location. It covered the front facade of the main Feathered Serpent Pyramid (Sugiyama 1998). One of the most significant discoveries was the more than 137 individuals found with abundant symbolic offerings of exceptional quality in and around the pyramid (Sugiyama 2005). Although we intentionally left some burials unexcavated, we believe that more than 200 individuals were buried during the construction of the pyramid (Cabrera Castro et al. 1991).

The unique distribution pattern of the mass-sacrificial graves clearly indicates a materialization of the Teotihuacan worldview by the state (fig. 6.1). The victims were carefully set in long rectangular pits excavated into the subsoil and were covered with stones and earth; the pits were symmetrically distributed outside and inside, along the E–W and N–S axes of the pyramid. The excavation contexts clearly indicate that the deceased were part of a mortuary complex dedicated to the erection of the pyramid. Significant numbers in Mesoamerican cosmology and calendric systems, such as 4, 8, 9, 13, 18, and 20, were used in organizing the burials. These would have explicitly symbolized the Mesoamerican cosmos, which consists of nine layers of underworld, four directions on earth, 13 layers of upper world, and a ritual calendar of 260 days (20 day signs × 13 prefix numbers), as well as a solar cycle of 365 days (20 days × 18 months + 5 days).

The burial complex was mainly composed of several sets of 18 (or 9 + 9) men in a long pit, and 8 (or 4 + 4) women in a shorter one located parallel to it. Their ages varied significantly (from 14 to 43 years old), but there were certain regularities in position, orientation, and other mortuary variables (Sugiyama 2005:96–121). Nearly 80 percent of the people buried at the pyramid had their arms crossed behind their backs, as if

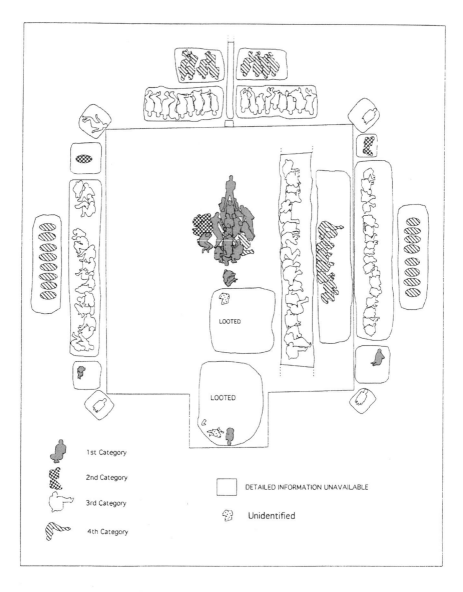

FIGURE 6.1. General plan of reconstructed body positions of the Feathered Serpent Pyramid burials, indicating possible affiliation of individuals suggested by burial patterns and associated offerings. The size of the graves has been enlarged out of proportion to the pyramid.

they had been tied. These data indicate that they were all sacrificial victims buried together in an anonymous fashion. Isotopic analysis suggests that most of them were brought from different regions in Mesoamerica (White et al. 2002).

The abundant offerings associated with them provide further information about their identification, the ritual meanings involved, and characteristics of the government. No ceramics were found at the monument, except for Tlaloc vessels that represented the Storm God. Virtually all the male skeletons were associated with abundant obsidian projectile points, slate disks attached to their hip bones, and shell pendants representing human maxilla; all of them can be identified as insignia of warriors. Some individuals carried pendants of real human or canid maxilla, which also symbolized Teotihuacano warriors. Female skeletons were also associated with projectile points, although the quantity was much smaller. The burial complex likely represented a mass sacrifice of warriors, who might have been brought voluntarily or forcefully as representatives of different ethnic/social groups or war captives and were attired as sacred Teotihuacano warriors.

Skeletons found in graves near the center of the pyramid, especially the central one containing 20 sacrifices (Grave 14), had much more varied offerings of higher quality. The offerings were found dispersed on or around the skeletons in certain patterns, as if a scattering ritual took place just before burying the individuals, as seen in several Teotihuacan murals (fig. 6.2). Offerings included greenstone ornaments, such as nose pendants symbolizing authority, figurines, and 18 enigmatic conical objects; shell pieces unworked and worked as ornaments; obsidian figures of humans and feathered serpents, blades, projectile points, knives, and "needles" ideal for autosacrifice; slate disks; and organic materials. Many of them were apparently symbols or tools for warfare, rulership, and human sacrifice or autosacrifice.

After covering the burials, the individuals responsible for the construction project finished the monumental building with a sculptural program, which was a much more explicit and permanent manifestation of the state religion for the public (fig. 6.3). The scene carved on the four facades carried a specific cosmogenic significance, again to proclaim the divine authority of state leaders to the public (López Austin et al. 1991; Sugiyama 1992, 2000; cf. Taube 1992). Two different high-relief sculptural

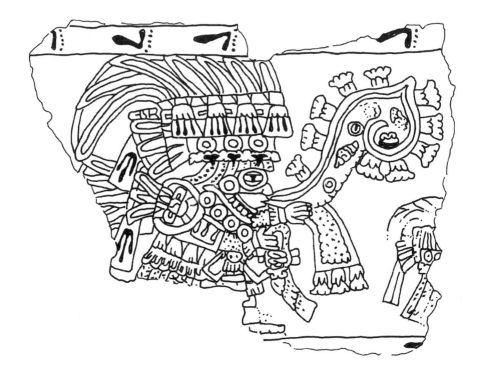

FIGURE 6.2. Individual carrying a bag of incense on a mural at Teotihuacan. He seems to be carrying out a scattering ritual, chanting the names of offerings like shells and greenstone objects.

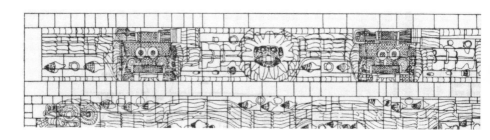

FIGURE 6.3. Sculptures on the main facade at the Feathered Serpent Pyramid.

motifs jutted out from the *"talud-tablero"* panels. The Feathered Serpent was obviously a central entity, being depicted with its entire body. This deity was believed in the Postclassic period to have been the great initiator of the calendric division, who brought the present world out from the watery underworld. Iconographic studies suggest that another central entity represented a headdress in the form of a primordial crocodilian monster, or what the Aztecs called Cipactli, which represented the first day of the ritual calendar, therefore symbolizing the beginning of time. A nose pendant, similar to those found inside the grave, was carved under this headdress. As a whole, the entire scene appears to have represented the creation of a new era brought by the Feathered Serpent, with the headdress symbolizing the genesis of the present world on its body (Sugiyama 2005).

We do not know exactly what this commemoration of a new era implied. It could have been for the celebration of a new 52-year period, another cycle of calendrical/astronomical significance, or a social event such as the celebration of a military victory. If we assume the powerful leadership needed to execute this grand-scale construction program that apparently involved the construction of the Sun Pyramid and an earlier incarnation of the Moon Pyramid as a kind of master plan, we can further hypothesize its significance from a sociopolitical perspective. It is more likely that the ruler established his divine status by constructing the FSP that depicted the creation of the world by the Feathered Serpent. This deity was carrying the headdress and nose pendant, personal items symbolizing the divine rulership that was to be granted to him (or her). Through the dramatization of mass sacrifice and the visualization of a new era, the Teotihuacan ruler may have orchestrated the succession-to-rulership ceremony authorized by a supreme creator. We know that headdresses and special nose pendants symbolizing the beginning of time were used traditionally by many Mesoamerican elites, especially contemporaneous Maya rulers, as emblems of political authority in depictions of succession to high office (Schele and Miller 1986:114–15). In Teotihuacan, the headdress and nose-pendant set was often depicted alone as an insignia, without the face of the person who used it. The mass-sacrificed warriors evidently formed a foundation in this dramatization of rulership, through which warfare was deliberately proclaimed and justified with divine reference.

The Moon Pyramid

Five grave complexes were recently excavated at the Moon Pyramid, adding substantial new data on the interaction of the sacrificial dead with living people (Sugiyama 2004; Sugiyama and Cabrera Castro 2003, 2007; Sugiyama and López Luján 2006, eds.; Sugiyama and López Luján 2007). As a result of systematic tunnel excavations into the pyramid, the long modification process of the monument has been revealed. Seven overlapping pyramidal platforms and five dedicatory or elite burials were detected inside. Each new building was constructed larger and covering earlier constructions; therefore, we designated the earliest and the smallest pyramidal structure found under the Adosada Platform Building 1, and the last and largest structure, known today as the Moon Pyramid, was named Building 7 (fig. 6.4). Five sacrificial burial complexes, called Burials 2, 3, 4, 5, and 6, were found with exceptionally rich offerings. In total we examined 37 individuals sacrificed and dedicated to different stages of monumental constructions. According to isotopic analysis, they were also probably brought from outside of the city (White et al. 2007), but were most likely special persons in their social status and/or in religious significance. Three burials, numbered 2, 3, and 4, were discovered at the subsoil level, while burials numbered 5 and 6 were uncovered in the upper section of the pyramid.

Burial 2 was found in the nucleus of Building 4. The grave was bordered on four sides by roughly made stone walls with no outside access or roof. Careful excavation revealed that one person was buried in a seated position near the eastern edge with his hands crossed behind his back as if they had been tied together. Therefore, we believe that this person, a male of 40 to 50 years at the time of death, was a sacrificial victim buried alongside offerings in dedication to the monument, although he could have been of high social status, as indicated by his high-quality ornaments.

The associated materials are exceptionally high-quality offerings. They include two greenstone anthropomorphic sculptures; nine obsidian human figures; 18 obsidian knives of exceptionally large size, and a large number of projectile points and prismatic blades of the same material; many shells, both unworked and worked in the form of ear spools, pendants, and beads; slate disks; and eight Tlaloc vessels, among

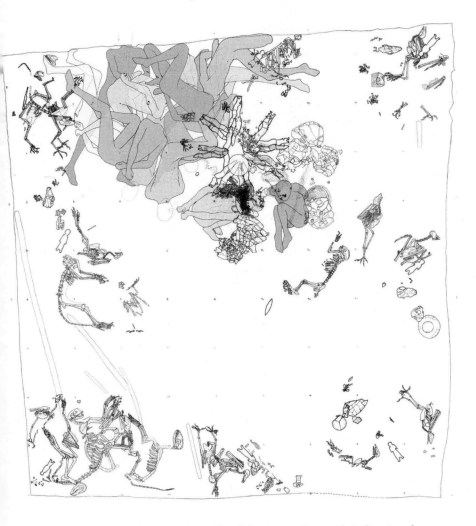

FIGURE 6.4. General plan and profile of the Moon Pyramid, indicating the location of seven overlapping architectural stages and five dedicatory burial/offering complexes.

other items. Most impressive were the skeletons of sacrificed animals: two pumas and one wolf (each found in an individual wooden cage), *nine* eagles, one falcon, one owl, and three small rattlesnakes (the species identifications of the animals found in Burials 2, 3, and 5 were made by Óscar J. Polaco of INAH). A wealth of martially themed objects and the animals, most probably buried alive during a mortuary ritual (since excrement was found in a cage), evidently symbolized military institutions, as iconographic data from later periods suggest.

Burial 3 constitutes another unique dedicatory burial complex associated with Building 5, although its contents are significantly different from those of Burial 2. Four individuals, possibly all males of about 14, 19, 22, and 42 years, evidently tied with their hands crossed behind their backs, were laid down carefully with offerings in a large pit. They were probably buried alive or killed just before being covered with rocks and earth to form the nucleus of Building 5. Quite different types of ornaments were found in direct association with each individual, as if each person represented a different origin or social category. General offerings scattered around them include shell trumpets, several clusters of obsidian projectile points, a large pyrite/slate disk, and an organic sheet forming a matlike object, which may have symbolized authority. Two clusters of offerings composed of many symbolic items were found in the central area. The most intriguing offerings were 14 wolf skulls, 4 puma skulls (in total 18 mammal heads), and 1 incomplete young owl skull.

Burial 4, found in association with Building 6, contrasted strongly with other burials uncovered in the Moon Pyramid. The builders apparently put or threw in 17 severed human heads without clear pattern along with rocks while constructing the north wall of Building 6. No offering was associated with them, except for the atlas of the *eighteenth* individual. This may suggest calendrical meanings attached to this dedication burial, although the rest of the individual was not found in a limited excavation area.

Burial 5 represents the first grave complex documented from the top level of a major monument at Teotihuacan. The burial pit was excavated near the northern edge of the upper floor of Building 5 on the N–S axis. Three bodies were set carefully on the pit floor in seated positions facing west with their legs crossed, a form associated with individuals of high political status in Mesoamerica. The fact that this form has never been found in Teotihuacan burials also indicates that they were special (Manzanilla and Serrano Sánchez 1999; Ruz Lhuillier 1968; Sempowski and Spence 1994). The hands of the individuals were not crossed behind their backs; rather, they were set together on their feet in front of the body. Two of the three individuals (5-A, 5-B) were seated side by side and adorned in almost identical greenstone ornaments, while another (5-C) was discovered significantly separated from them and adorned differently. According to Spence and Pereira (2007), individuals 5-A, 5-B, and 5-C were males of between 50 to 60, 45 to 55, and 40 to 45 years respectively at time of death. After mortuary ritual likely took place, the pit was filled, and immediately Building 6 construction began. Burial 5, therefore, served as both a termination of Building 5 and foundation ritual of Building 6. The fact that the burial was located in the three-dimensional center of Building 6 being constructed also implies that its builders planned it as part of new construction program.

Individuals 5-A and 5-B both wore special ornaments, including 20 to 22 jadeite beads, two large earspools, and large rectangular pectorals. All of the greenstone objects are exceptionally well polished, and of unusual size and luster for the city. The form of the two pectorals is completely unfamiliar to Teotihuacan art and ornamentation but is often represented in Classic Maya societies as a symbol of maximum political authority. Individual 5-C wore quite different ornaments; he had two large shell earspools combined with smaller greenstone earplugs, and a pendant complex composed of shell beads and shell discs. This type of necklace is represented only among Maya rulers, again suggesting the presence of a Maya connection to Burial 5.

The three individuals were associated with a large quantity of unusual offerings, including sacred animals such as eagles, pumas, and serpents, dispersed following certain spatial patterns. These data also indicate that all three individuals were extremely highly ranked and explicitly manifested symbols of Maya rulership, which may not have been familiar to the Teotihuacano public. Based on analytical studies of sacrificed individuals and offerings, I favor the idea that the three individuals were foreign dignitaries of extremely high status who had direct connections with contemporaneous Maya dynasties or were members of the Maya elite who visited or were brought to Teotihuacan to be buried, willingly or unwillingly, at the Moon Pyramid. The three bodies, perhaps buried in the most respected manner among all those found to date in Teotihuacan, were by no means buried in an anonymous or collective manner; rather, they were integrated into a cosmogram within one of the most sacred monument in the city. If they were victims of sacrifice from

Maya centers, the explicit indexing of their sociopolitical status must have been highly significant for Teotihuacan rulers to demonstrate to the public their divine authority and political power, perhaps also with strong connotation of interactions with certain Maya centers.

Burial 6 was discovered near the three-dimensional center of Building 4. Burial 6 stratigraphically corresponds to Building 4 and is therefore contemporaneous with Burial 2. The burial forcefully proclaimed the politico-religious power of the ritual by involving the sacrifice of 12 individuals, of whom 10 were decapitated and thrown in as headless bodies. Rich offerings of exceptional quality and more than 50 complete and incomplete animals (felines, canids, birds of prey, and serpents) were also buried following certain spatial patterns.

The 12 individuals tentatively identified as adult males were in varied positions, clearly with their arms tied behind their backs. Two individuals were located in the central area and possessed complete bodies, whereas 10 people were located in the northern section of the burial and were missing their heads and first cervical vertebrae. We therefore interpret the 10 individuals as the victims of a decapitation ritual carried out at a nearby site or inside the grave chamber (fig. 6.5). The material offerings included can be divided into two categories: personal objects associated with the two complete individuals, such as greenstone ornaments, jadeite needles possibly used for autosacrifice, and a shell pendant complex composed of imitation human maxilla; and general offerings distributed with certain patterns, mostly in its northern half.

The general offering placed in the center is one of the richest symbol sets yet discovered at Teotihuacan. The offering was composed of 18 large obsidian eccentrics set in a radial form (including nine curving knives and nine feathered serpents), underneath a large pyrite disk, an obsidian human figure, and a human figure with a wooden base covered with a mosaic of greenstone, shell, and obsidian plaques (fig. 6.6). Under this symbol set we uncovered a radial line drawing incised on the earthen floor of the grave that coincides with true N–S and E–W orientations. This suggests that the sacrificial ritual was structured with astronomical, probably equinox-related significance, of which 18 eccentrics set on these lines were also part. The sacrificial victims evidently formed a central component integrated in this foundation ritual with strong calendrical connotation.

FIGURE 6.5. General plan of Burial 6. Human bodies were reconstructed from the bone data, and a certain number of offerings are not shown to avoid overlapping.

The Sun Pyramid

Leopoldo Batres (1906) excavated the monument a century ago, finding burials of a young child in each of the four corners of the three lower pyramidal platforms, presumably a total of 12 children, as shown in his drawing. They were likely sacrificed (Millon 1992:363) and dedicated to the monument, since the bodies seem to have been incorporated into the building matrix. However, detailed excavation contexts are unavailable and recent reexcavations by Eduardo Matos Moctezuma (1995) and Alejandro Sarabia (personal communication 2007) indicate that there were not pits in *tepetate* at the corners; therefore, the children could have been buried during a later period and represent intrusive interments.

Krotser (1968) describes a burial at the southeast corner of the Sun Pyramid that Millon (1981:213, 1992) suspects was a sacrifice. It consisted

FIGURE 6.6. Eighteen obsidian eccentrics were found in Burial 6 at the Moon Pyramid.

of an adult male in an oval pit cut into the talud of the pyramid's lowest platform. Its location suggests that it also may postdate the original pyramid, perhaps having been associated with one of the modifications (Millon 1992:395).

Brief reports by Batres include the description of architectural features of the Sun Pyramid complex and some artifacts discovered in the vicinity of the pyramid during its excavation. There is no mention of offerings or caches associated with the sacrificial burials or the pyramid, and only an unpublished inventory of objects stored in the local museum may be used to complement these brief excavation reports. The inventory, written in 1934 by Enrique Díaz Lozano and Eduardo Noguera, states that the objects were found at the Sun Pyramid. It is not at all clear whether this list includes most or only a portion of the objects found by Batres at the Sun Pyramid. There are no detailed descriptions of the objects and no clear indication of their quantity, since collective terms were used in the inventory. Nonetheless, the list informs us that some of the objects found around the Sun Pyramid may originally have been parts of offerings or caches buried in the pyramid, as the unusually high quality and quantity of the objects suggest (Sugiyama 2005:204). The information in this inventory, together with data published elsewhere about symbolic objects found in the pyramid (Millon et al. 1965), suggests that child burials found at the corners (if they actually belonged to the original construction phase) were a part of a larger dedication program associated with the construction of the Sun Pyramid. No excavation looking for such a burial program had been carried out until Alejandro Sarabia (director) and I began intensive excavations in 2008.

Sacrificial Burials at Teotihuacan

The discoveries mentioned above and the pervasive representation of symbols of sacrificial rituals indicate that human sacrifice appears to have been widely practiced in Teotihuacano society. The data indicate that human sacrifice was a ritual behavior linked to both apartment compounds and monuments, particularly as foundation rituals, as it was in other Mesoamerican societies (Ruz Lhuillier 1965, 1968; Welsh 1988a, 1988b). In Teotihuacan, the percentage of sacrificial burials identified to date in domestic areas is small; however, the fact that bloody representations can be found virtually everywhere that iconographic data are available from living areas implies a strong concern of the city's residents with sacrifice.

The sacrificial complexes at the monuments can be distinguished from those of residential compounds. Graves found at the FSP, the Sun Pyramid, the Moon Pyramid, and perhaps the Oztoyahualco pyramid (Plaza One), comprise this category of state-sponsored violent rituals. The data allow us to recognize sacrificial complexes executed in diversified forms at the various locations of the major monuments in Teotihuacan. It was also revealed that victims of varying age, sex, and social category were typically buried on the axes or in symmetrical relationship in either the interior or exterior of the monuments. It is difficult to understand the specific meanings attached to each case; however, certain patterns and analogous features among them can help us to reconstruct some underlying ideological factors and social contexts in which they were created.

The interior space of the graves was always filled with the construction materials inside the pyramids or below the floors corresponding to the monuments; thus, in most cases the graves can be interpreted as parts of the foundation ritual of new monumental construction. Perhaps many sacrificial ceremonies took place at the monuments after the constructions concluded, though they can hardly be detected archaeologically. The instances uncovered simply suggest that the human sacrifices comprised one of the most important and grandest mortuary practices carried out by the state.

Certain burials discovered inside the Moon Pyramid are more analogous to those found at the FSP, although differences were also apparent. Burials 2, 3, and 6 at the Moon Pyramid contained individuals who evidently were sacrificed and buried in tied positions and accompanied by symbolic objects, some of which were quite similar to those of the FSP. This indicates certain links between the mortuary rituals conducted in the two monuments, and similarities in the motivations of the individuals who orchestrated the two monumental construction programs. In particular, the mass-sacrificial complex at the FSP and Burials 2 and 6 at the Moon Pyramid were contemporaneous (ca. AD 200–250), and likely constituted a major effort of citywide materialization promoting the state ideology.

At the same time, the distinctiveness of the FSP is also clear. Many more people were interred at the FSP than at the Moon Pyramid, and the complex of mass-sacrificed graves for paired male and female adults with abundant martial objects at the FSP seems to have been significantly different from other burial complexes found at other monuments. The erection of the FSP with a highly unique mortuary program may have derived from quite distinctive ritual meanings directly related to the Feathered Serpent symbolism, with strong emphasis on the rulership and military institution at Teotihuacan (Sugiyama 2005).

The Moon Pyramid contained 37 individuals, most of whom were evidently sacrificed and interred in association with Buildings 4, 5, and 6 (approximately corresponding to AD 200–350). The quality of abundant offerings associated with them was highest among those found to date at Teotihuacan. The three individuals in Burial 5 were buried in the most respected manner among all burials found to date, though they also may have been sacrificed. They were distinctively buried with particular offerings indicative of their social status, group identity, or individual attributes, and direct connection with Maya dynasties. Although there were no apparent name signs, it is clear that the people buried at the Moon Pyramid varied individually from such high social/symbolic status personages to very low, perhaps humiliated, individuals, in contrast to those buried differentially as a group in an anonymous fashion at the FSP. The result of isotopic analysis (White et al. 2007) indicates that most of the dead belonged to foreign groups. As suggested by the associated martial offerings, they may have been important people captured from antagonistic groups or provided by subjects or allies in different regions. The deceased sacrificial victims would have played central roles for living ruling groups to proclaim their sociopolitical authority, couched in religious metaphor, over the regions from which the victims may have originated. Similar social behavior to bring materials and people from subjugated regions and to incorporate them into the sacred architecture can be observed among other Mesoamerican societies, particularly in Mexicas (López Luján 2005).

Royal Burials in Teotihuacan

Besides sacrificial burials, another important type of dead for the living seems to have been elites buried at the monuments, although these two categories often cannot be distinguished clearly one from the other. Available archaeological information from Teotihuacan and Teotihuacan-related sites suggests that powerful divine authorities existed for more than three centuries, with strong influence over many regions in Mesoamerica. Powerful rulership enforced by strong military institutions was an integral part of state political organizations, as is evidenced by symbolic data (Sugiyama 2005). No royal graves, however, have been identified to date at Teotihuacan itself. Individuals of high social status can simply be suggested through comparative mortuary analyses of the bones and offerings (Sempowski 1994:237–247; Storey 1992). Specific types of mortuary items, personal adornments, and other grave offerings may have been correlated with the social identity of the buried individuals. However, we still lack sufficient data and an appropriate conceptual framework to identify the highest-ranked ruling groups. We also need to look for distinctive mortuary features to distinguish specially treated deceased individuals among highly ranked people and have to construct an explanatory model that takes into account the complicated relations of the dead (elites, sacrificed) and the living (responsible for the funerals, people influenced by the dead) with mortuary variables. Other factors, such as data from uneven excavation areas, techniques, or recording systems; iconography of abstract, mythical, ahistorical, or anonymous individuals; the un-deciphered writing system; and heavy looting activities also must be reinterpreted to identify rulers or royal family members in definitive form at Teotihuacan.

Cremations are among the mortuary treatments correlated with greater offering complexity (Sempowski 1994:251; Serrano Sánchez 1993:112). A positive correlation between incinerated burials and offering complexity was found in Xolalpan, Tetitla, Yayahuala, La Ventilla, and other compounds. In Postclassic periods, the bodies of elites, including Aztec kings, were normally incinerated and buried in association with monuments (Umberger 1987). Cremation was shown in a Teotihuacan mural, the so-called Temple of Agriculture near the Sun Pyramid (fig. 6.7). Beyer (1922:285–289) first interpreted the mural as a cremation scene of two persons, drawing an analogy with representations in Postclassic codices. Múnera Bermudez (1991:341) followed his interpretation by adding new information on a ceramic figurine probably representing a human mortuary bundle. The figurine was discovered in a burial context wearing a ceramic mask. In the mural, a burning mortuary bundle was represented with fire and smoke on the brazier at each side of the scene. The identification of the brazier is unmistakable, as its form is identical to a large Teotihuacan stone brazier (Batres 1906:26). Anthropomorphic figures are represented behind the burning bundles, as if they were visions of the deceased. Each one, without a face and identical to the other, wears a headdress, a nose pendant, two earspools, and necklaces, probably identifying his or her high social status. The scene suggests that the cremation was a means by which the deceased of a high social category interacted with commoners who worshipped them with a variety of offerings. If the cremation was involved in funerals for rulers, it would be more difficult to identify royal tombs archaeologically. Their recognition should be based more on the variables of offerings, graves, associated constructions, and the location in the sacred city layout, if royal graves ever existed in Teotihuacan.

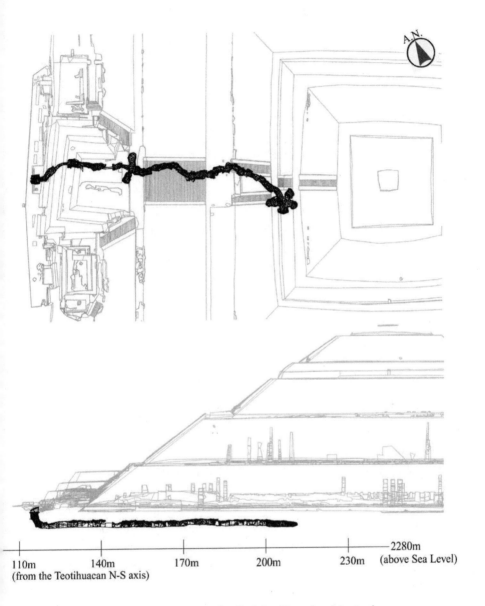

A.N.

110m   140m   170m   200m   230m   (above Sea Level)
(from the Teotihuacan N-S axis)

2280m

FIGURE 6.7. The Teotihuacan mural called the Temple of Agriculture.

Grave items found at monuments evidently contrast with those from residential compounds, as analyses by Sempowski and Spence (1994) indicate. Offerings in residences consisted predominantly of ceramics, while graves at monuments contained fewer ceramic vessels and more personal ornaments or ritual objects of exotic materials. A majority of the graves in residences seem to have been relatively simple and homogeneous, usually in a pit under the floors of residences without architectural preparation, and lack strong indication of outstanding individuals. The archaeological data described below also support the idea that the deceased of the highest social status seem to have been buried contrastingly at temple-pyramid constructions. However, royal graves have not been identified in definitive form at these monuments in Teotihuacan. We confirmed that the major monuments repeatedly integrated sacrificed people, but I also believe that royal graves can be suggested indirectly by recently obtained data and comparative analyses described below.

Feathered Serpent Pyramid (FSP)

As discussed previously, the central burial (Grave 14) contained symbolic offerings or tools for human sacrifice or autosacrifice. It is well known in Mesoamerica that these bloody rituals were among the most important events executed by rulers or royal family members and were frequently depicted in public space for the proclamation of rulership. Unique objects further include a complete wood baton or scepter, with its curved end depicting a Feathered Serpent head. The baton again seems to have symbolized individualistic political authority, as it did in other Mesoamerican societies (Nicholson 2000). It was found in one of the two looted pits inside and near the center of the pyramid (Grave 13) that might have contained sacrificial victims or a ruler's body. However, heavy looting activities impeded us from appropriately pursuing the question.

Another possible, stronger, candidate for a royal grave is a pit located in front of the staircase (Pit 5). The pit had been looted almost completely just before the main facade of the FSP was covered with the Adosada construction; therefore, we cannot be certain whether it once contained the dead rulers or again sacrificed people. However, the analogies with elite graves excavated at Mounds A and B in Kaminaljuyu and with a possible royal grave at the Sun Pyramid, in both cases located in front of or under the staircase, support the idea, as is discussed later. It is also possible that a royal grave might be located under the staircase of the FSP, since the side walls of the staircase were apparently broken and then repaired to put something under the staircase after the monumental construction was completed. The preparation of a royal grave, perhaps for a ruler who ordered the monumental construction and died later, may be a logical possibility. The spot has not been explored to date.

It is noteworthy that the FSP became a target of intensive looting activities from Teotihuacan's apogee in the fourth and fifth centuries (Sugiyama 1998). The graves that probably contained bodies of higher social status (Graves 12 and 13 and Pit 5) were exhaustively looted, while graves for warriors were never looted, although these were located closer to the walls and thus were easier to access. According to the fragmented remains recovered in the disturbed graves and the looters' tunnel, high-quality offerings and human bones were taken outside, probably to reuse them. Heavy looting activities were also recorded at the Moon Pyramid and the Sun Pyramid, indicating that the dead and their associated items were significant for the living during the following centuries until at least the Aztec time, probably as symbols of ancestral worship (López Luján 1988).

The Moon Pyramid

As discussed previously, Burial 5 found on the top of Building 5 might have contained very highly ranked individuals. Many of the associated offerings were of typical Teotihuacan style, while certain objects were contrastingly unique at Teotihuacan. In particular, jadeite pendants of this type have never been found at Teotihuacan nor depicted in Teotihuacan imagery, but they were frequently represented on the bodies of Maya rulers as symbols of rulership. This indicates that these individuals may have had a direct relationship with contemporaneous Mayan royal families. The questions of whether they were Teotihuacano rulers or elites, or Maya dignitaries, and whether they died naturally or were sacrificed should be discussed with the results of ongoing comprehensive studies, including isotope and DNA analyses in the near future. In any event, the implication is that the upper floor of the FSP and other monumental constructions might also have been used for elite burial; however, they would have been already destroyed or looted in most cases. Fragmented bones and offerings recovered from the upper fill of the FSP and the Sun Pyramid that Ignacio Marquina reported (Gamio 1922 [1979]:II:157–64) may have originally been offerings from an elite grave already destroyed.

The front facade of the earlier monuments at the Moon Pyramid had also been looted heavily into the last century and was another location where royal graves once might have been (Sugiyama and Cabrera Castro 2007:113). However, we confirmed that at the Moon Pyramid there was not a tunnel like the one that underlies the Sun Pyramid. We excavated a deep pit into the hard subsoil (7.3 m) at the center of Building 1, the earliest platform found under the Adosada, and did not find any artificial tunnel or natural cave on the N–S axis of the pyramid.

The Sun Pyramid

Millon et al. (1965:10, 13, 18, 19, and 90) discuss the possibility of a great tomb at the subsoil level near the center of the Sun Pyramid; however, our recent excavation in 2008 at the spot confirmed that there is no tomb or offering cache exactly at the center of the Sun Pyramid. The most probable place for the royal tomb is instead in the "cave" under the Sun Pyramid, accidentally found in 1971 and excavated by Jorge Acosta of INAH immediately following the discovery.

The "cave" beneath the Sun Pyramid has been interpreted as originally having been a natural cave that was later modified by Teotihuacanos to function as a sacred place for rituals (Heyden 1975:131, 1981; Millon 1981:231; Taube 1986). Although Heyden mentioned its possible use as a royal grave among other possibilities, it was mainly interpreted as a long-used holy ceremonial place even before the construction of the Sun Pyramid, because no clear evidence for a royal tomb, such as sarcophagi, human skeletons, or rich offerings, was found inside by the intensive excavation by Acosta, who soon died without leaving any publication about the exploration. Influenced by references in Postclassic and Colonial mythologies to the sacredness of Mesoamerican caves, the long space under the largest pyramid at Teotihuacan has been explained primarily as a legendary cave of origins, or Chicomoztoc, from which tribal groups were believed to have emerged (Heyden 1981; Manzanilla et al. 1994; Millon 1981). Although this interpretation was widely accepted among scholars, it is very weakly grounded on the archaeological data from the old city, and the fact that the "cave" was exhaustively looted since ancient times does not seem to have been appropriately taken into account.

Linda Manzanilla and her associates, in collaboration with the Institute of Geophysics and the Faculty of Engineering of the Universidad Nacional Autónoma de México, propose that virtually all the "caves" around the Sun Pyramid were completely man-made, primarily for the quarrying of construction materials at the level of a volcanic flow (Manzanilla et al. 1989; Manzanilla et al. 1994). Manzanilla further believes that the "cave" under the Sun Pyramid is one that was created for quarrying.

We carried out detailed inspection of the interior of the "cave" under the Sun Pyramid and elaborated a precise and detailed 3D map of it to complement the general plan of the Sun Pyramid complex and other public constructions in the city in 2007 (fig. 6.8). We also began in 2008–9 our intensive exploration inside the Sun Pyramid as a part of the Sun Pyramid Project directed by Alejandro Sarabia of the INAH, with which I am associated in charge of the interior excavations. It became clear that the previously published two-dimensional plan of the cave was not precise, and that we crucially lack the excavation data for appropriate interpretation. Moreover, the new study indicates clearly that the tunnel was completely man-made; it evidently would not have been created for quarrying, but very probably for funerary purposes, probably to deposit rulers or royal family members in a manner vastly different from the sacrificial burials integrated into the nucleus of the city's major monuments. The main evidence supporting this proposition follows.

The entrance of the tunnel (as in fig. 6.8) begins with an artificial pit excavated in *tepetate* in a standardized square form and following the Teotihuacan grid orientation with rounded corners (2.75 m N–S by 2.90 m E–W), a typical form for burial pits in the city. The tunnel then goes down vertically 6.5 m, partially breaking hard basaltic rocks. There was also a steep wall, or apparent "staircase with balustrade," exactly facing grid east that steps down to the tunnel floor. From that point the tunnel continues to the east horizontally.

The tunnel was probably accessible from the outside after the completion of the pyramid's construction. The vertical pit (the entrance)

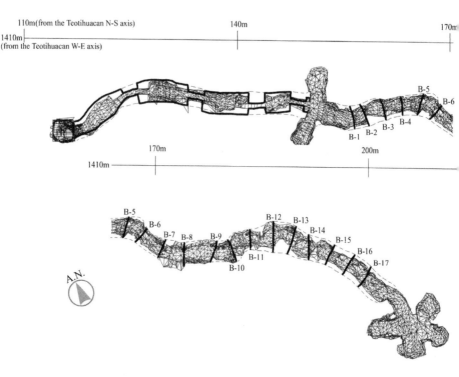

FIGURE 6.8. Detail of the plan of the tunnel found under the Sun Pyramid.

was apparently covered by stone blocks forming the main staircase of the Adosada platform; however, the data recovered inside suggest that the interior space (Section A) remained vacant. Namely, the tunnel was made with the intention of being used occasionally either for ritual or burial purposes after the pyramid or the Adosada construction was completed. The form of the tunnel is reminiscent of the conceptual layout of the shaft tombs of west Mexico or Oaxacan royal tombs, although the architectural style and the scale differ significantly. The "crypt" goes down vertically, then continues very horizontally, just as part of the shaft in shaft tombs descends.

The long interior space is proportionally distributed with rooms, walls, and floors, sometimes covered with a roof. It can be divided into three sections (named as A, B, and C; see fig. 6.8). The space in the first half of the tunnel (Section A) is composed of four long rooms originally connected to the others through narrow and low passages. This space does not appear to have ever been sealed completely, even after Section B was filled: the four rooms in Section A were open, possibly for esoteric rituals or funerary purposes (to deposit the deceased or offerings, for example). The second half of the tunnel (Section B) had a spatial distribution quite different from Section A; the interior segment and chamberlike rooms at the end of the tunnel (Section C) composed a long tunnel once filled out completely. The walls and the fill in these sections (B and C) were later destroyed and partially removed by looting activities during the following centuries (Heyden 1975). Strangely enough, Acosta left a significant portion of the original fill inside and constructed new walls with and without cement for consolidation in certain areas that gave the tunnel a natural or irregular "cave" appearance. Our 3-D digital map, however, indicates that the shape, width, and height of the space created, especially with regard to Section A, is too standardized and homogeneous to be a natural cave. The tunnel appears to have been excavated horizontally, with minimal variation for either the floor or the roof levels. The floor level proceeds through the tunnel at 2,287.80 m above sea level, with +0.5 m variation over its length, whereas the roof level proceeds for the full 97 meters at 2,289.90 m, with +0.6 m maximum variation. The N–S cut sections of the tunnel also demonstrate artificial round form and standardized size, probably designed for human activities (2.3 m wide and 2.1 m high on average, with +0.6 m maximum variation).

The tunnel has a serpentine form in plan, giving the impression that the tunnel was originally a natural cave modified partially by human activities, as Millon (1981) and others suggested. However, fairly straight segments in Section A and a more serpentine form with gentle curves in Section B seem intentional; the excavators may have preferred serpentine representation to excavating straight based on an indigenous concept of passage to the underworld. The tunnel has somewhat irregular curving only in a few spots where hard basaltic flows apparently impeded the excavators from continuing straight and forced them to proceed irregularly (e.g., b, c, and d in fig. 6.8).

Our excavation in 2009 confirmed that the "cave" or tunnel does not continue to the west (at the entrance); neither to the east (at the end); this also indicates that the space was completely man-made. The location of the entrance (the pit mentioned above) under the main staircase of the Adosada platform exactly on the E–W axis of the Sun Pyramid obviously indicates that the tunnel was an integral factor of the monumental construction. It has been said that the Sun Pyramid was constructed above a sacred natural cave that already existed (Heyden 1975:144; Millon 1993:23–24). However, since the cave orientation coincides approximately with the standardized E–W axis of the city that was determined by well-defined other (astronomical/calendrical) reasons (Millon 1993:35), it is a logical assertion that the cave was completely created following the standardized Teotihuacan canons. This interpretation also fits well with the idea that the whole city was designed with a consistent plan to materialize a Mesoamerican worldview at an early stage of its urbanization.

Two antechamber-like rooms bearing a symmetric relation to each other were dug at 35 m from the entrance in Section A (see fig. 6.8). Four rooms, or three rooms branched from the main tunnel (four rooms in all), were intentionally prepared at the end (fig. 6.8). Since heavy looting activities took place in these rooms, we critically lack the data suggesting functions of these special rooms. However, their location, shape, size, and distribution, as well as the rest of the walls forming antechamber- or chamber-like rooms, suggest the possible function of the tunnel as a royal grave complex. If the end of the tunnel once contained a royal burial, the two opposing chambers might have served to store offerings or sacrifices dedicated to the people buried farther inside, as other Mesoamerican royal tombs were accompanied by dedicatory burials/caches (e.g., Ruz Lhuillier 1965). This assumption can also be supported by the following data recovered farther inside.

Between the paired "antechambers" and four lobelike chambers at the end, the tunnel was once blocked with 17 stone walls that created 18 divisions, perhaps reflecting a cosmological/calendrical significance. All walls were roughly made, having a face only toward the entrance, and the space between them was completely filled with a homogeneous layer of rocks, stones, and earth. Section B was once stuffed from the end toward the entrance successively as if the builders wanted to seal something inside completely. All the walls were broken down by later looting activities (fig. 6.9) (Heyden 1975; Millon 1981).

These final rooms were heavily looted, probably when the wall blockages were deliberately destroyed. Possibly, Teotihuacanos in the fourth or

FIGURE 6.9. Inside view of the tunnel under the Sun Pyramid, around 81 m from the entrance.

a later century, the Aztecs in the fifteenth and sixteenth centuries, and any groups between them interested in the burial contents were responsible for looting, reuse, or reconsecration activities, as is suggested by materials found inside (Millon 1993:22). In fact, we have found in 2008 excavations fragments of unusually high-quality objects, such as large stone disks, greenstone beads, plaques, and figures, in the original deposit that Acosta left near the entrance of the "cave"; they apparently would have been part of an offering complex originally deposited farther inside. All this evidence of blockage and the looting activities point to the assertion that Section C was where a royal grave once existed. I suspect that the looters knew that the tunnel contained a royal grave and therefore looted it.

I propose from a purely archaeological point of view that the man-made tunnel was originally created to bury an important individual, probably a ruler, who died about the time of the construction of the Sun Pyramid. Although no direct evidence about the grave is available, the central location of the Sun Pyramid and the tunnel in the whole city layout supports the idea that the tunnel is the most logical place for a royal grave, rather than just for ritual purposes. We do not know whether the multichambered crypt was used only once or repeatedly for succeeding rulers and/or royal family members until the passage was completely blocked. Sometime after the tunnel was sealed, the looting activities began, and new ritual meanings and social functions were likely attached to it by Teotihuacanos and post-Teotihuacano visitors. The tunnel most likely later became a legendary "cave" for ancestral worship and ritual activities, as well as a sacred place in the search for legacy items by subsequent entities. In conclusion, it is plausible that the dead bodies and their symbols would have occupied the most central monumental place from an early stage of the city's foundation and continuously influenced living descendants in changing religious and political contexts during the following centuries.

Mounds A and B in Kaminaljuyú

I consider graves found at Mounds A and B in Kaminaljuyú the most similar instances of Teotihuacan elite burials abroad. Kaminaljuyú was one of the largest precolumbian cities in the Guatemalan highlands (Cheek 1971; Kidder et al. 1946; Sanders and Michels 1969; Shook 1951;

Shook and Kidder 1952). Chronologically, the graves at Kaminaljuyú can be understood as mortuary assemblages directly influenced by Teotihuacano burial traditions during the fourth and fifth centuries.

Kaminaljuyú has been interpreted as having been conquered, colonized, transformed into an enclave, and/or converted into a trade center by Teotihuacan (Cheek 1971; Coggins 1975; Sanders and Michels 1977). Many of the data substantiating a Teotihuacan-Kaminaljuyú connection are associated with mortuary practices at the major monuments. Teotihuacan-style offerings found in Kaminaljuyú, especially pottery and green obsidian objects (Spence 1977) in the tombs of Structures A and B, their associated iconography, and talud-tablero architecture at the pyramids containing these graves, indicate unquestionable relations of the site with Teotihuacan and certain lowland Maya centers (Coggins 1975).

Teotihuacan-influenced burial patterns are suggested by several other mortuary features besides offerings. In contrast to royal tombs in the Maya Lowlands, where graves of important personages were often placed in specially constructed masonry chambers in pyramids or under temples (Freidel and Suhler 1999; Ruz Lhuillier 1965, 1973; Welsh 1988a), the elites of Kaminaljuyú in the period of cultural contact were buried in simple earth-walled pits at ground level, a typical Teotihuacano grave form. The majority of the dead in the structures were set in a seated position, which was a common feature of Teotihuacano graves. In particular, the cross-legged seating position applied to the later burials of Structures A and B (after Tomb A-III) was rare at Kaminaljuyú and elsewhere in Mesoamerica, and the only known instances from Teotihuacan are the individuals found in Burial 5 at the Moon Pyramid, as discussed above.

At least six elite tombs were built during eight construction stages at Structure A (fig. 6.10), while six tombs were prepared during seven construction stages at Structure B. Except for the graves of Structures A-1, A-5, and B-1 to B-3, a distinct grave pattern was followed at each stage of architectural renovation; elite tombs were consistently located under the staircase or in front of it, evidently placed there at the time of the pyramid's modification.

Mound A contained eight structures, built one upon another. According to Kidder et al. (1946:10), "each one, except the earliest and perhaps one other, seems to have been erected after, and presumably in connection

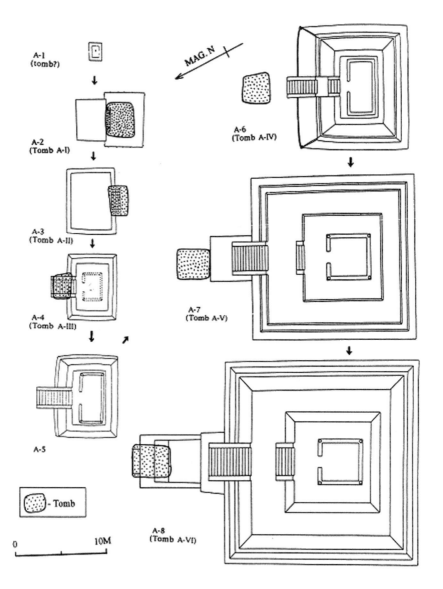

A-1
(tomb?)

A-2
(Tomb A-I)

A-3
(Tomb A-II)

A-4
(Tomb A-III)

A-5

MAG. N

A-6
(Tomb A-IV)

A-7
(Tomb A-V)

A-8
(Tomb A-VI)

⬛ - Tomb

0   10M

FIGURE 6.10. Drawing by Sugiyama, taking into account the data and interpretations of Kidder et al. (1946), to show the chronological sequence of the spatial relationships between the structures and corresponding tombs.

with, the entombment of an important personage." They appear to have been elite tombs, as suggested by the high quality, quantity, and variety of the associated offerings and monumental architecture. Each grave was evidently prepared in relation to a new construction and on the main axis of the pyramid.

The excavators believed that the earliest structure (A-1) may have stood completely on solid ground or partly upon the roofed pit of a tomb later reused as Tomb A-III (Kidder et al. 1946:11). This is the only structure that may have contained a tomb at the center, if one actually existed. Structures A-2 and A-3 were built consecutively, with the main facade facing west. It seems that the grave pits were dug on this side, at the foot of the pyramid, because the staircases were to be constructed on the same side. Tomb A-I was covered completely with the staircase and a low platform in front of it. Tomb A-II was also located under the corresponding staircase.

For some reason, the orientation of the building changed from west to east when Structure A-4 was constructed. A grave pit for Tomb A-III was made on the east side near the structure's edge, and the staircase was then built, covering the tomb on the same side. The modifications of Structure A-3 and A-4 demonstrate the close association of the graves with staircases at this Teotihuacan-influenced monument. During construction of Structure A-6, the grave pit of Tomb A-IV was laid, about 2 m east of the staircase. The excavators believe that the tomb had been covered by a low platform, which was removed when Structure A-7 was erected.

Tomb A-V is believed to have been prepared in association with Structure A-7, which had *talud-tablero* facades. Again, the grave pit was located in front of the staircase on the pyramid's E–W axis. The excavators believed the tomb was covered with a lower extension of its low platform oriented to the east. The last grave pit for Tomb A-VI was prepared farther east of the staircase when the final modification program, the construction of Structure A-8, took place. Again, the grave pit was sealed with stepped platforms that ascend the pyramid. The cases of Mound B also indicate similar spatial relations to those described above (Sugiyama 2005:216–217).

Royal Graves at Teotihuacan

At Mounds A and B in Kaminaljuyú, as Kidder et al. (1946:86) concluded, a major grave accompanied the construction phases of each mound, indicating direct association of the principal occupant in each grave with a corresponding architectural program. The grave contexts also inform us that the principal occupants were not sacrificial victims, but elites who had relations with Teotihuacan. In other words, architectural renovation likely took place because of the death of the principal occupant buried following Teotihuacano tradition, rather than in association with periodical/calendrical significance or other types of sociopolitical events.

In the case of both Structures A and B, simple pit graves for elites were located under the staircase or in front of it, along the axis of the corresponding pyramid. As we have seen, this architectural association of graves with the staircase is especially clear in the transition from Structure A-3 to A-4. Because the staircase was moved from the east side to the west, the location of the elite grave shifted correspondingly. In every case (with the exception of Structure A-6, for which there are insufficient data), elite burials were covered by either Adosada construction, a staircase, or a low platform attached to it, and always located on the front facade.

At the FSP, a somewhat parallel architectural trend can be suggested from field data. A grave pit, later looted, was prepared in association with a substructure found inside the pyramid (Grave 12). Sometime during the construction of the FSP or in a later period, a large pit was prepared in front of the staircase on the pyramid axis that probably served as a grave at one time and was covered with a masonry construction, perhaps a low platform or altar, like the cases of Tombs A-I, A-IV, A-V, A-VI, B-III, and B-IV at Kaminaljuyú. It is also possible that another grave might still exist under the pyramid's staircase. After the pit in front of the staircase was looted, it was finally covered by the Adosada platform, as in the cases of Tombs B-I and B-II. This parallel architectural coincidence between the two sites seems not to be accidental, given the detailed architectural and offertory similarities at both sites and their approximate contemporaneity. If the practice of renovating monuments in conjunction with elite graves in Kaminaljuyú derived from Teotihuacan, analogies would support the idea that pits found in front of the FSP, and a possible grave under its staircase, were elite tombs rather than a part of the sacrificial burial complex.

A similar spatial relationship between the staircases of monuments and elite graves in Teotihuacan is independently suggested by the new data from the Sun Pyramid. In the case of the tunnel under the Sun Pyramid, the way to prepare a royal grave (a tunnel in the form of a shaft tomb with an exceptionally long horizontal portion) is quite different from the case at the FSP (a vertical pit). However, analogy in the spatial relationship of elite graves with the staircase at both monuments seems to indicate that a shared concept was applied to these two major monuments in Teotihuacan. Elites or royal family members possibly had to be buried deep into the subsoil (toward the underworld) below the staircase on the axis that ascends to the top of the pyramid (toward the upperworld). The major pyramids were said to have symbolized the most sacred mountains or axis mundi connecting upperworld, present world, and underworld, where the royal members executed rituals and other sociopolitical events with divine power even after their death.

Like Mounds A and B in Kaminaljuyú, the Sun Pyramid, the Moon Pyramid, and the FSP (with their earlier incarnations) evidently coexisted for more than 300 years, as their modification phases and chronologies indicate. The relationships among elite graves integrated in them would have been complex and difficult to understand, since many rulers and royal family members were likely involved. Repeated intensive looting activities at the three major monuments began almost immediately after the sealing or blockage of the original graves during the following remodeling periods. However, the evidence of searches for their legacy by looting suggests at the same time a strong interest among the succeeding people who still might have had better knowledge about where influential individuals were buried. All the information presented above supports the idea that elite dead, as well as sacrificial victims integrated into sacred mountains (pyramids), were central factors in the local image of the "City of the Gods."[1] The dead became part of a larger legend, one that endured for almost a millennium after the original occupants of the site were no more. The pyramidal monuments provided the most conspicuous "theater" for this legend, where the living interacted with influential deceased, the deities, and divine forces through mortuary rituals at Teotihuacan.

Note

1. INAH (2010) has recently announced that a possible royal tomb in the Ciudadela has been discovered. Just like the "cave" beneath the Sun Pyramid, a wide and deep pit connecting to a long horizontal tunnel was accidentally uncovered under the Feathered

Serpent Pyramid through a "hole" sealed with the staircase of the Adosada Platform. The main entrance (pit) to the 11-meters-deep tunnel had been discovered between the Adosada and the central platform of the plaza in the Ciudadela by the INAH project in 1980–1982 (Rodríguez García 1992) and had been interpreted as a "well" until the "hole" was discovered. Sergio Gómez began to reexplore the "well" in 2010 and proposes that the tunnel was a royal tomb. If so, the excavation would support the idea that the "cave" under the Sun Pyramid was another royal tomb in Teotihuacan. It would also show that royal deceased were integrated into the city's cosmological presentation in a more complicated manner than we had thought.

Works Cited

Almaráz, Ramon
1865   Apuntes sobre las pirámides de San Juan. In *Memoria de los trabajos ejecutados por la comision científica de Pachuca en el año de 1864*, pp. 349–358. Ministerio de Fomento, Mexico, DF.

Armillas, Pedro
1950   Teotihuacan Tula y los toltecas: Las culturas post-arcaicas y pre-aztecas del centro de México: Excavaciones y estudios, 1922–1950. *Runa* 3:37–70.

Bastien, Rémy
1946   *Informe sobre las exploraciones hechas en "El Pozo de las Calaveras," Teotihuacan*. Estado de México, San Juan Teotihuacan, 1690–1891, 1918–1946. Archivo Técnico de la Dirección de Arqueología, Instituto Nacional de Antropología e Historia, Mexico, DF.

Batres, Leopoldo
1906   *Teotihuacán ó la ciudad sagrada de los tolteca*. Imprenta de Hull, Mexico, DF.

Beyer, Hermann
1922   Relaciones entre la civilizacion teotihuacana y la azteca. In *La población del Valle de Teotihuacán*, edited by Manuel Gamio, 3 vols., pp. 1:273–293. Secretaría de Agriculturaa y Fomento, Mexico, DF. (Republished in 1979. 5 vols. Instituto Nacional Indigenista, Mexico, DF.)

Cabrera Castro, Rubén, Saburo Sugiyama, and George Cowgill
1991   The Temple of Quetzalcoatl Project at Teotihuacan: A Preliminary Report. *Ancient Mesoamerica* 2 (1):77–92.

Carrasco, David
1982   *Quetzalcoatl and the Irony of Empire: Myths and Prophecies in the Aztec Tradition*. University of Chicago Press, Chicago.

Cheek, Charles D.
1971   Excavations at the Palangana, Kaminaljuyú, Guatemala. Ph.D. dissertation, Dept. of Anthropology, University of Arizona, Tucson.

Codex Chimalpopoca
1992   *History and Mythology of the Aztecs: Codex Chimalpopoca*. Translated by John Bierhorst. University of Arizona Press, Tucson.

Coggins, Clemency C.

1975　*Painting and Drawing Style at Tikal: A Historical and Iconographic Recon-struction.* 2 vols. Ph.D. dissertation, Harvard University, Cambridge. University Microfilms, Ann Arbor.

Cook de Leonard, Carmen

1957a　Proyecto del CIAM en Teotihuacan. *Boletín del Centro de Investigaciones Antropológicas de Mexico* 4:1–2.

1957b　Excavaciones en La Plaza #1, "Tres Palos," Teotihuacan. *Boletín del Centro de Investigaciones Antropológicas de Mexico* 4:3–5.

1971　Ceramics of the Classic Period in Central Mexico. In *Handbook of Middle American Indians,* edited by Gordon F. Ekholm and Ignacio Bernal, vol. 10, pp. 179–205. University of Texas Press, Austin.

Cowgill, George L.

1983　Rulership and the Ciudadela: Political Inferences from Teotihuacan Architecture. In *Civilization in the Ancient Americas: Essays in Honor of Gordon R. Willey,* edited by Richard M. Leventhal and Alan L. Kolata, pp. 313–343. University of New Mexico Press, Albuquerque, and Peabody Museum of Harvard University, Cambridge.

Freidel, David, and Charles Suhler

1999　The Path of Life: Toward a Functional Analysis of Ancient Maya Architecture. In *Mesoamerican Architecture as a Cultural Symbol,* edited by Jeff Karl Kowalski, pp. 250–273. Oxford University Press, New York.

Gamio, Manuel

1922　*La población del Valle de Teotihuacán.* 3 vols. Secretaría de Agricultura y Fomento, México, DF. (Republished in 1979. 5 vols. Instituto Nacional Indigenista, Mexico, DF.)

Gómez Chávez, Sergio

2000　La Ventilla: Un barrio de la antigua ciudad de Teotihuacán. Bachelor's thesis. Manuscript on file, Escuela Nacional de Antropología e Historia, Mexico, DF.

2002　Presencia del Occidente de México en Teotihuacan: Aproximaciones a la política exterior del estado teotihuacano. *Ideología y política a través de materiales, imágenes y símbolos: Memoria de la Primera Mesa Redonda de Teotihuacan,* edited by María Elena Ruiz Gallut, pp. 563–625. Universidad Nacional Autónoma de México and Instituto Nacional de Antropología e Historia, Mexico, DF.

González Miranda, L. A.

1993　Analisis de restos oseos humanos de Teotihuacan con presencia de huellas rituales. Paper presented at the 13th International Congress of Anthropological Ethnological Sciences, Mexico, DF.

González M., Luis Alfonso, and David Fuentes G.

1982　Informe preliminar acerca de los enterramientos prehispánicos en la zona arqueológica de Teotihuacan, México. In *Teotihuacan 80–82: Primeros resultados,* edited by Rubén Cabrera Castro, Ignacio Rodriguez García, and Noel Morelos García, pp. 421–449. Instituto Nacional de Antropología e Historia, Mexico, DF.

Heyden, Doris

1975   An Interpretation of the Cave Underneath the Pyramid of the Sun in Teotihuacán, Mexico. *American Antiquity* 40:131–147.

1981   Caves, Gods, and Myths: World-View and Planning in Teotihuacan. In *Mesoamerican Sites and World-Views*, edited by Elisabeth Benson, pp. 1–39. Dumbarton Oaks, Washington, D.C.

Instituto Nacional de Antropología e Historia

2010   Arqueólogos localizan entrada de túnel teotihuacano. Electronic document, http://www.inah.gob.mx/index.php?option=com_content&task=view&id=4538& Itemid=329, accessed August 3, 2010.

Jarquín Pacheco, Anna M., and Enrique Martínez Vargas

1991   Sacrificio de niños: Una ofrenda a la deidad de la lluvia en Teotihuacan. *Arqueología* 6:69–84.

Kidder, Alfred V., Jesse D. Jennings, and Edwin M. Shook

1946   *Excavations at Kaminaljuyu, Guatemala.* Publication No. 561. Carnegie Institution of Washington, Washington, D.C.

Krotser, G. Ramon

1968   Field Notes, TE 16B. Teotihuacan Mapping Project. Manuscript on file, Teotihuacan Archaeological Research Facility, San Juan Teotihuacan, Mexico.

López Austin, Alfredo, Leonardo López Luján, and Saburo Sugiyama

1991   The Feathered Serpent Pyramid at Teotihuacan: Its Possible Ideological Significance. *Ancient Mesoamerica* 2 (1):93–106.

1994   Geografía sagrada e inframundo en Teotihuacan. *Antropológicas* 11:53–65.

López Luján, Leonardo

1988   *La recuperación mexica del pasado teotihuacano.* Instituto Nacional de Antropología e Historia, Mexico, DF.

2005   *The Offerings of the Templo Mayor of Tenochtitlan.* University of New Mexico Press, Albuquerque.

Manzanilla, Linda, Luis Barba, René Chávez, Jorge Arzate, and Leticia Flores

1989   El inframundo de Teotihuacan. Geofísica y arqueología. *Ciencia y Desarrollo* 85:21–35.

Manzanilla, Linda, Luis Barba, René Chávez, Andrés Tejero, Gerardo Cifuentes, and Nayeli Peralta

1994   Caves and Geophysics: An Approximation to the Underworld of Teotihuacan, Mexico. *Archaeometry* 36 (1):141–157.

Manzanilla, Linda, and Carlos Serrano Sánchez (editors)

1999   *Prácticas funerarias en la Ciudad de los Dioses: Los enterramientos humanos de la antigua Teotihuacan.* Universidad Nacional Autónoma de México, Mexico, DF.

Martínez Vargas, E., and L. A. González Miranda

1991   Una estructura funeraria teotihuacana. In *Teotihuacan 1980–1982: Nuevas interpretaciones,* edited by Rubén Cabrera Castro, Ignacio Rodríguez García, and

Noel Morelos García, pp. 327–333. Instituto Nacional de Antropología e Historia, Mexico, DF.

Matos Moctezuma, Eduardo

1995   *La Pirámide del Sol, Teotihuacan*. Artes de México, Instituto Cultural Domecq, Mexico, DF.

Millon, René

1957   New Data on Teotihuacan I in Teotihuacan. *Boletín del Centro de Investigaciones Antropológicas de Mexico* 4:12–18.

1973   *Urbanization at Teotihuacan, Mexico: 1. The Teotihuacan Map. Part One: Text*. University of Texas Press, Austin.

1981   Teotihuacan: City, State, and Civilization. In *Supplement to the Handbook of Middle American Indians: 1. Archaeology*, edited by Victoria Bricker and Jeremy Sabloff, pp. 198–243. University of Texas Press, Austin.

1992   Teotihuacan Studies: From 1950 to 1990 and Beyond. In *Art, Ideology and the City of Teotihuacan*, ed. Janet C. Berlo, pp. 339–429. Dumbarton Oaks, Washington, D.C.

1993   The Place Where Time Began. In *Teotihuacan: Art from the City of the Gods*, edited by Kathleen Berrin and Esther Pasztory, pp. 17–43. Thames and Hudson, New York, Fine Arts Museums of San Francisco, San Francisco.

Millon, René, Bruce Drewitt, and James A. Bennyhoff

1965   The Pyramid of the Sun at Teotihuacán: 1959 Investigations. In *Transactions of the American Philosophical Society*, n.s. 55, pt. 6. American Philosophical Society, Philadelphia.

Millon, Rene, Bruce Drewitt, and George L. Cowgill

1973   *Urbanization at Teotihuacan, Mexico: 1. The Teotihuacan Map: Part Two. Maps*. University of Texas Press, Austin.

Mogor, J.

1966   Pit report: Cut N17E1 in Oaxaca barrio excavations. Manuscript on file, University of the Americas, Puebla.

Múnera Bermudez, Luis Carlos

1991   Una representación de bulto mortuorio. In *Teotihuacan 1980–1982: Nuevas interpretaciones*, edited by Rubén Cabrera Castro, Ignacio Rodríguez García, and Noel Morelos García, pp. 335–341. Instituto Nacional de Antropología e Historia, Mexico, DF.

Nicholson, Henry B.

1971   Religion in Pre-Hispanic Central Mexico. In *Archaeology of Northern Mesoamerica*, edited by Gordon F. Ekholm and Ignacio Bernal, pp. 395–446. Handbook of Middle American Indians, Vol. 10, general editor Robert Wauchope. University of Texas Press, Austin.

2000   The Iconography of the Feathered Serpent in Late Postclassic Central Mexico. In *Mesoamerica's Classic Heritage: From Teotihuacan to the Aztecs*, edited by David Carrasco, Lindsay Jones, and Scott Sessions, pp. 145–164. University Press of Colorado, Boulder.

Rattray, Evelyn C.

1992   *The Teotihuacan Burials and Offerings: A Commentary and Inventory.* Publications in Anthropology No. 42. Vanderbilt University, Nashville.

Rodríguez García, Ignacio

1992   Frente 2. In *Memoria del Proyecto Arqueológico Teotihuacan 80–82*, edited by Rubén Castro, Ignacio Rodríguez García, and Noel Morelos García, pp. 55–73. Instituto Nacional de Antropología e Historia, Mexico, DF.

Rodríguez Manzo, Veronica

1992   Patrón de enterramiento en Teotihuacán durante el período clásico: Estudio de 814 entierros. BS thesis. Manuscript on file, Escuela Nacional de Anthropología e Historia, Mexico, DF.

Ruz Lhuillier, Alberto

1965   Tombs and Funerary Practices in the Maya Lowlands. In *Handbook of Middle American Indians: 2. Archaeology of Southern Mesoamerica*, pt. 1, edited by Gordon R. Willey, pp. 441–461. University of Texas Press, Austin.

1968   *Costumbres funerarias de los antiguos mayas.* Universidad Nacional Autónoma de México, Mexico, DF.

1973   *El Templo de las Inscripciones Palenque.* Coleccion Cientifica 7, Arqueología. Instituto Nacional de Antropología e Historia, Mexico, DF.

Sahagún, Fray Bernardino

1950–   *Florentine Codex: General History of the Things of New Spain.* Translated by
1982   Arthur J. O. Anderson and Charles E. Dibble. School of American Research and the University of Utah, Santa Fe.

Sanders, William T., and Joseph W. Michels (editors)

1969   *The Pennsylvania State University K'aminaljuyu Project: 1968 Seasons, Part I: The Excavations.* Occasional Papers in Anthropology No. 2. Pennsylvania State University, University Park.

1977   *Teotihuacan and Kaminaljuyu: A Study in Prehistoric Culture Contact.* Pennsylvania State University Press, University Park.

Schele, Linda, and Mary Ellen Miller

1986   *The Blood of Kings: Dynasty and Ritual in Maya Art.* G. Braziller, New York.

Sempowski, Martha L.

1994   Mortuary Practices at Teotihuacan. In *Mortuary Practices and Skeletal Remains at Teotihuacan*, edited by Martha L. Sempowski and Michael Spence, pp. 1–314, University of Utah Press, Salt Lake City.

Sempowski, Martha L., and Michael W. Spence

1994   *Mortuary Practices and Skeletal Remains at Teotihuacan.* University of Utah Press, Salt Lake City.

Serrano Sánchez, Carlos

1993   Funerary Practices and Human Sacrifice in Teotihuacan Burials. In *Teotihuacan: Art from the City of the Gods*, edited by Kathleen Berrin and Esther Pasztory, pp. 108–115. Thames and Hudson, New York, Fine Arts Museums of San Francisco, San Francisco.

Serrano Sánchez, Carlos, and Zaid Lagunas Rodríguez

1975   Sistema de enterramiento y notas sobre el material osteológico de La Ventilla, Teotihuacan, México. *Anales del Instituto Nacional de Antropología e Historia*, Epoca 7a (4):105–144.

Shook, Edwin M.

1951   The Present Status of Research on the Preclassic Horizon in Guatemala. In *The Civilizations of Ancient America*, edited by Sol Tax, pp. 93–100. Selected papers of the 24th International Congress of Americanists, University of Chicago Press, Chicago.

Shook, Edwin M., and Alfred V. Kidder

1952   *Mound E-III, Kaminaljuyu, Guatemala*. Publication No. 596. Carnegie Institution of Washington, Washington, D.C.

Spence, Michael W.

1977   Teotihuacan y el intercambio de obsidiana en Mesoamerica. In *Los procesos de cambio: XV Mesa Redonda*, pp. 293–300. Sociedad Mexicana de Antropología, Mexico, DF.

Spence, Michael W., and Grégory Pereira

2007   The Human Skeletal Remains of the Moon Pyramid, Teotihuacan. *Ancient Mesoamerica* 18 (1):147–167.

Storey, Rebecca

1992   *Life and Death in the Ancient City of Teotihuacan: A Modern Paleodemographic Synthesis*. University of Alabama Press, Tuscaloosa.

Sugiyama, Saburo

1989   Burials Dedicated to the Old Temple of Quetzalcoatl at Teotihuacan, Mexico. *American Antiquity* 54 (1):85–106.

1992   Rulership, Warfare, and Human Sacrifice at the Ciudadela, Teotihuacan: An Iconographic Study of Feathered Serpent Representations. In *Art, Ideology, and the City of Teotihuacan*, edited by Janet C. Berlo, pp. 205–230. Dumbarton Oaks, Washington, D.C.

1993   Worldview Materialized in Teotihuacan, Mexico. *Latin American Antiquity* 4 (2):103–129.

1998   Termination Programs and Prehispanic Looting at the Feathered Serpent Pyramid in Teotihuacan, Mexico. In *The Sowing and the Dawning: Termination, Dedication, and Transformation in the Archaeological and Ethnographic Record of Mesoamerica*, edited by Shirley Boteler Mock. University of New Mexico Press, Albuquerque.

2000   Teotihuacan as an Origin for Postclassic Feathered Serpent Symbolism. In *Mesoamerica's Classic Heritage: From Teotihuacan to the Aztecs*, edited by David Carrasco, Lindsay Jones, and Scott Sessions, pp. 117–143. University Press of Colorado, Boulder.

2005   *Human Sacrifice, Militarism, and Rulership: Materialization of State Ideology at the Feathered Serpent Pyramid, Teotihuacan*. Cambridge University Press, Cambridge.

2009   Teotihuacan City Layout as a Cosmogram: Preliminary Results of the 2006 Measurement Unit Study. In *The Archaeology of Measurement: Comprehending Heaven, Earth and Time in Ancient Societies*, edited by Iain Morley and Colin Renfrew, pp. 130–149, Cambridge University Press, Cambridge.

Sugiyama, Saburo (editor)

2004   *Viaje al centro de la Pirámide de la Luna: Recientes descubrimientos en Teotihuacan*. Instituto Nacional de Antropología e Historia/Arizona State University, México, DF.

Sugiyama, Saburo, and Rubén Cabrera Castro

2003   Hallazgos recientes en la Pirámide de la Luna. *Arqueología Mexicana* 11 (64):42–49.

2007   The Moon Pyramid Project and the Teotihuacan State Polity: A Brief Summary of the 1998–2004 Excavations. *Ancient Mesoamerica* 18 (1):109–125.

Sugiyama, Saburo, and Leonardo López Luján (editors)

2006   *Sacrificios de consagración en la Pirámide de la Luna*. Instituto Nacional de Antropología e Historia/Arizona State University, México, DF.

Sugiyama, Saburo, and Leonardo López Luján

2007   Dedicatory Burial/Offering Complexes at the Moon Pyramid, Teotihuacan: A Preliminary Report of 1998–2004 Explorations. *Ancient Mesoamerica* 18 (1):127–146.

Taube, Karl

1986   The Teotihuacan Cave of Origin. *RES: Anthropology and Aesthetics* 12:51–82.

1992   The Temple of Quetzalcoatl and the Cult of Sacred War at Teotihuacan. *RES: Anthropology and Aesthetics* 21:53–87.

Umberger, Emily

1987   Events Commemorated by Date Plaques at the Templo Mayor: Further Thoughts on the Solar Metaphor. In *The Aztec Templo Mayor*, edited by Elizabeth H. Boone, pp. 411–449. Dumbarton Oaks, Washington, D.C.

Welsh, W.B.M.

1988a   An Analysis of Classic Lowland Maya Burials. BAR International Series No. 409. British Archaeological Reports, Oxford.

1988b   A Case for the Practice of Human Sacrifice Among the Classic Lowland Maya. In *Recent Studies in Pre-Columbian Archaeology*, edited by Nicholas J. Saunders and Olivier de Montmollin, Part I, pp. 143–165. BAR International Series No. 421(i). British Archaeological Reports, Oxford.

White, Christine D., T. Douglas Price, and Fred J. Longstaffe

2007   Residential Histories of the Human Sacrifices at the Moon Pyramid, Teotihuacan: Evidence from Oxygen and Strontium Isotopes. *Ancient Mesoamerica* 18 (1): 159–172.

White, Christine D., Michael W. Spence, Fred J. Longstaffe, Hilary Stuart-Williams, and Kimberley R. Law

2002   Geographic Identities of the Sacrificial Victims from the Feathered Serpent Pyramid, Teotihuacan: Implications for the Nature of State Power. *Latin American Antiquity* 13 (2):217–236.

CHAPTER 7

Concepts of Death and the Afterlife in Central Mexico

ELIZABETH BAQUEDANO

WE HAVE ABUNDANT information on the beliefs of the people who lived in central Mexico at the time of the Spanish conquest, one of whose major preoccupations was death and the afterlife. The Mexica, as the Aztecs are more properly called, had a practical idea of the afterlife as being determined by the manner of a person's death. Once that person was dead, there was a disintegration of the components of the human being: the body, the blood, and the animistic forces (*teyolia, tonalli,* and *ihiyotl* in Nahuatl, according to the study of López Austin [1988:1:313–16]). The soul abandoned the individual and went to one of several different resting places in the afterlife, the destination sometimes being foreordained, while at other times the circumstances of death were determinant. The Mexica had a complex religion, one element of which, a calendar of 260 days, was used for divining the future and the fate of individuals as decreed at their birth by the gods. This almanac, together with the solar calendar, also helped the ancient Mexica plan their agricultural cycles and conquest activities for the wet season and dry seasons respectively (Torquemada 1943:2:299). The one provided sustenance for their capital, the city of Tenochtitlan, while the other brought tribute to the rulers of the city. Death was omnipresent, as is made clear by abundant historical references, but to understand the beliefs and practices of the time we need to supplement the written evidence with archaeological data. This paper will therefore look at the concepts of death and the afterlife as described in the ethnohistorical sources, as well as at the relevant material remains.

The written and material record is extremely complex, and the best modern scholars differ somewhat on its interpretation. León-Portilla (1982:127), for example, tells us that the Mexica believed that man's final destiny was determined by the nature of his death, not on the basis of his moral conduct in life. To Christians, who believe that moral conduct at least partially determines the nature of the afterlife, the Mexica view may seem strange, for there was no suggestion of punishment or reward in the hereafter. In contrast to this view, López Austin (1988:1:338) suggests that:

> Behaviour was important in winning ultraterrestrial glory. Even though the fate of the *teyolia* (1) did not depend entirely on a person's conduct, access to Tlalocan and to Tonatiuh Ilhuicac was easier if a person cultivated the virtues of valour, purity, and devotion; behaviour was not separate from the fate of the dead. A privileged death was also seen as either a punishment or a reward, apart from other factors beyond the will of man. The marked contrast between a good death and an inglorious one had the characteristics of an ideological instrument to lead men along the socially established routes.

There are elements of truth in both these views, for which there is supporting evidence in the historical sources. On one hand, the Mexica were fatalistic in recognizing that the chance of dying whilst doing something worthy was no more likely than that of dying in one's sleep. On the other hand, the vision of the several paradises to which the souls of the deceased might go implied that there was some choice and that there were rewards for dying worthily on the sacrificial stone or on the battlefield. In attempting to clarify these issues, I rely on Sahagún as my main source, since his descriptions of death, burial, and the afterlife are much the most complete. However, I will supplement him with details from other contemporaneous chroniclers and from the archaeological evidence, as well as with certain ideas about the soul that persist in ethnographic reports of the twentieth century.

The Historical Sources

The Spanish and native chroniclers recorded many ideas concerning the places inhabited or visited by the dead. Sahagún (1950–1982:3:41–49) described three such destinations: Mictlan, Tlalocan, and the Home of the Sun. The cause of death was the determinant of the final destiny of the *teyolia*, as well as of the way in which the corpse was treated. The first destination, Mictlan, was, according to *Codex Vaticanus* 3738 (Codex Vaticanus A), reserved for those who died a natural death. Durán

(1971:392) states that *Mictlampa* means "the infernal region" and was believed to lie in the north. Sahagún (1950–82) and other sources explain that this region comprised nine subterranean levels. These were (López Austin 1988:1:333]:

1. "the earth," understood to be the outer limit of the underworld,
2. "the passageway of water,"
3. "the place where the hills are found,"
4. "the obsidian hills,"
5. "the place of the obsidian wind,"
6. "the place where the banners fly,"
7. "the place where people are killed by arrows,"
8. "the place where people's hearts are devoured," and
9. "the obsidian place of the dead" or "the place that has no outlet for smoke."

Sahagún (1950–1982:3:41) explained that this place of the dead was presided over by Mictlantecuhtli (or Tzontemoc) and Mictlancihuatl, his consort: "there to the place of the dead went all those who died on earth, who died only of sickness: the rulers, the commoners. People who died of a common illness (*tlalmiquiztli*, or 'earthly death') were cremated." This uniform treatment of rulers and commoners seems to have been the predominant view, but, typical of the many inconsistencies in the sixteenth-century accounts, López Austin (1988:328), quotes another passage of Sahagún suggesting that the fate of rulers was different from the commoners': "And the ancients believed, in their self-deception, that when the lords died, they became gods. So they would be feared and obeyed the rulers said that some became a Sun, others the Moon, and still others planets." Dead rulers were depicted in the codices as either a bundled body on a throne or prepared as a warrior for cremation (Dibble 1947:11). Cremation in fact, was the most common funerary practice of the Mexica. One example can be seen in *Codex Magliabechiano* (Boone 1983:67v) and several in *Codex Vaticanus 3738* (e.g., Ahuitzotl bundled and identified by the hieroglyph behind him [84r]).

On their way to Mictlan, people who had died a natural death had to overcome a number of obstacles or tests. Therefore, the deceased was granted the company of an auburn dog, cremated along with the corpse, to "take the deceased person across the place of the nine rivers in the

FIGURE 7.1. Fragment of mural painting from Tepantitla, Teotihuacan, known as Tlalocan, a pre-Mexica version of the paradise of the Rain God. Here people disport themselves in an idyllic landscape amid birds and butterflies, perhaps representing the souls of the dead or unborn children (photograph by James L. Fitzsimmons).

place of the dead" (Sahagún 1950–1982:207, my translation). Confirmation of this belief was found in the excavation of Tenochtitlan's Templo Mayor (Great Temple), where Offering 44 included a plumbate ceramic dog containing cremated human remains. The Mexica believed that this testing period lasted four years, after which the wandering existence of the dead came to an end. Sahagún (1950–1982:44) reports that when the four years had ended, the dead person went to the nine places of the dead, where lay a broad river. Then, at Chiconamictlan, the ninth place as described in *Codex Vaticanus A*, the deceased finally entered his or her rest.

The second destination of the dead was the Tlalocan, the "earthly paradise" (fig. 7.1). Here, there was "great wealth, there were great riches. Never did one suffer. Never did the ears of green maize, the gourds, the squash blossoms, the heads of amaranth, the green chilis, the tomatoes, the green beans, the cempoalxochitl, fail. And there dwelt the Tlalocs"

(Sahagún 1950–1982:47). This pleasant destiny befell those chosen by Tlaloc, the Rain God. He summoned his elect to a death that clearly indicated his personal intervention—drowning, lightning, hemorrhoids, dropsy, or gout. Individuals thus selected by the rain deity were not cremated but buried, and there are hints of possible reincarnation. León-Portilla (1982:125), for example, notes: "Concerning the destiny of those who went to Tlalocan, certain verses from the Tlaloc *icuic* seem to imply, as Seler noted, 'a subsequent development of the souls of those who die through the intervention of Tlaloc.' It hints at another existence on earth for those who have gone to Tlalocan." Again, according to Sahagún (1950–1982:1:276), "in four years, in the beyond, there is a rebirth. People here [on earth] no longer remember, for . . . long they have lost count. In the place of the fleshless, in the house of the quetzal plumes, there is a transformation of what belongs to the one who restores people to life."

Inhumed, Tlaloc's elect "acted as a seed that germinated under the earth" (López Austin 1980:1:366–67, my translation). Burial was a way to return to Tlaloc a kind of humus, this being consistent with the meaning of his name: he who was made of earth (*tlalloc*). The notion that dead bodies contribute to regenerate the soil is shared by the Melpa, for whom the flesh of the living is a product of the fertility brought about by the putrescence of the dead, whose bodies regenerate the soil and feed the plants on which the living subsist and which creates their substance (Bloch and Parry 1982:30).

Consistent with the notion of burial as the mode of disposal for Tlaloc's elect, the only complete human skeletons found in the Great Temple excavations were in Offering 48, located at the northeast corner of the Great Temple on the side dedicated to the Rain God. Matos Moctezuma (1988:94) reports that "skeletal remains of at least forty-two infants were discovered" there; and above them were found 11 Tlaloc effigy vessels, painted blue, the same color used to represent the Rain God in the codices. These are undoubtedly child sacrifices offered to the deity, such sacrifices being an unmistakable element in the ritual ceremonies in his honor. Typically, such sacrifices took place during the dry season. According to López Luján (2005:152), children were sacrificed to assure abundant rain for the next agricultural cycle. The petition for water was addressed to Tlaloc and his helpers, who supposedly lived in the mountains and hills, where they controlled springs and rainfall

(Broda 1987). Chroniclers mention that boys were sacrificed at hilltops, while girls were decapitated and their bodies cast in a whirlpool. As one example, Durán (1971:164) recorded that the high priests and dignitaries carried forth a little girl seven or eight years old in a covered litter. She was dressed in blue, representing the great lake and other springs and creeks. The girl was taken off in a canoe, and when they arrived at the place called Pantitlan, they slit her throat with a small spear and her blood was allowed to flow into the water. Once [the blood] had flowed, she was cast into the waters, right into the whirlpool.

The Great Temple find is rather different in its ritual context, both boys and girls being sacrificed and the number of victims far exceeding the figures recorded by the chroniclers. López Luján (2005:155) suggests that the glyph One Rabbit is associated with Stages IV and IVa of the construction of the Great Temple. If so, this date would correspond to the year 1454, when the Basin of Mexico suffered a great famine during the rule of Motecuhzoma Ilhuicamina (ca. 1440–1469). Hassig (1981:175) states that although the climatic conditions affected everyone, their consequences were demographically and socially skewed. Death from malnutrition stalked the land as the earth failed to yield its bounty. I suggest that this mass child sacrifice at the Great Temple was in fact a desperate plea for rain. It is recorded in the historical sources that the tears of children about to be sacrificed were a promising omen of rain. Having so many children crying would have been fittingly symbolic. Furthermore, there are several sculptures bearing the date One Rabbit, for example, the monumental sculpture depicting the earth goddess Coatlicue and the so-called Yollotlicue. These sculptures have carvings on the underside depicting Tlaloc-Tlaltecuhtli, a further allusion to the earth and rain.

The third destination of the souls of the dead was in the heavens, in the dwelling of the Sun, Tonatiuh Ilhuicac. This was considered a place of glory—"a place of wealth, a place of joy" (Sahagún 1950–1982:3:49). The ones chosen for this heaven were those who died in battle, captives who had died at the hands of their enemies, and sacrificial victims. In the house of the Sun, they rejoiced forever. Sahagún (ibid.) described these chosen ones: "Perchance one was slain in gladiatorial sacrifice, or cast into the fire, or pierced by darts, or offered up on the barrel cactus, or shot by arrows, or encrusted [and burned] with pieces of resinous wood: all [these] went to the home of the sun." Women who died in childbirth also went to the Sun's paradise. These women were equated to male warriors, for in dying with a child in their womb, they were taking a "prisoner" into the next world with them. Women who died from bearing a first child were called *mociuaquetzque* and, with those who died in battle, went to the house of the Sun to reside in the western part of the sky (Sahagún 1950–1982:1:318).

Sahagún (1950–1982:6:161–2) gives more information about the mociuaquetzque:

> And as it became night they bore this little woman to bury her there before the images of their devils whom they named Ciuapipiltin, celestial princesses. And when they had borne her, then they buried her, they placed her in the earth. But her husband and still others helped to guard her for four nights, that no one might steal her. . . . Her parents and the husband rejoiced therefore even more, for it was said she went there to the heavens, to the house of the sun. . . . And these little women who thus had died in childbirth, those said to have become *mociuaquetzque*, when they died, they said, became goddesses.

After four years, the mociuaquetzque were transformed into a variety of birds (ibid.:3:49): "those who had died in the war, then . . . changed into precious birds—hummingbirds, orioles, yellow birds, yellow birds blackened about the . . . eyes, chalky butterflies, feather down butterflies, gourd bowl butterflies; they sucked honey [from the flowers] there where they dwelt." In prehispanic times, the Mexica believed that the adult *yolia* (soul) of women who died in childbirth as well as the yolia of warriors took the form of winged creatures; the souls of dead children became birds or butterflies. As mentioned above, Sahagún wrote in the *Florentine Codex* that four years after death, the souls of the dead became hummingbirds, or a variety of butterflies that sucked the nectar of flowers, as did the hummingbirds. Warriors, specifically, were transformed into *huitzilopochtlis* (hummingbirds). This was an apt symbol: there are over fifty species of this type of bird in Mexico (Wheeler 1987:19).

The idea of the soul-as-bird is common today throughout Mexico and has considerable time depth. At Tepantitla, one of Teotihuacan's apartment complexes, there is a wall painting known as the Tlalocan, a pre-Mexica version of the paradise of the Rain God. Here people disport themselves in an idyllic landscape amid birds and butterflies, perhaps

FIGURE 7.2. Excavations carried out by Rubén Cabrera at the site of La Ventilla, Teotihuacan, showing part of the cemetery with fetuses placed on earthen bowls.

representing the souls of the dead or unborn children (McKeever 1995). The excavations at La Ventilla in Teotihuacan carried out by Rubén Cabrera and his team revealed a special cemetery for unborn babies (fig. 7.2). There were rows of fetuses placed in earthen bowls buried with goods for the afterlife such as metates and *manos* (grinding stones). Slightly later in time, at the Toltec site of Tula in the modern state of Hidalgo, both the atlantid columns from Pyramid B as well as the chac-mool sculptures wear pectorals in the form of highly stylized butterflies (fig. 7.3). In some Toltec sculptures the same butterfly motif is repeated on the headdress. This stylized butterfly is also used in Mexica sculpture, including the state-commissioned monumental carvings known as the *cuauhxicalli* of Moctezuma (Matos Moctezuma and Solís, 2004) and the Stone of Tizoc. I have observed that in both monuments every successful captor wears a butterfly pectoral, including of course Tizoc himself.

FIGURE 7.3. Atlantid Warrior Column from Pyramid B, Tula, displaying stylized butterfly pectoral (photograph by James L. Fitzsimmons).

The use of this pectoral in scenes of capture of prisoners of war suggests that this kind of pectoral is restricted to those who attained success in the battlefield. Likewise, the placement of this iconographic motif near the heart (the yolia) points to what the Mexica considered the organ of ability and strength par excellence—a prerequisite for success in war.

Codex Vaticanus A mentions yet another destination of the dead, Chichihuacuauhco, which was in the house of Tonacatecuhtli (Lord of our Flesh). This name, according to León-Portilla (1982:127), means "in the wet-nurse tree" (fig. 7.4). To this place went children who died before attaining "the age of reason." This tree had branches with breasts, and the children fed from the milk that dripped from its leaves. "It is said that the little children who died, like jade, turquoise, and jewels, do not go to the frightful and cold region of the dead [Mictlan]. They go to the house of Tonacatecuhtli; they live by the 'tree of our flesh.' They nourish themselves on the tree of our sustenance; they live near the 'tree of our flesh'; from it do they feed themselves" (Sahagún 1950–1982:6:96.).

In present-day Mexico during the Day of the Dead celebrations in November, the Nahua communities make offerings to the souls of children who died before they learned to speak (Sandstrom 1991:282).

Burial Practices

The burial practices of the Mexica, like the afterlife destination of the defunct person, varied according to the nature of a person's death, except for a common purification rite: no matter what the cause of death, the corpse had to be washed with water. Durán (1971:267) recorded: "As soon as someone died, whether a man, a woman, or a child, whether or not a great nobleman, whether a rich man or a pauper, the first thing that was done after his death was to strip him naked and wash him carefully. After he was washed, he was again dressed in all his clothes, to be buried or incinerated. They said that water served them for death."

Otherwise the disposal of the body, its clothing, and related ritual were dictated by the circumstances of the individual's death. Those who died naturally were cremated, their passage to Mictlan being facilitated by offerings of vessels, clothing, and other objects necessary for the ordeal, as well as a dog to help its master make the journey less perilous (López Austin 1988:1:320).

FIGURE 7.4. Chichihuacuauhco, the place destined for the souls of children who died before attaining the "age of reason." *Codex Vaticanus A* (after López Austin 1980:1:384).

Cremation was also the lot of those who died in honor of the Sun. The hearts of those who were sacrificed to the Sun, and they were many according to Sahagún, were placed in the *cuauhxicalli* (eagle vessel) (Sahagún 1950–1982:2:48). And they named the hearts of the captives "eagle-cactus fruit." By contrast, those who died in honor of Tlaloc and were destined for Tlalocan were buried and the heart was cast into the whirlpool or drain called Pantitlan in the Lake of Mexico (Sahagún 1950–1982:2:11).

According to several of the chroniclers, commoners were customarily buried in house courtyards. More specific details are provided by Acosta (1973:2:315):

> The places where they buried them was in their gardens, and in the courts of their own houses; others carried them to the places of sacrifices which were done in the mountains; others burnt them, and after buried the ashes in their Temples, and they buried them all with whatsoever they had of apparel, stones, and jewels. They did put the ashes of such as were burnt into pots, and with them the jewels, stones, and earrings of the dead, how rich and precious soever.

Sahagún (1950–1982:8:3) too provided a detailed description: "When a woman died of sickness, she was buried in her courtyard and they laid stones over her grave. The placenta of a baby girl was buried in the house too. And the midwife forthwith cut the umbilical cord of the baby; she took its umbilical cord. And she removed that which is called the after-birth; in which the baby came wrapped, in which it came enveloped. This she buried in a corner [of the house]." The umbilical cord of a boy was saved: "It was dried; later it was left in the battlefield" (ibid.:6:169).

Only burials of special significance appear to have been placed in major civic structures. For example, in the excavations at the Great Temple, Tenochtitlan, human remains were found in three types of situation that reflect the three ways in which the Mexica conceived of the afterlife. First, cremated remains of persons (presumably destined for Mictlan following a natural death) were deposited in urns such as those found beneath the platform of the Temple, at the earliest excavated level (Stage II), on the side of the shrine dedicated to Huitzilopochtli. An obsidian funerary vessel depicting a skull and containing incinerated bones was found in Offering 34, and two other urn burials were found in Offering 10 and Offering 14 near a cremation pit. Umberger (1983:412) speculates that their contents may have been the remains of Moctezuma I, who died in the year 3 House (1469), the date associated with the phase of the temple where they were found. However (subsequently she revised her ideas in light of new evidence and critiques), this interpretation seems implausible, since the dates assigned to the Great Temple's structural phases are

open to serious question (Graulich 1988), and it is unlikely that Moctezuma would have been buried in one of two similar but unexceptional
ceramic pots: Nezahuapipiltin, the king of Texcoco, was buried in a gold
coffin. Perhaps we will never know the truth.

The second type of situation involved deposits of decorated skulls with
sacrificial knives inserted in the mouth and/or nose, typical of sacrifices
to Huitzilopochtli. The third type comprised complete skeletons, mainly
of children, doubtless dedicated to Tlaloc and destined for Tlalocan.
Burial 1 contained the only unburned, complete adult skeleton found
during the excavations of the Great Temple project (López Luján 2005).

Special Features of Elite Burials

As noted above, the main purpose of funeral rites was to prepare the
deceased for life after death. Hence, their elaborate nature and rich associated offerings. Several chroniclers record that, when a ruler or nobleman
died, it was customary to kill his slaves and women to accompany him in
the afterlife, to take care of him, to prepare his chocolate, and to cook for
him. Torquemada says that as many as 200 slaves were sacrificed when
a ruler died, including household slaves, dwarves, jesters, and slaves presented by visiting dignitaries. Writing of Nezahualpipiltin's death, Ixtlilxochitl (1965:2:328) says: "He was cremated, his body attired with many jewels
of gold and silver and fine stones ('pedrería'), and with a variety of headdresses and feathers; and they sacrificed in his honour two hundred male
slaves and a hundred female slaves; and his ashes were kept in a golden
coffin which was taken to his burial place in the Great Temple in the city
of Texcoco, the temple of the idol Huitzilopochtli" (my translation). It is
likely that this practice of killing retainers to accompany the deceased was
of ancient origin, having been verified in several multiple burials dating
back to the Preclassic period. Such burials have also been excavated at the
site of Tlatelolco, Tenochtitlan's twin city, where large urns containing cremated remains and small funerary urns depicting skulls have been found.

Another outstanding feature of the burials at the Great Temple in the
case of presumed nobles or rulers is the nature of the objects accompanying them. (For a detailed description of a cluster of funeral deposits from
Complex E of the Great Temple see López Luján [2005]. This cluster is
particularly meaningful, as it was deposited over four different phases in

the construction of the temple.) Among the objects deposited were items of gold and precious jewels. Masks and greenstones seem to have played a special role in burial ritual. There are few references to the first in the historical records, but the latter are well documented. In a rare mention, Torquemada (1986:2:521) states that a painted mask was placed over the bundle: "sobre la mortaja le ponían una mascara pintada"; in the 1988 excavations at Tlatelolco, several masks were found buried with human skeletal remains in large pottery urns.

A precious stone (jade, other greenstones, or obsidian) symbolized and replaced the human heart as an essential element in burials. Sahagún (1950–1982:3:45) and Torquemada (1986:2:521) recorded that when rulers and noblemen died, genuine greenstones were placed in their mouths. And if they were only commoners, then greenish stones or obsidian sufficed. "It was said that they became their hearts. The greenstone was a substitute of the heart giving vitality to the deceased" (fig. 7.5). López Austin (1980:1:373) speculates that these stones served as payment for services on the way to the afterlife, but, as Digby (1972:11) has remarked, it is more likely that jade was regarded as having life-giving properties, the spirit or essence of which would be absorbed by the spirit of the deceased and ensure his or her continued spiritual survival.

This concept of jade as a symbol of life and regeneration applied to both humans and animals. López Luján (2005:149) records that, in Offering 48 at the Great Temple, greenstone beads were found in the mouths of five individuals, while in Chamber 2 of the temple the skeleton of a puma was found with a jade bead between its fangs (López Luján 2005:246). The puma was placed on top of offerings to Tlaloc, thus associating it with life and water. This symbolism is eloquently expressed in a prayer to Tlaloc:

> The gods, Our Lords, the Providers,
> the Lords of Rubber,
> the Lords of the Sweet-Scented Marigold,
> the Lords of Copal,
> have sealed themselves in a coffer,
> they have locked themselves in a box.
> They have hidden the jade and turquoise
> and precious jewels of life.
> (Sullivan 1965:43)

FIGURE 7.5. Jade, other greenstones, or obsidian symbolized and replaced the human heart as an essential element in burial. British Museum (photograph by Elizabeth Baquedano 1989:pl.24).

Sculpture and Death

Despite the importance attributed to death and the afterlife by the Mexica, the god and goddess of the underworld, Mictlantecuhtli and Mictecacihuatl, are rarely depicted in the otherwise ample corpus of sculpture associated with death. One of the few effigies is a vessel from Offering 17 in the Great Temple. It is characteristic of representations of Mictlantecuhtli in the codices, with a fully fleshed body and a skull in place of the head. Another example, in the British Museum, portrays a similar figure (fig. 7.6). It bears several dates, the meaning of which is unclear: Two Death on the headdress, Four House below the head, and Five Vulture on one shoulder. Posthumous portraits, particularly portrait heads, are more common, there being a fine and rather startling example in

FIGURE 7.6. The Lord of the Underworld, Mictlantecuhtli, is not often represented in sculpture. British Museum (after Baquedano 1984:pl. 26).

the British Museum. It has mother-of-pearl inlay for the whites of the eyes and a mouth that sags open. Other examples are to be found in the National Museum of Anthropology, Mexico City.

Ritual objects are another category of death-related sculpture. The most notable are the *cuauhxicallis* (eagle vessels) of stone or wood (fig. 7.7). They are usually described as receptacles for sacrificed human hearts and blood, but they have a wider usage. Some codices depict them as containers of the limbs of sacrificial victims (e.g., Codex Magliabechi-ano, 61v.), one such a vessel from Santa Cecilia Acatitlan (fig. 7.8) being decorated around its circumference with dismembered limbs, a heart, and other symbols (Baquedano 1989; Solís 1976:35). Both Sahagún and Durán report that these vessels were used in yet other ways, for example to burn items such as flowers during rituals. The chroniclers suggest indeed that incineration may have been one of the most important uses of the *cuauhxicalli*. By analogy, Quauhxicalco means "burning place" and Sahagún (1950–1982:2:168, 170–71) mentions that there were four places so named in the temple square where brave warriors were burned (Sahagún 1950–1982:12:57). However, I have not found a *cuauhxicalli* with signs of burning. This ritual vessel was also used as a depository for relics such as the hair of sacrificial victims and those who had died a natural death. Reporting on the ceremony of casting hair, Sahagún (1950–1982:9:63–64) writes:

> And when they had fed them . . . they came taking some hair from the crowns of their heads. A man came blowing, sounding a whistle; it came saying "chic." He came with it only in order that they swiftly proceed to remove hair from the crown of one's head: if [there were] two, if three, if four bathed ones, as many times did he do so. At once [the whistler] [came circling slaves], carrying the eagle vessel, in which he went casting the hair.

Another deity whose images were found in the burial offerings of the Great Temple is Xiuhtecuhtli, the god of fire. His association with the death complex is less evident than that of the death gods and ritual objects mentioned above and may perhaps be explained as being a source of warmth and comfort in the otherwise frigid regions of the dead. This would be consistent with reports of the chroniclers that it was customary to wrap a corpse before burial in several *mantas* (blankets) so as to keep it from feeling the cold.

FIGURE 7.7. Greenstone *cuauhxicalli*. This sacrificial vessel depicts stylized hearts, feathers, and precious jade symbols. The inside shows a sun disk and the 4 "Movement" Glyph. The Lord of the Earth (Tlaltecuhtli) is carved in the underside of the vessel. Museum für Völkerkunde, Berlin (photograph by Elizabeth Baquedano).

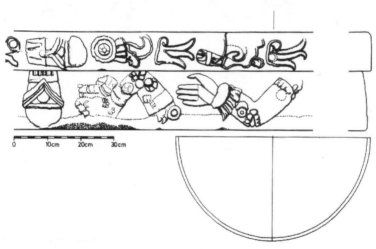

FIGURE 7.8. The circumference of the vessel from Santa Cecilia Acatitlan depicts the dismembered limbs of a sacrificial victim, a heart, and other symbols. Santa Cecilia Museum, Estado de México (after Baquedano 1989:pl. 15a, b).

FIGURE 7.9. Relief sculpture of Coyolxauhqui with "demon faces" at the ankle, knee, and shoulder joints. Great Temple of Tenochtitlan (drawing by Laurie Umberger).

Other sculptures found during the Great Temple excavations throw further light on Mexica beliefs concerning death and the afterlife. The great relief figure of the dismembered goddess Coyolxauhqui, malevolent sister of Huitzilopochtli, depicts her with what scholars have called "demon faces" at the ankle, knee, and shoulder joints (fig. 7.9). This curious feature is surely not accidental. It appears on colossal depictions

FIGURE 7.10. The Lord of the Earth, Tlaltecuhtli, with "demon faces" carved at the level of the joints. Museum für Völkerkunde, Hamburg (after Taube 1993:36).

of several deities such as Coatlicue and Yollotlicue, and on sculptures associated with Tlaltecuhtli, Lord/Lady of the Earth (figs. 7.10 and 7.11). The "demon face" is also depicted on objects used in death rituals such as decorated knives from the Great Temple (see, for example, Nicholson and Quiñones Keber [1983:40]).

Its usage and symbolism may derive from Mckeever Furst's contention (1995:69) that the *tonalli* (soul) seems to be concentrated in those parts of the body, particularly around the joints, where the blood pulses most strongly. For his part, López Austin (1988:I:215) mentions that the joints were regarded as especially vulnerable to attack and penetration by the invisible forces that seek to steal a person's vital force. This general concept is reflected in our time in the beliefs of the modern Nahuas of Hueyapan, Morelos, who assign particular importance to the wrists, whose pulse they observe during illnesses. They recognize its progressive

FIGURE 7.11. The Lord of the Earth seems to show pronounced "demon faces" at the areas where the *tonalli* concentrated the most, around the joints. British Museum (after Baquedano 1984:pl. 59).

withdrawal from the wrist to the elbow and thence to the shoulder as the end approaches. When the soul shrinks to the heart, the person is dead (Alvarez Heydenreich 1987:103 in Mckeever Furst [1995]).

I would suggest that the "demon face" is yet another representation of the notion of death whose precise meaning is determined by context and the nature of the sculpture or the object under consideration. In essence it is the visual manifestation of the *tonalli*, present as heat in life or as its absence at death. Agricultural fertility, war, and human sacrifice are important contextual parameters in the case of the cult of Tlaltecuhtli (Baquedano 1989, 2001), while war, needless to say, is a major factor in the presence of a "demon face" on a flint knife at shoulder level on a warrior sculpture reminiscent of the Toltec atlantid (fig. 7.12).

Interpretation and Conclusions

The ineluctable intervention of the gods in the life and afterlife of humankind is a remarkable and irresistible feature of Mexica religion and has, as I have suggested, ambiguous implications for human conduct and morality. The gods proposed and disposed within the limits of their powers and jurisdictions. People reacted and, within the imprecise area of free will left to them by the forces of predestination so deeply entrenched in Mexica ideology, strove to forge their own destiny both in this world and in the next. The ultimate destiny of choice, if one wished to avoid the miseries of Mictlan and the perils of Tlaloc's unpredictability, lay in the home of the Sun, Tonatiuh Ilhuicac, where Huitzilopoctli offered glory, transformation (into winged creatures), and the prospect of rebirth to warriors killed in battle, sacrificial victims, and women who had died in childbirth. It is interesting to note that death by sacrifice seems, from the accounts of the Spanish chroniclers and indigenous imagery, to have most preoccupied the minds of native peoples and the conquistadores. There are no accounts of what happened to the souls of the sacrificer priests, but Graulich (1982:264) has suggested that they were notionally incorporated in their victims and thus ended up in Tlalocan or Tonatiuh Ilhuicac, but not in Mictlan.

Tlalocan, the destination of the elect of the Rain God, was hardly less attractive, but the unpredictability of death related to water must have been a serious impediment for the aspirant to a comfortable eternity.

FIGURE 7.12. Warrior reminiscent of the Toltec style atlantids. Side depicting a sacrificial knife with a "demon face" at shoulder level. National Museum of Anthropology, Mexico City (after Pasztory 1983:pl. 146).

The vast majority of citizens died tranquilly of old age and ended up in the least desirable of destinations, Mictlan, a frightful, cold region, described by Sahagún (1950–1982:3:42): "Here is wherewith thou wilt pass the place of the obsidian-bladed winds; and in . . . the place of the obsidian-bladed winds, it was said that there was much suffering." That these destinations in the afterlife should vary so much and that the differential awards for courage on the battlefield and other acts of civic interest should be so marked suggests manipulation of religious ideology by a state notorious for its expansionist policies. Citizens were encouraged by the system to seek a peerless afterlife by doing something worthy in life, be it death in battle, giving birth to the next generation, or even, perhaps, catching fish on waters subject to Tlaloc's wrath.

It seems clear that the views developed by the Mexica about life, death, and the afterlife were profoundly influenced by their immediate environment. The lakes and mountains that surrounded the Basin of Mexico, and the sky above became the dwellings of the gods and the destination of human souls. Death faced the Mexica on the battlefield, where they strove to maintain the supremacy of Tenochtitlan in the name of their patron deity, Huitzilopochtli. It faced those whose vocation was on the lakes subject to storms, whirlpools, and lightning at the whim of Tlaloc, and it faced those of more modest circumstances who tended fields dependent for their fertility on fickle rainfall. Those who died naturally without distinction returned to the soil, regenerating the life cycle and restoring the productive equilibrium of the universe (López Austin 1988:1:418).

Acknowledgments

I would like to thank James Langley for reading and making insightful comments on my chapter. I would also like to thank Susan Milbrath for her editorial comments on an earlier draft. Chris Winter, Ian Bryden, and my son José were patient in formatting and scanning my figures more than once.

Works Cited

Acosta, Joseph de
1973   The Natural and Moral History of the Indies. 2 vols. Lenox Hill, New York.
Alvarez Heydenreich, Laurencia
1987   La enfermedad y la cosmovisión en Hueyapan, Morelos. Serie de Antropología Social 74. Instituto Nacional Indigenísta, Mexico.

Baquedano, Elizabeth

1984   *Aztec Sculpture*. British Museum Publications, London.

1989   Aztec Death Sculpture. Ph.D. dissertation. Institute of Archaeology, University College, University of London.

2001   Earth Deities. In *The Oxford Encyclopedia of Mesoamerican Cultures: The Civilizations of Mexico and Central America*, edited by Davíd Carrasco, Vol. 1, pp. 350–351. Oxford University Press, Oxford.

Bloch, Maurice, and Jonathan Parry

1982   Introduction: Death and the Regeneration of Life. In *Death and the Regeneration of Life*, edited by Maurice Bloch and Jonathan Parry, pp. 1–44. Cambridge University Press, Cambridge.

Boone, Elizabeth H. (editor)

1983   *Codex Magliabechiano and the Lost Prototype of the Magliabechiano Group*. University of California Press, Berkeley.

Broda, Johanna

1987   Templo Mayor as a Ritual Space. In *The Great Temple of Tenochtitlan: Center and Periphery in the Aztec World*, edited by Johanna Broda, Davíd Carrasco, and Eduardo Matos Moctezuma, pp. 61–123. University of California Press, Berkeley.

Corona Núñez, José

1964   *Codex Ríos (Vaticanus A or 3738)*. Antiguedades de México, Secretaría de Hacienda y Crédito Público, Mexico.

Dibble, Charles

1947   *An Ancient Mexican Hieroglyphic Picture Manuscript*. Monographs of the School of American Research No. 11. University of New Mexico Press, Albuquerque.

Digby, Adrian

1972   *Maya Jades*. British Museum Publications, London.

Durán, Diego

1971   *Book of the Gods and Rites and the Ancient Calendar*. University of Oklahoma Press, Norman.

Graulich, Michel

1982   *Mythes et rituals du Mexique ancien prehispanique*. Academie Royale de Belgique, Palais des Academies, Brusells.

1988   Les incertitudes du Grand Temple. In *Les aztèques: Tresors du Mexique ancien*, pp. 121–131. Catalogue de la Exposition aux Musées Royaux d'Art et d'Histoire, Brussels.

Hassig, Ross

1981   The Famine of One Rabbit: Ecological Causes and Social Consequences of a Pre-Columbian Calamity. *Journal of Anthropological Research* 37:172–182.

Hertz, Robert

1907   Contribution à une ètude sur la representation collective de la mort. *Année Sociologique* 10:48–137.

1960   A contribution to the study of the collective representation of death. In *Death and the Right Hand*, edited by Rodney and Claudia Needham, pp. 27–86. Cohen and West, New York.

Heyden, Doris
1998   *México, orígenes de un símbolo.* Consejo Nacional para la Cultura y las Artes. INAH, Mexico.
Ixtlilxochitl, Fernando de Alva
1965   *Obras históricas.* 2 vols. Edited by Alfredo Chavero. Editora Nacional, Mexico.
León-Portilla, Miguel
1982   *Aztec Thought and Culture: A Study of the Ancient Nahuatl Mind.* 6th ed. Translated by Jack Emory Davis. University of Oklahoma Press, Norman.
López Austin, Alfredo
1980   *Cuerpo humano e ideología.* 2 vols. Universidad Nacional Autónoma de México, Instituto de Investigaciones Antropológicas, Mexico City.
1988   *Human Body and Ideology.* 2 vols. Translated by Thelma Ortiz de Montellano and Bernard Ortiz de Montellano. University of Utah Press, Salt Lake City.
López Luján, Leonardo
2005   *The Offerings of the Templo Mayor of Tenochtitlan.* Translated by Bernard R. Ortiz de Montellano and Thelma Ortiz de Montellano. University of New Mexico Press, Albuquerque.
Matos Moctezuma, Eduardo
1988   *The Great Temple of the Aztecs.* Thames and Hudson, London.
Matos Moctezuma, Eduardo, and Felipe Solís
2004   *The Aztec Calendar and Other Solar Monuments.* Conaculta. INAH, Mexico.
Mckeever Furst, Jill Leslie
1995   *The Natural History of the Soul in Ancient Mexico.* Yale University Press, New Haven.
Nicholson, H. B., and Eloise Quiñones Keber
1983   *Art of Aztec Mexico: Treasures of Tenochtitlan National Gallery of Art.* National Gallery, Washington, D.C.
Pasztory, Esther
1983   *Aztec Art.* Harry N. Abrams, New York.
Sahagún, Fray Bernardino
1950–1982 *Florentine Codex: General History of the Things of New Spain.* Translated by Arthur J. O. Anderson and Charles E. Dibble. School of American Research, Santa Fe, N.M.
Sandstrom, Alan
1991   *Corn Is Our Blood: Culture and Ethnicity in a Contemporary Aztec Indian Village.* University of Oklahoma Press, Norman.
Solís, Felipe
1976   *La escultura mexica del Museo de Santa Cecilia Acatitlan.* INAH, Mexico.
Sullivan, Thelma
1965   *A Prayer to Tlaloc. Estudios de Cultura Nahuatl* 5:39–55.
Taube, Karl
1993   *Aztec and Maya Myths.* British Museum Press, London.
Torquemada, Juan de
1943   *Monarquía indiana.* 3 vols. 3rd ed. Chávez Hayhoe, Mexico.
1986   *Monarquía indiana.* 3 vols. Porrúa, Mexico.

Umberger, Emily
1983   Events Commemorated by Date Plaques at the Templo Mayor: Further Thoughts on the Solar Metaphor. In *The Aztec Templo Mayor*, edited by Elizabeth Hill Boone, pp. 411–449. Dumbarton Oaks, Washington, D.C.
Wheeler, Margaret
1987   *A Bird Watcher's Guide to Mexico*. Minutiae Mexicana, Mexico.

CHAPTER 8

Toward a Hermeneutics of Death

Commentary on Seven Essays Written for Living with the Dead

PATRICIA A. MCANANY

WE ARE ACCUSTOMED to a western, medicalized approach to death as something that can be recorded down to the minute—an acute moment when the breath of life ceases. But like most things in life, this view is historically and culturally situated and differs from ideas about death that involve a slow transformation from one state to another or a complex interplay between physical and social existence that can endure and be celebrated long after corporeal death. In one form or another, the authors who contribute to this book grapple with the hermeneutic of death and, in the process, provide deep insights into the fundamentally different ways in which life and death—and the aftermath of death— were entangled in Mesoamerica.

In many respects, the study of Mesoamerican mortuary practices is about transcending death. As Fitzsimmons notes here and elsewhere (2009), in social contexts in which selected persons retain a social persona after death, those individuals can be said to have transcended death. The charged manner in which a single bone (*b'aak* in Maya Classic texts) can stand for the entire body and materialize social identity (as Blomster and several others here describe for a range of Mesoamerican societies) connotes a transcendence of death, regardless of whether the skeletal parts were those of a revered ancestor, a political captive, or both. In a sense, to be remembered—to be reanimated from a carved femur or other mnemonic object—is to triumph over death. Those whose names, titles, or life details were carved into a Zaachila genealogical registry or Tikal Altar 5 have entered the annals of monumental time (Ricoeur 1985:106). Likewise, for those whose place of burial was reopened, revisited, or transformed (as per Chase and Chase), the progressive anonymity of death was forestalled. Empirically, those whose remains have been exhumed by archaeologists have assumed a resurgent biological and social identity in a kind of scientific apotheosis that ironically and uniquely can stand apart from the desires of descendant kin groups.

I take transcendence as the starting point for this exploration of the hermeneutics of death. From this place, I build upon several key ideas proposed by contributors beginning with discussion of a topic that is pervasive throughout this book—biological death as opposed to social death. From this point, I move to consider the linkage between memory and mortuary ritual, particularly iterative and politically motivated mortuary practices and commemorations that promote stasis or change. Next, the problematic of violence and the ambiguity of archaeological assignations in reference to the human body is considered. As the final rite of passage, death provides a portal to the afterlife and is a concept of demonstrated plurality in Mesoamerica that has been shown to exist in relation to age, gender, and life experience. Given the enduring tradition of social difference within Mesoamerica, the hermeneutical extendability of a knowledge base accrued from royal and elite contexts—such as the archetypal tomb of K'inich Janahb Pakal of Palenque (Tiesler and Cucina 2004)—to less illustrious mortuary remains is examined. Commentary on these linked topics aims to contribute to an emergent archaeological study of the hermeneutics of death within Mesoamerica and elsewhere (e.g., Rakita et al. 2005).

Regardless of its social ontology, death is definitive and always a loss to the living. It represents the most fundamental of existential crises— the meaning of the absence of life—and can engender political crisis and danger (and probably did so in many of the examples provided here of the death of Mesoamerican royals). Although social persona can be deeply entangled with notions of power, for the moment, I consider simply the separability of biological and social death. For heuristic purposes, a two-way table can be constructed:

State of Being		
Categories of Persona	Death	Survival
Biological	Ancestors *relics* *trophies*	Captives
Social	Captives	Ancestors *relics* *trophies*

The cells of this matrix are informed by an analysis of Classic Maya royal epigraphy and iconography (Houston et al. 2006) in which the humiliation of captives is interpreted as a killing of the social persona even though the individual continued to live as a biological organism, albeit greatly compromised. The opposite would be the situation for those we classify as ancestors, "relics," or "trophies"—categories in which human remains from biological death are used to assert the continued potency and influence of a person. To my mind, the latter two terms—relics and trophies—are imprecise ones that reflect our limited conceptual vocabulary in reference to skeletal partibility and the ways in which religious beliefs, political power, and social memory can be materialized in reference to skeletal remains. Nonetheless, the hermeneutic of all three states of being—revered ancestor, political trophy, or commemorated relic—(and all are deeply informed by archaeological context) encompass states of biological death and social survival. Certainly, categories of this contingency table are not meant to be exhaustive, could be expanded to include an economic, spiritual, or political persona, and may not exist invariably as dichotomous states.[1] Nevertheless, this opening gambit demonstrates the complex parsing of human identity in reference to social and biological dimensions.

In Mesoamerica, human remains embodied life, vitality, ancestral identity, and social space (the last discussed by Blomster, this volume), even in a disembodied and biologically deanimated state. An ironic concept for the dichotomy-prone western mind, the coupling of vitality with human decay is exemplified by the Mexican celebration of *Dia de los Muertos* in which ancestral spirits of the dead are remembered, fed, and otherwise nourished amid raucous vitality. Although Blomster refers to the premise that this ritual practice may not have deep taproots in Mesoamerica, nourishing and remembering are strong characteristics of traditional Mesoamerican cosmologies (Monaghan 2000). The expectation that the living will remember the dead—and that a debt is owed to ancestral spirits—can assume covenantal or contractual dimensions, as discussed here by Chase and Chase. On the other hand, the majority of essays address a type of linkage between memory and mortuary ritual that transcends the two-to-three-generation, short-term memory of social collectivities and rather is lodged in the social memory and collective eulogium of the longue durée, along with creation narratives, culture heroes, and social/natural catastrophes. Iterative mortuary ritual creates culture heroes who become fixed in telescopic social memory of longue durée as those whose lives held particular significance. In this way, social memory and transcendence over death are actualized through mortuary ritual and anniversary celebrations.

Politicization of the dead often conforms to this trajectory. Both Fitzsimmons and Weiss-Krejci (this volume) discuss royal Maya iterative mortuary ritual timed to the anniversary of death. Often involving a tomb reentry ceremony, any given death commemoration could be separated temporally from the biological death of the celebrated person by several decades. This stretching of the temporal fabric of human life often occurs within a charged political milieu of either attempted stasis or dramatic change. In his introductory essay, Fitzsimmons emphasizes how memory of the drama of death can be managed by the politically powerful—via ritual pageantry—in a manner that assuaged and commemorated loss and assured continuity in the face of fundamental change (that is, loss of a politically powerful person). Weiss-Krejci, on the other hand, emphasizes how exhumation of a human burial—as attested by the text of Tikal Altar 5—can indicate political change, a new network of alliances, or a redrawing of political boundaries. Within a less political and more family-crypt context, Chase and Chase also emphasize cyclic tomb reentry, either for the traditional purpose of interring another family member or for transformational purposes that may have been linked to altered political landscapes. Codical, epigraphic, and increasingly archaeological information suggests that shifts in political power within Mesoamerica were not complete without reckoning with the places of ancestors—whether that reckoning took the form of reanimating or deanimating highly charged burial places. Increasingly, archaeologists are aware of the political significance of scattered human remains marked as elite by virtue of dental inlays (Harrison-Buck et al. 2007) or of emptied tomb chambers, as Sugiyama describes for Teotihuacan. Representational imagery of ancestral rulers—Maya stelae, Olmec colossal heads, or Mixtec genealogical registers—received similarly intense attention and often underwent modification as political landscapes changed.

The extent to which actual human remains (or representational media) are deployed as a mnemonic that materializes apotheosis from deceased human to culture hero or deity is highly variable. Certainly, both human remains and iconography/epigraphy were deployed in this fashion in the

Maya region, where femora or crania in particular embodied identity and, as Fitzsimmons notes, also narrative and history. A tool such as an awl made from a human femur held special significance, just as the use of skeletal "relics" of bona fide Catholic saints were said to consecrate a Catholic house of worship. But human remains also can be deployed in reference to the dark violence of political domination and revenge. The problematic of violence and ambiguity of archaeological assignation of violence is nowhere more apparent than in Sugiyama's chapter on axial interments placed within the Pyramid of the Moon at Teotihuacan, ostensibly to dedicate new construction phases. An apparent contradiction between the lavish funerary items and the placement of Burial 5 (composed of three seated males adorned with jadeite and interred with eagle, puma, and serpent remains) indicates the complexity that resides within the terms "dedicatory burial" and "ritual sacrifice." The strontium "signatures" of alterity for most interments from both the Moon and Feathered Serpent pyramids suggests that a measure of exoticism increased the efficacy of dedicatory interments. Were these interments part of an ensoulment of a newly built structure that was activated by the *transference* of the animate (interred persons and animals) to the inanimate (stone pyramid)? While loss of life occurred as part of structure dedication ceremonies, did this constitute "sacrifice" if interred persons were foreign to the city? This seems very different from sacrificing a finger to be placed in what appears to have been votive offerings to the dead at Caracol. Violence at Teotihuacan is indicated by the fact that many interments (but not those of Burial 5) were placed with their hands tied behind their back. The martial overtones of dedicatory interments within both the Feathered Serpent Pyramid and the Pyramid of the Moon—specifically, projectile points and faunal remains of animals that later came to represent martial sodalities—provide a contrast to Classic Maya dedicatory and tomb burials in which projectile points rarely are present and never in the quantities reported by Sugiyama for Teotihuacan. Here again, we seem to be bumping against the limits of our conceptual vocabulary and ability to cross-thread notions of death and violence with their use in Mesoamerica for the purpose of commemoration.

As a number of contributors emphasize, deathways are all about the living, about mourning, loss, and survival of descendants and how the dead can facilitate the continued vitality of a family, community, or dynastic line. But deathways also represent the final rite of passage for the deceased, a ceremony that bridges the passage of death—as noted in earlier mortuary studies by Hertz (1960) and Metcalf and Huntington (1991). Mortuary ritual provides a context of social meaning through which a corpse might be transformed into an ancestor, a deity, or fertilizer for future generations of crops. Part of grappling with the loss entailed by death involves wrestling with the deeply philosophical question of what comes after life and whether or not there is an afterlife. Among highland Mexica people, the journey of the soul after death was embodied as a hummingbird in flight.

But if death is the final passage, where does that passage lead? Although concepts of afterlife differed across Mesoamerica, there was uniform acceptance of the notion of afterlife—be it a place of paradisical apotheosis or a cold and frightening place that posed daunting challenges. Baquedano details the plurality of Mexica concepts of afterlife and the role of age, gender, and circumstances of death in routing one down a particular passage. There was a good way to die within Mexica society, in which the value of warriors and pregnant women to imperial expansion and biological reproduction was much exalted. The bundled concepts of gender, warfare, and reproduction seem to have been foreshadowed at Teotihuacan, where Sugiyama reports the presence of females buried with projectile points under the Pyramid of the Feathered Serpent. A similar plurality of afterlife experiences—beyond the oft-noted Xibalba and including passage to a fragrant and flowery mountain—is documented for the Maya region (Taube 2004). But only for a select few did the passage of death result in transcendent apotheosis, ancestor status, or residence on Flower Mountain. Status and identity in life probably served as a remarkable predictor of who was destined to become an ancestor, and the concept of ancestorhood probably has been overextended by archaeologists, as James Whitley (2002) alleges. Yet Sugiyama argues convincingly that Teotihuacan—often suggested to have been a place of a faceless theocracy with no investment in ancestor commemoration (but see Headrick 1999)—contained royal burials under both the Feathered Serpent Pyramid and the Pyramid of the Sun. These places were so thoroughly remembered and so thoroughly looted in antiquity that the long, sinuous chamber beneath the Pyramid of the Sun could be interpreted by modern researchers as an allegorical cave rather than a royal tomb chamber.

The diversity of afterlife experiences and the social diacriticality of mortuary places and practices indicate that care must be taken in reference to hermeneutical extendability. In short, can notions of afterlife and mortuary ritual so well documented through iconography, tombs, and epigraphy be extended to nonroyal and nonelite contexts? Where are the relevant social limits beyond which notions of self and afterlife lacked equivalencies? This question tends to be masked by monolithic and homogenizing expressions such as "the Ancient Maya" that connote a unity and uniformity that, in fact, never existed. Were deathways shared across the profound social differences that existed among status and wealth sectors within Classic Maya societies? Was the notion of head *jol* as a seat of royal identity extended to heads of households? Could *b'aah* (one's individuality and personal qualities) refer to characteristics of a royal as well as those of a commoner? These are difficult questions, but they require attention if our understanding of Classic Maya times is to attain the comprehensiveness of social history. Likewise, mortuary context and social difference appear to have been highly relational; both Blomster and Chase and Chase comment that residence size was correlated with the size of tombs and elaboration of accompanying items at Monte Albán and Caracol respectively; only an estimated 10 percent of the population within the residential complexes of Caracol were buried therein; the remaining 90 percent were disposed in a manner that is archaeologically invisible. Social difference is a deeply rooted and enduring feature of Mesoamerica, where elite and possibly royal tombs date back as early as 500 BCE at San José Mogote. There also existed pronounced long-term stability in commoner house forms and burial practices, as Blomster notes for Oaxaca. Regardless of status, subfloor burial practices in Mesoamerica exhibit a pervasiveness that did not pass unnoticed by Spanish colonizers, who are reported to have excavated under the house floors of Mixtec elites during the idolatry trials of the 1540s. Thus, a remarkably enduring armature of social reproduction and of social difference framed the liminal space between the living and the dead of Mesoamerica.

The adage that "nothing in life is certain save death and taxes" is a fascinating expression, because it naturalizes and universalizes two human experiences—dying and paying taxes—that surely differ dramatically from place to place and time to time. It is this difference—the culturally positioned existentiality of death—that forms a unifying theme of these essays. Carr (1995) notes that deathways are deeply philosophical practices that are shaped most proximately by religious beliefs. In a wider context, Insoll (2004:37) has called for the development of an archaeology of religion. But as we have seen in the foregoing chapters, the manner in which we perceive the dead and mobilize resources to memorialize them is both constrained and amplified by wealth and political circumstance. Several authors provide insightful analyses of this interpenetration and the resultant and potent constellation of religion and power. Although the philosophical heritage of Mesoamerica is profound, it is perhaps nowhere more complex and layered than in beliefs and practices concerning the transcendence of death and the fixing of a person within long-term social memory. As the hermeneutics of death mature within Mesoamerican archaeology, it will, hopefully, include expanded discussion of topics introduced in the pages of this book and exhibit a general trend toward a fuller meshing of the theological with the material.

Note

1. I am indebted to the reviewer who brought to my attention the tragic case of Terry Schiavo, which exemplifies the power of western medicine to forestall indefinitely biological death. In the process, kin members, legislators, and the judiciary grapple with new contingencies in which a nonagentive social persona can exist alongside a biological persona whose existence has been extended through life-supporting technology.

Works Cited

Carr, Christopher
1995   Mortuary Practices: Their Social, Philosophical-Religious, Circumstantial, and Physical Determinants. *Journal of Archaeological Method and Theory* 2(2):105–200.
Fitzsimmons, James L.
2009   *Death and the Classic Maya Kings*. University of Texas Press, Austin.
Harrison-Buck, Eleanor, Patricia A. McAnany, and Rebecca Storey
2007   Empowered and Disempowered During the Late to Terminal Classic Transition: Maya Burial and Termination Rituals in the Sibun Valley, Belize. In *New Perspectives on Human Sacrifice and Ritual Body Treatments in Ancient Maya Society*, edited by Vera Tiesler and Andrea Cucina, pp. 74–101. Springer Science+Business Media, LLC, New York.
Headrick, Annabeth
1999   The Street of the Dead . . . It Really Was: Mortuary Bundles at Teotihuacan. *Ancient Mesoamerica* 10:69–85.

Hertz, Robert
1960/   *Death and the Right Hand: A Contribution to the Study of the Collective Repre-*
[1907]   *sentation of Death.* Glencoe Press, Glencoe, Ill.
Houston, Stephen D., David Stuart, and Karl Taube
2006   *The Memory of Bones: Body, Being, and Experience among the Classic Maya.*
        University of Texas Press, Austin.
Insoll, Timothy
2004   *Archaeology, Ritual, Religion.* Routledge, New York.
Metcalf, Peter, and Richard Huntington
1991   *Celebrations of Death: The Anthropology of Mortuary Ritual.* 2nd ed. Cambridge
        University Press, Cambridge.
Monaghan, John
2000   Theology and History in the Study of Mesoamerican Religions. In *Handbook
        of Middle American Indians:Supplement 6.Ethnology.* University of Texas Press,
        Austin.
Rakita, Gordon, Jane E. Buikstra, Lane A. Beck, and Sloan R. Williams (editors)
2005   *Interacting with the Dead: Perspectives on Mortuary Archaeology for the New Mil-
        lennium.* University Press of Florida, Gainesville.
Ricoeur, Paul
1985   *Time and Narrative,* vol. 2. Translated by Kathleen McLaughlin and David Pel-
        lauer. University of Chicago Press, Chicago.
Taube, Karl A.
2004   Flower Mountain: Concepts of Life, Beauty, and Paradise Among the Classic
        Maya. *RES: Anthropology and Aesthetics* 45:69–98.
Tiesler, Vera, and Andrea Cucina (editors)
2004   *Janaab' Pakal de Palenque: Vida y muerte de un gobernante maya.* Universidad
        Nacional Autónoma de México and Universidad Autónoma de Yucatán, DF,
        and Mérida, Yucatán, Mexico.
Whitley, James
2002   Too Many Ancestors. *Antiquity* 76:119–126.

About the Editors

James L. Fitzsimmons (PhD 2002, Harvard University) is an assistant professor of anthropology at Middlebury College. He is an anthropological archaeologist whose research interests include the anthropology of death, Maya epigraphy, and archaeological method and theory. Fitzsimmons has worked on several projects in Mesoamerica and North America, including fieldwork at Piedras Negras, Guatemala, and Copan, Honduras. For the past several years he has directed excavations at Zapote Bobal, Guatemala, part of a polity that in the Classic period was called Hix Witz, or "Jaguar Hill." Fitzsimmons has recently published a book for the University of Texas Press entitled, *Death and the Classic Maya Kings* (2009), which explores ancient Maya attitudes toward death and reconstructs the mortuary rites of Classic Maya elites. His work has also been published in book chapters as well as numerous scholarly journals, including *Ancient Mesoamerica, Latin American Antiquity*, and *Mexicon*. Currently, Fitzsimmons is working on his second sole-authored book, entitled *The Archaeology of Death in Ancient Mesoamerica*.

Izumi Shimada (PhD 1976, University of Arizona) is a professor and Distinguished Scholar in the Department of Anthropology at Southern Illinois University. His research interests include complex prehispanic cultures of the Andes, technology and organization of craft production, experimental archaeology, mortuary archaeology, and the archaeology of religion. Shimada has directed a number of long-term projects designed to compare Andean religious and ceremonial centers, including Pachacamac, Pampa Grande, and Sicán. He has published over 150 journal articles and book chapters, and has authored or edited several books, including *Craft Production in Complex Societies* (2007), *Andean Ceramics: Technology, Organization, and Approaches* (1998), *Cultura Sicán* (1995), and *Pampa Grande and the Mochica Culture* (1994). Shimada has received numerous awards and grants over the course of his academic career and was given the Gran Official medal from the Peruvian government in 2006 for his archaeological fieldwork at Sicán.

About the Contributors

Elizabeth Baquedano received her PhD at the Institute of Archaeology, University College London, and teaches at University College London and at the Institute for the Study of the Americas, University of London, England. Her main research interest is Aztec (Mexica) archaeology and ethnohistory. She is particularly interested in death symbolism and has been conducting fieldwork in Mixquic, Mexico, where the cult of the dead has been important since precolumbian times. Baquedano is also currently working on the importance of gold among the Mexica, focusing on archaeology, codices, and ethnohistory. Some of her works have been published in *Estudios de Cultura Nahuatl* and *Papers of the Institute of Archaeology*, and by the University Press of Colorado.

Jeffrey Blomster is an anthropological archaeologist specializing in social complexity, interregional interaction, and approaches to style, ritual, and ideology. His regional and spatial research interests lie primarily in Mesoamerica, where he has focused on Mixtec, Zapotec, and Olmec cultures. For nearly a year, he conducted archaeological fieldwork in the Mixteca Alta of Oaxaca, Mexico. This fieldwork, and subsequent laboratory analysis in Oaxaca, examines the emergence of social complexity in the Nochixtlán Valley and explores the impact of interregional interaction in this area. His academic writings have focused on manipulation and movement of style, looking at both traditional stylistic analyses and compositional sourcing. His most recent book, *After Monte Albán: Transformation and Negotiation in Oaxaca, Mexico* (University Press of Colorado, 2008), is an edited volume that examines urban and social transitions that occurred with the Late Classic collapse of the Monte Albán state. Blomster received his PhD from Yale University and is an assistant professor at George Washington University.

Arlen F. Chase (PhD 1983, University of Pennsylvania) is a Pegasus professor and the chair of anthropology at the University of Central Florida. His research interests focus on archaeological method and theory in the Maya area, with particular emphasis on contextual, settlement, and ceramic analysis, and secondary interests in urbanism, ethnicity, and epigraphic interpretation. For more than a quarter century, he has codirected excavations at Caracol, Belize; before that he worked on a seven-year project at Santa Rita Corozal in the same country. He has authored over a hundred articles and book chapters, as well as *The Lowland Maya Postclassic* (1985; edited with P. M. Rice), *Investigations at the Classic Maya City of Caracol, Belize* (1987; with D. Z. Chase), *A Postclassic Perspective* (1988; with D. Z. Chase), *Mesoamerican Elites: An Archaeological Assessment* (1992, 1994; edited with D. Z. Chase), and *Studies in the Archaeology of Caracol, Belize* (1994; with D. Z. Chase). PDF files of his writings may be found at www.caracol.org.

Diane Z. Chase (PhD 1982, University of Pennsylvania) is a Pegasus professor and the vice provost of academic affairs at the University of Central Florida. Her primary focus of research is the ancient Maya of Central America. Her research interests center on archaeological method and theory in the Maya area, with particular emphasis on complex societies and hermeneutics, ethnohistory, and osteological and mortuary analysis. For more than a quarter century, she has codirected excavations at Caracol, Belize; before that she directed a seven-year project at Santa Rita Corozal in the same country. She has authored over a hundred articles and book chapters, as well as *Investigations at the Classic Maya City of Caracol, Belize* (1987; with A. F. Chase), *A Postclassic Perspective* (1988; with A. F. Chase), *Mesoamerican Elites: An Archaeological Assessment* (1992, 1994; edited with A. F. Chase), and *Studies in the Archaeology of Caracol, Belize* (1994; with A. F. Chase). Currently, she is working on a book with A. F. Chase entitled *Maya Archaeology: Reconstructing an Ancient Civilization*. PDF files of her writings may be found at www.caracol.org.

Patricia A. McAnany is Kenan Eminent Professor of Anthropology at the University of North Carolina–Chapel Hill. A Maya archaeologist, she serves as principal investigator of the Xibun Archaeological Research Project and the Maya Area Cultural Heritage Initiative, and formerly of the K'axob Project (www.bu.edu/tricia and www.machiproject .org). She is the editor/author of several books, including *Ancestral Maya Economies in Archaeological Perspective* (2010); *Questioning Collapse: Human Resilience, Ecological Vulnerability, and the Aftermath of Empire* (2009), coedited with Norman Yoffee; *Dimensions of Ritual Economy* (2008), coedited with E. Christian Wells; *K'axob: Ritual, Work, and Family in an Ancient Maya Village* (2004); and *Living with the Ancestors: Kinship and Kingship in Ancient Maya Society* (1995). Her journal articles include "Rational Exuberance: Mesoamerican Economies and Landscapes in the Research of Robert S. Santley," *Journal of Anthropological Research* 64 (2008), coauthored with Christopher A. Pool; "America's First Connoisseurs of Chocolate," *Food and Foodways* 15 (2007), coauthored with Satoru Murata; and "Reclaiming Maya Ancestry," in *Look Close, See Far: A Cultural Portrait of the Maya*, photographs by B. T. Martin (2007) and coauthored with Shoshaunna Parks.

Saburo Sugiyama was born in 1952 in Shizuoka, Japan, and has lived in Mexico for more than eight years, working for the Mexican institution INAH. He moved to the United States in 1987 and obtained a PhD from Arizona State University in 1995. He has worked at many Mesoamerican sites, including Palenque, Becán, Xpuhil, Cacaxtla, Cocula (Guerrero), and Templo Mayor of the Aztecs; his strong research interest, however, has been Teotihuacan, an enormous, ancient planned city. He was a member of the INAH Teotihuacan project in 1980–1982, the assistant director of the Feathered Serpent Pyramid project in 1988–1989, and codirector of the Moon Pyramid project from 1998 to date, and is currently an invited researcher of the Sun Pyramid Project. He is also finishing a 3-D architectural map of the whole city. He is a professor at Aichi Prefectural University, Japan, and also associate research professor of the School of Human Evolution and Social Change, Arizona State University. Among his numerous publications is *Human Sacrifice, Militarism, and Rulership* (Cambridge University Press, 2005).

Estella Weiss-Krejci received her PhD in anthropology from the University of Vienna, Austria, and is teaching at the University of Vienna. Her main research interests are ancient Maya water-storage features as well as cross-cultural investigations of mortuary behavior with emphasis on the ancient Maya, medieval and postmedieval Europe, and Neolithic and Copper Age Iberia. For many years she has conducted archaeological fieldwork in northwestern Belize around the ancient city of La Milpa, in collaboration with Boston University's La Milpa Archaeological Project and the Programme for Belize Archaeological Project of the University of Texas at Austin. Weiss-Krejci has been a recipient of grants awarded by the Fulbright Commission, the Portuguese Science Foundation, and the Austrian Science Fund. Her research results have been published in *Antiquity*, *Latin American Antiquity*, the *Journal of Social Archaeology*, and various book chapters.

Index

Page numbers in italics refer to illustrations.